The Transmuta
and Avant-Ga

MODERN AND CONTEMPORARY POETICS

The Transmutation of Love and Avant-Garde Poetics

JEANNE HEUVING

THE UNIVERSITY OF ALABAMA PRESS
Tuscaloosa

The University of Alabama Press
Tuscaloosa, Alabama 35487–0380
uapress.ua.edu

Inquiries about reproducing material from this work should be addressed to the
University of Alabama Press.

Typeface: Scala and Scala Sans

Manufactured in the United States of America

Cover photograph: Rayograph, 1922, gelatin silver print.
Man Ray (1890–1976), Museum of Modern Art, Gift of James Thrall Soby;
© ARS, NY, used by permission
Cover design: Michele Myatt Quinn

∞

The paper on which this book is printed meets the minimum requirements of
American National Standard for Information Sciences—Permanence of Paper for
Printed Library Materials, ANSI Z39.48–1984.

Library of Congress Cataloging-in-Publication Data

Names: Heuving, Jeanne, 1951– author.
Title: The transmutation of love and avant-garde poetics / Jeanne Heuving.
Description: Tuscaloosa : The University of Alabama Press, 2016. | Series:
Modern and contemporary poetics | Includes bibliographical references and index.
Identifiers: LCCN 2015039997| ISBN 9780817358433 (pbk. : alk. paper) | ISBN
9780817389093 (ebook)
Subjects: LCSH: Love in literature. | American poetry—20th century—History
and criticism. | Experimental poetry, American—History and criticism.
Classification: LCC PS310.L65 H38 2016 | DDC 811.009/3543—dc23
LC record available at http://lccn.loc.gov/2015039997

For James

For those who have loved much

Contents

Preface

In the *Phaedrus* Plato declares that poets do not create poetry by "technique" alone but through the "madness of the Muses" (103; 245a). In *The Transmutation of Love and Avant-Garde Poetics* I pursue a similar insight with respect to avant-garde poetry, but replace "the Muses" with the inspiriting phenomenon of sexual love. Throughout the twentieth century and into the twenty-first, avant-garde poets and intellectuals repeatedly have inveighed against sexual love as being thoroughly in bed with the capitalist and bourgeois orders they contest.[1] In this book, I articulate a different vein of avant-garde activity as the transmutation of love. The poets I discuss change the form of love poetry through the synergistic relations between being in love and writing love. Ezra Pound, H.D., Robert Duncan, Kathleen Fraser, and Nathaniel Mackey all create their innovative verse in large measure through changed love writing. These poets replace the lover of yore with an impersonal or posthuman subjectivity that is their means for conveying the *gloire* and chiaroscuro of love. As Duncan writes, "There is a love in which we are outcast and vagabond from what we are that we call 'falling in love'" (*The H.D. Book* 578).

As did love poets before them, these poets write their verse in the throes of being in love and prolonged states of limerence, but whereas preceding love poets bind these erotic energies to a poetic speaker as self-professing lover, these avant-garde poets engage these energies in what I develop here as a projective love and libidinized field poetics. Unified emotional stances are rejected for ecstatic explorations in which one perception leads directly to the next, one language phrase to another, and all aspects of the poem are generative of meaning. These poets write an Edenic verse, not because of an innate identity between word and thing, but because they do not separate their libidinal investments from language as a full-spectrum symbolic, visual, and aural medium. While

Rimbaud's phrase *"Je est un autre"* ("I is an other") has been defining for avant-garde poetics, I locate a different version of these poetics succinctly theorized by Julia Kristeva: "In love, 'I' has been an *other*" (4).[2] Pound's "radiant" verse; H.D.'s "clairvoyant" image; Duncan's "grand collage"; Fraser's "falling into the page"; and Mackey's "song so black" are all connected to these poets' writings of love.

In scores of biographies, the presumption that a writer's love life has a powerful effect on his or her artistic or literary production is a constant. Yet in most textual or poetics studies, a writer's love relations are regarded, and usually disregarded, as unseemly. In *The Transmutation of Love and Avant-Garde Poetics*, I claim that these poets' innovations are unthinkable apart from sexual love as a generative force and subject matter. I query the bifurcation between sex and love that is endemic to modern thought and theorize the relationship between being in love and writing love. I focus on the historical struggle of individual poets as they came to write love differently and address their use of language as a medium—as conveyor and material.

Early in her career, H.D. pronounced, "There is no great art period without great lovers" (*Notes on Thought* 21). By this statement, H.D. did not mean to indicate that all significant art is created by great lovers, but rather that each era needs artists and poets to engage this powerful source as defining for the work they create. The transmutation of love—the transformation of the profound experience of "being in love" into changed love writing—has not been incidental or secondary to poetic innovations in the twentieth and twenty-first centuries but a basis for the amplified and electrified innovative poetry scenes that by their very numbers of poets are becoming mainstream.

This book has had a long and involved genealogy. It has an important instigation in critiques of romantic and heterosexual love and of the gendered, sexed, and raced makeup of lyric poetry, especially love poetry. It was at once the explanatory power and limitations of these critiques that first gave rise to this project. In Anglo American and European societies the ways that white male heterosexual poets can assume the position of lover and how this position is not available to others in the same empowered way, whether in lyric poetry or in other venues, signaled much to me not only about the inscription of love but about the ways society itself functions. The cultural, social, and historical constitution of sexual love defines not only how its rhetorics and dynamics position men and women, heterosexual and queer, white and nonwhite, but also the very way these formations enable or prohibit sexual energies in public roles and performances, whether of poets or politicians. While recent decades have provided an array of responses to these issues, they have almost always operated under the sign of sexual desire and not sexual love, or through a bifurcation of these.

It was either "his sexual love" or no sexual love at all.[3] My response to this particular set of issues was initially to ask what women poets had done to write love.

In the course of pursuing this version of the book, I found that by framing my book on women's love poetry that I foreground gender and other positionalities at the expense of the confusing, complex phenomenon of sexual love. Indeed, it was my intent in beginning this project not only to understand and critique cultural formation but somehow to find a different sexual love. By concentrating exclusively on female poets, I was falling short of my subject, the transmutation of love. I had begun this project by focusing on H.D. because of the power of her love poetry. H.D.'s poetics led me to Pound and to Fraser, and then to Duncan and Mackey, all poets whose poetry is defined through their love writing and who share aspects of their poetics. At the same time I was researching Pound, I happened to pick up Fraser's *when new time folds up*. Expecting to find marked differences between them, I found instead surprising similarities. It was something in their writing's illumination and opacity, deliberateness and swash.[4] Through this conjunction, the current direction of this book began to take shape. By attending to the poetics that links these poets I aimed to keep my focus on their writing of sexual love, making secondary what separates them, their different positionalities. As such I would be closer to the poet's own writing, their poetry *as* poetry, for it seemed to me that these poets were more compelled by writing love than by inscribing their social identities per se, or at the very least sought some fruitful exchange between these.

My pursuit of this project was also motivated by related questions about poetry itself in an ascendant cultural studies in which poetry is at best a tolerated example. When poetry is consulted, it is often read as just one more discourse or text, and rarely as a specific kind of cultural production. Indeed, in cultural studies, poetry's very capacity to initiate an inceptive speech, poetry as poesis, has been little accounted for. Yet, as Ron Silliman has aptly analyzed, official and academic culture is saturated with what he terms an "absent-but-neutral" voice that issues from no one and for which no one takes responsibility, much less one that elicits sexual desire or sexual love (361). Indeed, in a not so distant past, various theorists and poets made large claims for poetry and for love poetry as generative of and attendant on cultural change, equating love with literature itself. As Kristeva pronounces, "Literature . . . is love" (1). At the outset of this project I found that much which had garnered for poetry power and interest had fallen into a cultural vacuum. Sexual love was alive and living in often troubling ways in a popular culture, spreading with much alacrity across the globe, and its heralded decline in the academy seemed to me to be part of a new cultural hegemony and management rather than a cultural poesis. Indeed, as Plato observed in the *Phaedrus* as he witnessed his world shifting from a pri-

marily oral into a written culture, love hardened by a new regime into rhetorical argument was not adequately presented. To convey love one would need to
respect the powers of love and perhaps be in love.

If this book has an involved critical genealogy, it also has a basis in my poetry writing. The first time the subject of this book suggested itself to me was
long before I engaged it critically. Rather, I first encountered it in my early poetry as a kind of felicity and transport in perception and language when I was
in love and put my pen to paper. I was hardly in command of my writing, much
less of laying claim to the lover role, to have been able to describe myself as a
love poet, yet I did note with pleasure and curiosity this sense of language transport when I experienced being in love. This awareness was soon met by more
complicated affairs and relationships and the critique of love and romance in
the culture at large. My creative books, *Incapacity* and *Transducer*, were written
through the firings and misfirings of these complications. I initiate *Incapacity*,
a work I designate as poetry, fiction, autobiography, and biography, with an epigraph quoting myself as not being able simultaneously to write myself and to
write my desire—or, more exactingly, just "this piece." The epigraph emerged
out of my writing in the early 1980s at a time when the epistemology of sexual
desire and the desiring subject were foremost on my mind.[5] *Transducer* begins
with a quotation from Robert Duncan's "A Poem Beginning with a Line from
Pindar": "The light foot hears you and the brightness begins." *Transducer* is a
version of the poetics examined here and antedates my work on this book. It replaces epistemology with ontology—the phenomenon of sexual love. While this
critical book may not attain a "light foot," it is my hope that its engagement with
its elected subject is at least partially illuminating.

Acknowledgments

This book would never have existed except for the people and communities dedicated to interchange among poetry, theory, and scholarship. I am grateful to Charles Bernstein, Hank Lazer, Dan Waterman, and the Modern and Contemporary Poetics series at the University of Alabama Press for their encouragement of my work, their insights, and their fortitude in responding to my lengthy commentary during the review stage. The texture and argument of this book gained much from these exchanges. I wish to express gratitude to Charles Altieri for his example, these many years, of unstinting intellectual work to make manifest the richness and value of art and poetry, and for his reading of this manuscript. For direct and indirect contributions to the shaping of this book, I thank Charles Alexander, Lee Ann Brown, Laynie Browne, Joseph Donahue, Rachel Blau DuPlessis, Randy Hayes, Ted Hiebert, Suzanne Jill Levine, Robert Mittenthal, Peter O'Leary, Kathleen Woodward, Lissa Wolsak, and the late Herbert Blau and Leslie Scalapino.

Both Kathleen Fraser and Nathaniel Mackey have been very generous in their interactions with my work and me. Nate contributed the full acumen of his capacious intellect in the interview I conducted with him; my ear, already attuned to his work and to jazz, was made that much more acute. Kathleen and her invitation to serve on the editorial board of the electronic journal *HOW2* made my passage into the twenty-first century far more challenging, rewarding, and joyful than it would have been without her and *HOW2*. Her work and her friendship are rare gifts. An exchange with Susan Howe and Joan Jonas in a three-way conversation conducted by the Queens Museum of Art curator Valerie Smith about Joan's performance piece *Lines in the Sand*, which draws on H.D.'s *Helen in Egypt*, provided grist and thrill.

For reading and commenting on parts of this book in manuscript or in presentations, I am grateful to Constantin Behler, Bruce Burgett, Amaranth Borsuk, Rebecca Brown, Michael Davidson, Sarah Dowling, Lynarra Featherly, Claudia Gorbman, Ted Hiebert, Cynthia Hogue, Linda Kinnahan, Gregory Laynor, Kari Lerum, Ron Krabill, Joe Milutis, David Morris, Brian Reed, Leonard Schwartz, Ron Silliman, and Barrett Watten. I am also beholden to the anonymous reviewers at the University of Alabama Press for their detailed readings. I wish to thank the editorial department at the press, especially Joanna Jacobs, for the care they took of my book during the copy-editing stage. For valuable interactions and advice, I thank Tyler Babbie, Emily Beall, Merrill Cole, Stephen Collis, Tim Dean, Robert Gluck, Carla Harryman, Paul Jaussen, Ezra Mark, Shannon McRae, David Morris, Peter Quartermain, Susan Schultz, Nico Vassilakis, Fred Wah, Tyrone Williams, and Lidia Yuknavitch. I also wish to express much gratitude to the Subtext Collective and the many readers in our New Writing from Seattle Reading series. Many thanks to Susan Jeffords and others at the University of Washington Bothell for the opportunity to create a MFA in Creative Writing and Poetics degree that made pursuit of this book all the more lively.

My research was aided and financed by several grants and institutions. I wish to thank Nancy Kuhl and Patricia Willis for their invaluable help in researching H.D. and Pound when I was the H.D. Fellow at Yale's Beinecke Library. The classics scholar Stephen Hinds provided an incisive perspective on the classical legacy of love poetry through a University of Washington Simpson Center for the Humanities Collaborative Scholarship grant. I am also grateful for a National Endowment for the Humanities summer fellowship and a Fulbright grant to Sweden at the inception of this project. A Royalty Research grant and a Simpson Humanities Center Society of Scholars fellowship from the University of Washington, in addition to sabbatical research leave, were much appreciated. Several summer residencies at the Whiteley Center at the University of Washington Laboratories on the San Juan Islands allowed me uninterrupted research and writing time. The beautiful Puget Sound setting and the Whiteley Center staff—Kathy Cowell and Aimee Urata—created much-needed tranquility.

Numerous adventures out in the world to converse about my scholarship and to read my creative work were supported by these entities: University of California, Berkeley, English Department; University of California, Santa Barbara, English Department; Evergreen State College; Gothenburg University, English Department; Uppsala University, English Department; Reed College, Leslie Scalapino Memorial Reading; Cornell University, Laura (Riding) Jackson Symposium; Yale University, Beinecke Library, Biography Conference; University of Washington, Henry Art Gallery; University of Washington, Bothell Research Colloquium; Charles Olson Centennial Conference; Belladonna and CUNY's Advancing Feminist Poetics and Activism conference; Duquesne's "Lifting Belly High": Women's

Poetry since 1990 conference; Barnard's Innovation in Contemporary American Poetry by Women; University of Maine, Poetry of the 1960s and 1970s conferences; American Literature Association; Modern Language Association; Modernist Studies Association; Associated Writing Programs; Fordham University, Poets Out Loud series; Arizona State University, Writers Conference; Beyond Baroque; Kootenay School of Writing; Hedreen Gallery; Non-Site Reading series; Open Books; Pilot Books; Spare Room; and Unnameable Books.

Finally, I wish to thank James Reed for his companionship, support, and love. When I reached a nadir a few times in working on this book, he encouraged me onward: "This is your intellectual life." James's dedication to his art, music, and writing is inspiring and his unerring recollection of names, sounds, and information keeps me connected. I am most grateful to my mother and father, Yvonne Loe Heuving and the late Ralph Heuving. Both traveled great distances in their lifetimes and the example of their good will and courage have been invaluable.

I formally acknowledge permission to quote poems from Nathaniel Mackey's *Four for Trane*; *Eroding Witness*; *School of Udhra*; and *Whatsaid Serif*, as granted by the author, and permission to quote poems from Kathleen Fraser's *il cuore: the heart*; *Little Notes to You, from Lucas Street*; *New Shoes*; *Something (even human voices) in the foreground, a lake*; and *when new time folds up*, as granted by the author. Thanks to *Contemporary Literature* and the University of Wisconsin Press, especially their excellent editorial staff, with much gratitude to Mary Mekemson, for publishing two works important for this book: "Kathleen Fraser and the Transmutation of Love," *Contemporary Literature* 51.3 (Fall 2010): 532–64; and "Nathaniel Mackey: Interview, Conducted by Jeanne Heuving," *Contemporary Literature* 53.2 (Summer 2012): 207–36. An initial engagement with the subject of this book, existing as only traces here, appeared as "The Violence of Negation or 'Love's Infolding,'" in *The World in Time and Space: Towards a History of Innovative Poetry 1979–2000*, edited by Ed Foster and Joseph Donahue (Aberdeen: Talisman House, 2002), 185–200.

The Transmutation of Love
and Avant-Garde Poetics

Introduction

Erotic-emotional innovation is comparatively rare.
     —H.D., "Notes on Euripides, Pausanius, and Greek Lyric Poets"

In the twentieth century and now in the twenty-first, there has been much cynicism and skepticism about love. The flourishing of love in Western poetry is thought to be in decline. Love itself is understood to be a mere ideological overlay or imaginary formation for a more "real" desire and sex. *The Transmutation of Love and Avant-Garde Poetics* attests otherwise. In this book I claim that the achievement of the poetry of Ezra Pound, H.D., Robert Duncan, Kathleen Fraser, and Nathaniel Mackey lies significantly in their writing of sexual love. All of these poets begin with a love poetry in which a poetic speaker as lover writes to or about his beloved, and all change this writing to a projective love and libidinized field poetics. Moreover, I contend that this love writing is critical for avant-garde innovations that partake of its changed energies and relationships even when the poetry is not specifically about sexual love. These authors shift the dramatic locus of their poetry away from a poetic speaker as lover and to their poems' others and to language. They espouse a powerful love that overtakes their egoistic selves, and they engage language as a medium. As H.D. writes, "yet to sing love, / love must first shatter us" (*Collected Poems* 175).

Throughout different epochs, poets have testified to the synergistic relations between being in love and writing love.[1] While being in love leads to poetry writing, writing love poetry intensifies love, causing poets to write more poetry. Ovid, initially setting out to write an epic based on the heroics of war, is overcome with the experience and writing of love. He complains to Cupid, "Is it true that everything everywhere is yours?" (1.1.15; qtd. in Kennedy 44). Dante writes in *La Divina Commedia*, "I am one who, when / Love inspires me, takes note, and / goes setting it forth after the fashion / which he dictates within me" (24: 52–54; Agamben *End* 94).

The poets I study are no less definite about the importance of sexual love to their writing. Pound explored the interrelation between sexual love and poetic vision early in his career, asserting, "the servants of Amore saw visions quite as well as the servants of the Roman ecclesiastical hierarchy." But rather than being troubled "by a dark night of the soul," their rite of passage was through "delightful psychic experience" (*Spirit* 91, 92). Robert Duncan writes: "The meaning of things seems to change when we fall in love, as if the universe were itself a language beyond our human language we had begun to understand. It is the virtue of words that what were forces become meanings and seek form" (*The H.D. Book* 82–83).

Almost all histories of the formation of Western love have concentrated on the development of an introspective lover and the increase in this disposition over time.[2] In *Lyric Texts and Lyric Consciousness: The Birth of a Genre from Archaic Greece to Augustan Rome* Paul Allen Miller claims that it is through the love sequences initiated by Catullus that the introspective subject of lyric poetry is born, arguing that Sappho's poetic speaker does not possess the same introspective qualities (52–77).[3] In *The Culture of Love: Victorians to Moderns* Stephen Kern suggests that the transformations of the modern epoch involved a greater sense of "introspection" or "self-reflexivity" "as men and women [have] come to reflect more profoundly on what it means to be in love" (1). In *Tales of Love* Julia Kristeva asserts that an introspective love is defining for Western love, beginning at least as early as Ovid and culminating in Freud, "the most internalized moment in Western historicality." But she also finds that in the twentieth century this introspective love begins to decline since patriarchal structures that allow for relatively stable forms of identification are weakened: "When the social consensus gives little or no support to such idealizing possibility, as may be observed at the present time . . . the derealization that underlies amatory idealism shows up with its full power." While Kristeva, in part, welcomes the diminishment of the introspective subject as an "end to codes," she also notes that without love relationships the subject is dead: "the amatory principle is indispensable for a body to be living rather than a corpse under care." In this crisis of the subject, this situation of flux, she calls for perpetual relationships of the imaginary, "of love as a builder of spoken spaces" (276, 381–82).

For the poets I investigate here, the rejection of an egoistic or introspective lover as the locus of their poetry enables their projective love and libidinized field poetics. But instead of ascribing everything to the "imaginary," as does Kristeva, they create a poetry that transforms received ideas, representations, and languages through the movement of the writing itself. While these poets' poetics are frequently understood through references to modernist impersonalism or posthuman subjectivity, I inquire into how their subjective orientation evolves in relationship to their intent to write love. I ask, using Charles Olson's apt descriptions from "Projective Verse," how this intention catapults them into a writing which gets "rid of the lyrical interference of the individual as ego" and in which "ONE PERCEPTION MUST . . . DIRECTLY LEAD TO A FURTHER PERCEPTION" (*Selected Writings* 24, 17). These poets make the process of the composition of their poetry determining for the love they write. For instance, while Pound in his early poem "Praise of Ysolt," likely written to H.D., constitutes his poetic speaker as a lover who seeks a woman who "holdeth the wonder words within her eyes," in *Canto I* he presents Aphrodite through a set of concatenating languages: "Aphrodite, / Cypri munimenta sortita est, mirthful, orichalchi . . . / thou with dark eyelids" (*Personae* 17; *Cantos* 5). Pound's love writing shifts the dramatic focus from the poetic speaker as lover to his poems' others and languages, enabling him to invoke but also to alter existing signification. Pound's choice of the Latin for "held sway over the Cyprian heights" (Terrell 3) atypically produces a love figure through consonance rather than assonance and ascribes "mirth" to this figure while sustaining her allure through "dark eyelids."

In an early poem, Fraser's poetic speaker as lover laments knowing her lover only in "the dim light" when her need and desire "shine / the way the sun does on those fat blue days / with sky everywhere" (*Change* 3). In a later poem, replacing her questing poetic speaker with an *ex stasis*, a standing outside of herself, she celebrates:

> (mare pulling into *mare*)
>   horse plowing sea
>   Maremma (*when new time folds up* 20)

Here, the poetic speaker rejoices in her love through a "horse plowing sea," such that mare becomes *mare*, a penetrated and moving sea, carrying forward its eros through mobile italics and into the sounding of the Italian place name "Maremma." The emphasis is on the action of "plowing," a feminized, if also traditionally a masculine prerogative, rather than on subject and object.

On the surface, the poets' movement away from a mimetic rendering of the drama of love, of a lover pursuing a beloved, might be wrongly perceived as a lessening or weakening of love writing. But for these poets, it is an intensification. In forgoing a poetic speaker as an individuated or egoistic lover, they have replaced this controlling figure with erotic energies which cathect directly to their poems' others and languages. They write an Edenic language because their libidinal investments and language as a full-spectrum semantic, visual, and aural medium concatenate. Or, as Pound describes, this poetry "is language charged with meaning to the utmost possible degree" (*Literary Essays* 23).

Throughout the twentieth century and into the present, sexual love has been much maligned in accounts rejecting what is perceived as its idealizing hypocrisy. One of the mainstays of these critiques has been to divide love from sex, deploring love while celebrating the salutary effects of sex. In 1928, for instance, J. W. Krutch in *The Modern Temper* comments that love is a "superstructure of poetry" built on a "biological urge" (Selinger 77). Eric Selinger in *What Is It Then between Us?: Traditions of Love in American Poetry* takes on this same dichotomy, characterizing the entire twentieth century as a time in which "love's reductively sexual origins" undermined "its expansive cultural flourishing" (81). In *Desire: Love Stories in Western Culture* (1994), Catherine Belsey claims that "true love" is the ideological formation that "Western culture has created between two kinds of feeling, caring on the one hand and desire on the other" (13). She concludes, "True love is a mode of policing the gaze, excluding errant desires, bringing the subject into line" (148).

Some of the earliest to attack love were avant-garde writers, most notably Mina Loy and F. T. Marinetti. Loy, in her indictments of "Pig Cupid . . . Rooting erotic garbage" in *Songs to Joannes*, asserts in her "Feminist Manifesto," "Women must destroy in themselves, the desire to be loved." And she notes, "there is nothing impure in sex—except the mental attitude to it" (*The Lost Lunar Baedeker* 53, 154, 155). In his manifestos, Marinetti links "woman" and "*amore*," calling *amore* an "invention of the poets": "We scorn woman conceived as the sole ideal, the divine reservoir of *Amore*, the woman-poison, woman the tragic trinket, the fragile woman, obsessing and fatal" (72).

Laura (Riding) Jackson, drawing together a critique of love and gender, advocates a recreated love and sex. In its civilized version, sexual love is produced as a kind of rare brew of bodily impulses, scientific phrases, and literary sentiments, which all conspire to keep women in a passive state. Jackson shows just what this "diffusion which modern society calls love" consists of by revealing what a man's "I love you" speech means:

> My sexual glands by the growing enlargement of my sex instincts since childhood and its insidious, civilized traffic with each part of my mental and physical being, are unfortunately in a state of continual excitement. I have a very good control of myself, but my awareness of your sexual physique and its radiations are so acute that I could not resist the temptation to desire to lie with you. Please do not think this ignoble of me, for I shall perform this act, if you permit it, with the greatest respect and tenderness and attempt to make up for the indignity it of course fundamentally will be to you (however pleasurable) by serving you in every possible way and by sexually flattering manifestations of your personality which are not strictly sexual. (*Anarchism* 189)

In Jackson's analysis, this civilized sexual love is a product of a literature of the "individual real," in which the self "authenticates" itself in relationship to a compromising social order. In contrast, Jackson advocated a poetry of the "individual unreal," of a corrective response, to make way for an actual love (*Anarchism* 46, 47). For Jackson, sex and love have been horribly misconstrued by a civilization in which women serve primarily as a "prop" "for the solemn masculine machine" (196). "Woman" can only look to herself and must become "the death in whom / Love must disaster" (*Poems of Laura Riding* 264).

In claiming that the innovative poets of this book are involved in transmuting love poetry into a projective love and libidinized field poetics, I do not mean to suggest that their individual motivations or issues are the same. However, I do begin with the observation that all of these poets come to find lover-beloved forms—a lover writing to or about his beloved—problematic. Moreover, all of the writers in their mature poetry affirm love and engage its power, even when they address its failure or loss. And while each poet composes his or her love differently, each is sensitive to social and cultural changes that directly challenge conceptions of the lover of yore. Changing gender norms disrupt the traditional engendering of love lyrics—of an active masculine lover and a passive feminine beloved. Newly emergent concepts of sexuality, which include theorizations of bisexuality and homosexuality, render the presumed heterosexuality of traditional love poetry problematic. Critiques of racial discrimination and improved conditions for "advancement" give nonwhite lovers new possibilities for saying their love publicly to a mixed-race audience.

Throughout North American, European, and Latin poetic history, love poetry has been empowering for white heterosexual men, but rarely for others.[4] From Gaius Catullus to Robert Creeley, white male heterosexual love poets have created a rich trove of rhetorical dynamics and semantic meanings. Although poets of diverse identities and orientations have sometimes engaged or travestied these forms, this tradition of lover-beloved poetry remains largely a white, male production.[5] Indeed, these forms are silencing for other poets both on and off the page—and are implicated in a complex set of negotiations about who can make a public display of their love and to what effect. By transmuting love poetry into a projective, libidinized field poetics, the poets I am analyzing here make way for diverse poets to say their love publicly.

Although these poets occasionally have been studied with respect to their love writing, their shared contribution to changing the form of love writing has not been recognized nor has this change been linked to their avant-garde poetics. In claiming that these poets are involved in a shared transmutation of love, I do not mean to suggest that their love writing is the same, but rather to draw attention to the ways they have shaped a changed poetry economy. The critic Margaret Homans, noting that unrequitedness was the primary condition of love poetry in the nineteenth century and earlier—a poetry in which hierarchical lover and beloved relations pertain—remarks, "attainment would remove the motive for future poems" (570). For the love poetry of the authors included in *The Transmutation of Love and Avant-Garde Poetics*, while unrequitedness and requitedness, disappointment and hopefulness may give rise to their poetry, the focus is almost always on the power of love, not on the unavailability of the beloved. Although H.D. often composed her works in reference to failed love relations, only occasionally in her writing does she take on the position of the lover questing after an unobtainable beloved; rather, she seeks to explore love itself. Addressing the loss of love, Mackey in "Song of the Andoumboulou: 5" in *Eroding Witness* has a muse figure tell the poetic speaker: "beware the beauty of loss." She further enjoins: "The least eye's observance of / dawn will endanger what / of love // you take with 'love's bite'" (44).

I have chosen poets whose sustained engagement with sexual love is formative not only for their poetry but for others' poetry. All of these poets convey sexual love with a concerted intensity commensurate with love poets of the past—Sappho, Propertius, Cavalcanti, Shelley, Keats. They seek out the synergistic exchange between being in love and writing love, and create their poetry in significant ways through these energies. I begin with Pound and H.D. because their Imagist poetics are an emergent projective love and libidinized field poetics, which they develop in their long poems *The Cantos*, *Trilogy*, and *Helen in Egypt*. I then turn to Duncan as he initiates his projective love and libidinized field poetics in *The Opening of the Field*. Both Fraser and Mackey have early insights into this transmutation—Fraser in *Little Notes to You, from Lucas Street* and Mackey in *Four for Trane*—and work to engage and develop these poetics in subsequent writing. Although there are other poets whose love poetry has contributed to this transmutation, for the poets considered in this book it is a defining question asked and answered in multiple books and over decades of their writing. In the afterword, I take up the issue of other writers for whom projective love and libidinized field poetics are important and the relation of these poetics to a more broadly practiced projective verse and field poetics. In the last decades, there has been a widespread and electric amplification of field poetics—indeed, a poetry that, if not always a projective love writing, often evinces a libidinized field—which simply would not have occurred had sexual love either been ignored by these earlier generations or existed as an aside to a more narrowly construed avant-gardism.

The Transmutation of Love and Avant-Garde Poetics presents a revisionist history of twentieth- and twenty-first-century poetry by paying close attention to the chronological development of the poets' work as they came to write love differently. For them the transmutation of love is a synergistic endeavor embedded in the formation of their poetry. They operate within the tradition well expressed by Propertius in which loving and the writing of love are inseparable: "I, as I have been accustomed to do, get on with my—*amores*" (1.7; qtd. in Kennedy 24). So troubled has been the writing of love in the twentieth and twenty-first centuries, and so clear has been the clarion call for a poetry that will meet the hard demands of modernity or the insistent complexities of postmodernity that these poets' transmutation of love simply has gone unrecognized. In this book I tell a "long history" of avant-garde activity that concentrates on continuities across several generations of poets, rather than on the differences announced in manifestos and poetic statements, in which in their eagerness to articulate their present moment often deny entanglements with the past. The way a society structures and formalizes (puts into form) its sexual relations is a key to its multiple institutions and casual interactions. By discovering a different way to write love—by shifting their erotic energies away from a poetic speaker as lover and to their poems' others and languages—the poets create a changed eros that replaces a pervasive economy of active lovers and passive beloveds. They close down the gaps, the great distances that yawn, in love poetry itself—and approach an eros or "erotism" that subtends existence and has been theorized variously throughout the ages.[6]

In focusing on sexual love, I distinguish it from sexual desire and erotic play. While it is impossible to distinguish these in any absolute way, I seek to locate how sexual love is uniquely motivating and generative for poetry writing. The state of being in love is usually experienced as more extreme and disturbing than mere sexual desire or erotic play and creates rather different effects in the subject. In love, the poet experiences a subjective dispensation that in Freudian theory greatly reduces "ego-libido" in exchange for "object-libido." For Freud, "being in love" is the "highest phase of object-libido" and is the state in which subjects are most inclined to relinquish their egoistic orientation and to open themselves up to an infusion of otherness (547). These poets exhibit a marked "negative capability" or self-abandonment—as opposed, say, to the often willful agency exhibited in poems primarily of sexual desire or erotic play. These poets move beyond the mimetic form of lover-beloved poetry, outside a limited lover-beloved economy, and engage the ecstatic free fall of sexual love, joining centuries of poets and philosophers who have celebrated an ecstatic love or erotic mania—or what postmodern theorists have referred to somewhat differently as a jouissance.

The poets in this book do not change love at the level of love tropes that, abstracted from the writing, provide new definitions, but rather through the ways they initiate shifting and mobile relations in a form previously dominated by lover-beloved oppositions and subject-object dichotomies. Indeed, while my larger argument in this book is that changes in gender, race, and sexuality have made the white male heterosexual prerogatives of prior love poetry no longer viable, I also explore how these poets have changed love poetry by insisting on their own different dispensations. That is, with the exception of Pound, all of these poets find themselves positioned outside of the dominant love economies of the past, and their differences of gender, sexuality, or race enable them to shift representation once they are no longer tied to the previous form. They change poetry not by going at loggerheads with the Lord Byrons and Don Juans of the past but by altering the form of love poetry so that it is no longer dependent on the dramatization of a poetic speaker as lover but rather produces its love in relationship to a wider libidinized horizon. Who says what almost always changes the what—and no more so than in a highly gendered, raced, and sexed love poetry. These poets open up languages that were anchored in the past to particular kinds of poetic speakers.

In this book I define "sexual love" as a sustained attraction for a specific beloved that is compelling and cannot be let go easily, and I understand sexual love to be a physical, emotional, and cognitive (and therefore language) phenomenon. Susan Stewart has argued for poetry's special role of poesis, of making as cultural formation, but she has also commented on how difficult poesis may be to locate. She understands significant formal change as something that emerges out of a necessity and to be a precise response to an unarticulated need. Thus, an important function for poetry is to bring somatic and social experiences into alignment (*Fate* 116–17). But once created, a successful poem often covers over the space of its necessity, and the historical demand for its formation is rendered mute. Stewart notes that therein lies a "tragedy" for the poet, in "the fading of the referent in time, in the impermanence of whatever is grasped" (*Fate* 2). She adds, "The poet's recompense is the production of a form that enters into the transforming life of language" and, more broadly, the culture (*Fate* 2). Stewart suggests that a transforming poetry as well as other aesthetic forms should be taken as "central to the epistemological and ethical possibilities of culture's emergence" ("State" 95)

To inquire into relations that are inherently difficult to locate, in this book I explore three interrelated postulations. The first are the splits between sex and love and between desire and love that emerge in the twentieth century, which obfuscate these poets' efforts to write sexual love.[7] While the emergence of discourses of sexuality leads to these divisions, sexual love has persisted as a powerful and integrated phenomenon. This is no more apparent than in the sex theorists themselves. Freud, who is credited with creating the concept of sexuality, regularly blurs distinctions between sex and love: when he says one, he often means both. Foucault in debunking the cultural importance placed on sex and sexuality as a means of liberation also notes how sexuality has become the *ars erotica* of our time (*History* 156). Second, these poets' writings of sexual love are directly connected to the formal innovations for which they are known. In the cases of Pound, H.D., and Fraser their writing of love leads to their new poetics; in the cases of Duncan and Mackey they integrate sexual love with poetic practices that attract them—and only in doing so are they able to realize the poetry they sought to write. In all cases these poets' most important and defining poetry is significantly derived through their discovery of how to engage sexual love and its energies. While they write love often in the throes of being in love, they also engage it as a sustained limerence or *gloire* activated by writing itself. This heightened emotional state is directly conducive to a metamorphosing of form and representation. Third, this poetry is better addressed by conceiving of the poet and language itself as mediums. While the idea of the poet as a medium is sometimes brought into discussions of these poets, the ways that language itself functions mediumistically has been little explored. The concept of the poet as a receptive medium is an important corrective to the emphasis on willful agency in avant-garde poetics, with the poets discussed here operating both as agents and as mediums. The concept of language as a medium allows for a sense of language as possessing material properties, but it also draws to the forefront its mediumistic attributes—as at once mediating the larger society and the poet's somatic response but also serving as a means of transportation by which these are freshly addressed and thereby referenced. As Mackey puts it, "Writing is a mix of saying what I mean to say and finding out what else the writing might say" ("Interview" 214).

Two large historical conditions of modernity have directly contributed in decisive ways to this changed poetry. The emergent discourses of sexuality not only radically change the dispensation of love but they demand to be answered. Foucault has theorized that these discourses arise as part of a larger modern regime distinguished by its need to regulate biopower, and he has explicated how the liberatory promises that have accompanied the exposé of sexuality come with their own disciplinary logics. For Foucault all disciplining is at once limiting and productive—and he notes how sexuality in the twentieth century came to be identified with the very truth and meaning of our existence. A relative paucity of attention has been paid to the effects of discourses of sexuality on poetry or on modern literature more generally, apart from a wholesale celebratory substitution of an epistemology of sexual desire for one of sexual love. Indeed, discourses of sexuality since their emergence have had beneficial effects for populations for whom the role of lover is gendered, racialized, and sexualized in hostile ways. While only some people can position themselves as lovers—as Don Juans or Creeley's elusive masculine poetic speakers—everyone "has" sex, "has" sexuality. (Indeed, in one of my graduate seminars, a student eager for the openings that lesbian sexuality and queer theory provided, who was alternately fascinated and perplexed by the subject of the course, asked me, "Why are you going back to love when we have only just begun to have sexuality?") All of the poets covered in this book are motivated to understand and to engage with the discourses of sex and sexuality. But they also address sexual love itself, in part through classical conceptions that refuse the division between sex and love, namely eros and amour. They challenge modernity with its regulatory and categorical imperatives by seeking what Bataille calls "erotism": "a substitution of isolated discontinuity" for a "feeling of profound continuity" (15).

While this poetry is attentive to large changes in the disciplining and understanding of sex and love, it is also responsive to a changing orientation to language. Although the turn to language is located historically in the second part of the twentieth century, articulated most forcefully by poststructuralism and by the Language or L=A=N=G=U=A=G=E movement, the experience of language as an object occurs throughout the twentieth century and before. Indeed, the rise of advertising and commodity culture along with a comparative study of cultures and languages (with a strong value placed on the activity of translation) at the outset of the twentieth century produced a sense of language as a medium, conveyor and thing. For example, at the outset of her career, H.D. describes the process of translating Greek words as one of engaging them as "portals, as windows, or port-holes . . . that look out . . .onto a sea that moves and changes" ("Essays on Euripides, Pausanius, and Greek Lyric Poets" 9). Only in the last several decades has a widespread intellectual, academic, and artistic regime elected to become assertive about just what this changed orientation to language may entail, but in doing so it also has tended to reify language. Indeed, with the incorporation of this new understanding into multiple arenas of endeavor, including poetry, an exclusionary emphasis on language has abated. Marjorie Perloff, throughout her career, has been most attentive to mapping out distinctions in how language has been engaged by poets and artists in the twentieth and into the twenty-first century, although she has at times insisted on the materiality of language to the exclusion of more complex meditations with respect to how language functions.[8] Her 1981 *Poetics of Indeterminacy* comes closest to the sense of language I elaborate on in this book because of how she engages language as a set of shifting significations. But while she emphasizes "indeterminacy," I stress a motivated and libidinal engagement with language which separates language from its habitual significations for the purpose of writing love otherwise.

This book is divided into two parts: "Love Poetics" and "Love Poesis." Although there is considerable overlap between poetics and poesis, in general as well as in the exposition of this book, the two designations demarcate a shift in emphasis. In "Love Poetics," I provide a generalized description of the poetics of my selected poets and a theoretical investigation into the synergistic relations between being in love and writing love. And I establish Pound's and H.D.'s Imagist poetry as an initial and emergent projective love and libidinized field poetics. In "Love Poesis," I focus on each poet's chronological process as they come to write—or to make—love differently. Although I pay attention to commonalities between the poets, I propose that each poet is engaged in a singular transformation of love poetry, neither entirely generalizable nor paraphrasable, but involving all the mystery and particularity of his or her love and of poetic formation itself. This focus involves considerable close reading, but it is a close reading in service not of interpretation per se but of demarcating the poets' changed love writing in relationship to the poetry that has earned them their reputations. I give some consideration to biographical events, but I predominantly focus on the poets' changing poesis. Indeed, in postulating that these poets change the writing of love through an immanent writing that acts on itself, there is no more exacting attention than the tracing of their progress as they engage specific languages and tropes within the context of their evolving oeuvres and individual poems. These poets change love by writing love.

In chapter 1, "Projective Love and Libidinized Field Poetics," I begin with two examples that have been definitive for avant-garde poetics generally: Pound's *Canto IV* (which led to his revision of his earlier *Three Cantos* and the writing of his *Cantos* proper) and Duncan's "Often I Am Permitted to Return to a Meadow," the initial poem in his revolutionary *The Opening of the Field*. In taking my primary terms for this book from Olson's "Projective Verse," I argue for a different understanding of Olson's poetics than is commonly attributed to him as well as for broadening the sense of these poetics with respect to a much wider historical use. Rather than Olson's "push" and "INSTANTER," I suggest that a projective writing can also occur through a slowed-down and introjective set of relations. That is, if a defining aspect of the projective is that one perception must lead directly to the next, there is an implicit introjective moment in this associative composition that Olson does not typically account for. Suggesting that something akin to a projective writing may well have been initiated in the nineteenth century by Whitman and Shelley, and rather differently by Rimbaud and

Mallarmé, I consider how, for the poets examined in this book, the increased sense of language as an object or thing within the compositional process alters their sense of that process. While Olson postulates that "a poem is energy transferred from where the poet got it" and may have "several causations," I address projective poetics when the causal energy is specifically sexual love (*Selected Writings* 16). I explore how for love poets past and present, language itself becomes mediumistic or, as Wilde puts it: "Do you wish to love? Use Love's Litany, and the words will create the yearning from which the world fancies that they spring" (399; qtd. in Kopelson 2). For the poets covered in this book, altered relations to language means that this mediumistic encounter occurs not only cognitively and emotionally but also in relationship to the aural and visual aspects of language itself.

Chapter 2, "Being in Love and Writing Love," inquires into the generativity of sexual love for poetry writing. I begin with Plato's *Phaedrus* and *Symposium* and Socrates's theories about how erotic energies based in love for a beloved have special properties of extension. Although Plato's ideas are frequently allied with the modern concept of sublimation, I point out the radical difference between them, both as Freud theorizes sublimation and in its common usage.[9] I then turn to Freud's theories for an understanding of how subjects in love become differently disposed. His concepts of "mourning" and "melancholia," along with the related concepts of "enchantment" and "mania," are queried with respect to his basic distinctions between "ego-libido" and "object-libido" and to the ways they account for rather different subject dispositions (545–61, 548–89). Overall, this book favors Freudian over Lacanian theories because of Lacan's insistence on separating out "symbolic" and "imaginary" realms, a division that enforces the bifurcation of sexual desire and sexual love. Yet it finds Lacan's distinction between "empty" and "full" speech most useful in validating poetry itself (*Ecrits* 30–113). Indeed, both psychoanalysis and projective love writing give considerable importance to the subject's constitution of his or her speech through an associative delivery. But although each of these historically new practices locates much merit in process-based knowledge formation, psychoanalysts aim for the "cure" of an individual subject whereas the poets put their efforts into creating and altering meaning itself.

Chapter 3, "Imagism as Projective Love," locates a nascent projective love and libidinized field writing in Pound's and H.D.'s Imagist verse. Little attention has been paid to how the poems Pound selected for his 1914 *Des Imagistes* to represent H.D.'s and his own work are almost all based in erotic relations and texts. I take up the argument developed by Cyrena Pondrom and others that H.D.'s poems served as formative examples for Pound's poetry and for his exposition of Imagist poetics.[10] H.D. discovered instigating models for her Imagist poetry in J. K. Mackail's *Select Epigrams from the Greek Anthology* and wrote several of her Imagist poems as creative translations of epigrams written by poets of different sexual orientations. These poets often referred to themselves in the third person and spoke their love with unabashed aplomb.[11]

In "Love Poesis," each chapter examines the trajectory of an individual poet as they came to write their version of a projective love and libidinized field poetics. In each case, the tenor of the poetry and the challenges the poets faced with respect to their social positionalities are different. All of the poets' initial engagement with earlier love poetry encouraged them to create unified and recognizable emotional stances. As they developed poetic speaking positions that were not based on "the lyrical interference of the individual as ego" (Olson, *Selected Writings* 24), their poetry was increasingly ecstatic or, to use a term from Mackey, "strung out" ("Interview" 214). All of the male poets initially engaged the power of melancholic stances, a staple of men's love poetry, but they came to replace melancholic regimes with more complex erotic renderings. Although neither H.D. nor Fraser had access to the established stance of the poetic speaker as male lover and to his melancholic modes, they each managed early on an emergent projective love and libidinized writing only to be plummeted into decades of inquiry into what H.D. called the "sex-gender system" before regaining this writing relatively late in life. Indeed, while Pound and Mackey were drawn to impersonal or posthuman poetics, H.D., Duncan, and Fraser found a greater access to their writing through transpersonal or transhuman economies. And while Pound could shift patriarchal representations in decisive ways given his privileged place in these economies, H.D., Duncan, Fraser, and Mackey had to significantly revise their representational fields. All of the poets not only were involved in a personal quest to write their love differently but also were engaged with the public valuations, judgments, and languages that doing so entails. As Agamben puts it, all of these poets sought a writing in which "the object sought by love would correspond with the very language in which [the work] is written" (*End* 60).

Each of the poets faced different historical realities with respect to changing dispensations of gender, sexuality, and race and their relations to these. Pound and H.D. wrote their poetry alert to the implications of emergent discourses of sexuality and changing gender norms. They had to find their ways in a society in which gender was in flux and sexuality challenged love, conditions which at once necessitated and enabled their poetic explorations. Duncan began writing at the cusp of the formation of identity politics and arguably led the way, while rejecting identity formations. His groundbreaking 1944 essay, "The Homosexual in Society," can be seen as an emergent version of these politics that is also alert to their problematics. Although Duncan advocated for the recognition and inclusion of homosexuals in the larger society, he also wrote of experiencing diminishment of his full emotional responses within the exclusive coteries that created separate homosexual cultures. Fraser and Mackey began their writing in the 1960s and 1970s at a time when identity politics were becoming pronounced. While both attended closely to the need for changed gender, sexual, and racial definitions, they sought a writing that exceeded the delimiting demands of identity politics. Fraser understood feminism's need for "a binding voice of women's strength," but she recoiled from the limited registers of what counted as "personal experience" (*Translating* 31). Mackey has remarked on the debasement that occurs through a reception of a poet's work that looks only for what marks it racially. He further notes, "There has been far too much emphasis on accessibility when it comes to writers from socially marginalized groups" (*Discrepant* 17).

While these poets addressed diverse historical moments that affected their relationship to positionality itself, they also engaged divergent traditions and poetry movements. For instance, Pound, alert to modernism across the arts, insisted on making his poetry new, and Fraser brought to modernist and New American poetics a simultaneous involvement with the playful energies of the New York School. Thus, her poetry might be described as "affectional ecstatic," whereas Mackey, who came to his poetics primarily through New American and Black Mountain poetics, creates a "posthuman ecstatic." Mackey—attentive to the ways that African Americans have been left out of the social contract and denied kinship in what amounts to a social death—has been highly alert to how language constitutes "unevenly alloted orders of agency." He accordingly creates an outsiders' outside, an ecstatic that is in service of a love not found elsewhere (*Discrepant* 284). To do so, Mackey has turned specifically to African and Caribbean traditions and myths and to African American jazz to relocate his field of endeavor.

The poets also have related to the projective and introjective strophes of a projective poetics in markedly different ways, and they have manifested much variation in the degree to which they have located their libidinal fields in recognizable cultural or historical figures or in a disruption of language itself. In the highly introjected poetry of H.D. and Mackey, and sometimes Duncan, the same historical and mythical figures are replicated and transformed in books and poems written over several decades. Fraser and Pound, who primarily emphasize projective elements, change their fields of reference more frequently. Indeed, one of the reasons that Pound's early *Cantos* are a more enlivened engagement with the projective love poetics discussed here is that in his later *Cantos* he replicates preordained ideograms and figures without sufficient rebooting. H.D. and Duncan only occasionally disrupt language through visual and aural materialities that counter sense-making, whereas Pound, Fraser, and Mackey do so more frequently.

In the chapters on the individual poets, I trace how each one came to write love otherwise. Chapter 4, "'Circe's This Craft,'" addresses Pound's radical change from nineteenth-century modes of love writing to projective love as the result of not only his changing poetics but his changing attitudes toward love. His early love writing vacillates between enchantment and melancholia and between celebrating and reviling love, dispositions which he syncretizes in *The Cantos*. Pound's disappointment and disgust with love are particularly evident in his 1917 *Three Cantos* (his ur-cantos). By 1919 and the writing of *Canto IV*, which led to a rewriting of *Three Cantos*, his ambivalence about love is gone. Ronald Bush remarks about the transition between *Three Cantos* and *Canto IV*: "*Three Cantos* . . . describes. *Canto IV* presents" (200).[12] Even more critically, *Three Cantos* describes love. *Canto IV* presents love. Pound created his characteristic writing in *The Cantos* by projecting a semantic field of obtruding visual and aural materialities that act on his poetic speaker through their concatenating symbolics and materialities in a production that Richard Sieburth, drawing from Deleuze, calls his "schizopoetics" (xxxiii).

H.D. never questioned the power of love nor its relationship to her writing. However, while she extended her early successful Imagist writing in her first volume of verse, *Sea Garden*, a long love poem, she did not regain this projective love writing until relatively late in her career, in her long works *Trilogy* and *Helen in Egypt*. In chapter 5, "'Love Is Writing,'" I consider the reasons for H.D.'s prolonged and radical revision of her "content" or representational field that enabled her to extend the implicit lessons of what she called her poetics of "clairvoyance" in contrast to Pound's ability to carry through on his initial Imagist discoveries comparatively quickly. In Pound's *Cantos* the forward movement of a projective love writing is prominent, but in H.D.'s work introjection is intense. H.D.'s process-based writing finds a rich trove of palimpsestic meanings that surfaced through sets of interacting aural and semantic relations. As she writes in *Trilogy*: "I feel / the meaning that words hide; // they are anagrams, cryptograms, / little boxes, conditioned to hatch butterflies" (*Collected Poems* 540).

In chapter 6, "The First Beloved," I explore how Duncan, initially attracted to Pound's and H.D.'s poetics, did not discover how to write a projective love and libidinized field poetics until his 1960 volume, *The Opening of the Field*. Writing his early poetry often through willful poetic speakers whose mournful and melancholic stances served to entrench his poems' subject-object dichotomies, Duncan turned to imitations of Gertrude Stein in his 1953 *Writing Writing* in a deliberate effort to change his poetry. Bringing together the troubled emotions of his initial work and the playful, loosened writing of the intervening period, he then wrote *The Opening of the Field*, which evinces a poetics described by Duncan as "total freedom in interaction " ("Interview" by Faas 4–5). Throughout his writing, he subtly shifts meanings through his changed relationship to the languages he employs. For example, he writes of falling in love with the manhood in a man, something that is "only there" through "the way we then make love" ("Interview" by Abbott and Shurin 94).

Fraser discovered a projective love writing as early as her 1972 *Little Notes to You, from Lucas Street* but did not return to it until the 1990s. In chapter 7, "Kathleen Fraser and 'Falling into the Page,'" I consider how Fraser, alert to feminism's critique of what Adrienne Rich called "compulsory heterosexuality" and Rachel Blau DuPlessis named "romantic thralldom," undermined her own early poetic conviction that without "lust" poetic transport does not happen (Rich 203–23; Friedman and DuPlessis 406–29; Fraser, *Change* 15). During this time she attempted to write love differently but did not achieve the effervescence of her earlier poetry. In the 1990s she rediscovered a projective love writing and the possibilities of an ecstatic writing, and she linked these discoveries to Olson's poetics in her essay "Translating the Unspeakable: Visual Poetics as Projected through Olson's 'Field' into Current Female Writing Practice." She writes that the poet is "a field charged with sound. The page begins revising its surface" (*Translating* 10). Beginning initially with a poetry that expressed much dissatisfaction with her beloved, a poetry of absence, she came to write a poetry in which absence and presence are not mutually exclusive, but interpenetrate.

Mackey, initially drawn to Petrarchan melancholic economies, turns from these to combine New American open field poetics with an improvisational jazz aesthetic. If there is an aesthetic, ethical, and political dilemma that threads its way through Mackey's work, it is how to engage loss and desire, failure and aspiration, without giving short shrift to either. In chapter 8, "Nathaniel Mackey and 'Black Sounds,'" I explore how he responds to this dilemma by engaging art forms that synergistically combine these oppositions—most importantly jazz, as a love-inflected, African American invention and as a dissonant, syncopated arrangement of sounds that depends on recalling previous musical passages as these are caught up in forward movement.[13] He turns to African and African diasporic cultural fields to locate a different set of cultural figures than are found in the Western traditions that the other poets engage. Throughout Mackey's poetry, a sense of ecstasy, a standing outside of himself, prevails. He creates a poetry in which loss and aspiration are syncretically joined: "Some / ecstatic elsewhere's / advocacy strummed, / unsung, lost inside / the oud's complaint" (*Whatsaid Serif* 3). To achieve an "articulacy" for his poetics, Mackey engages homonymic and punning aspects of language in a word "splay" that "subject[s] words to bends, breaks, deformation, reformation—othering" (*Discrepant* 272).

The poets covered in *The Transmutation of Love and Avant-Garde Poetics* take considerable risks—not only in going against dominant literary and intellectual modes and thereby risking the reception of their work but also in their cultivation of various states of embrace and abandon. They take on potentially threatening or accelerated psychological states, as suggested by Sieburth's term "schizopoetics" and Norman Finkelstein's evaluation of Mackey's work as "shamanistic."

I

Love Poetics

Projective Love and Libidinized Field Poetics

By bad verse, whether "regular" or "free," I mean verse which pretends
to some emotion which did not assist at its parturition.
                        —Ezra Pound, "Affirmations: As for Imagisme"

Love poetry has been definitive for Western poetry and for love in Western cultures since classical times. And while this love writing has shifted through diverse historical epochs—Latin elegists, Provençal, *dolce stil nuovo*, and Romantic traditions, among others—it has occurred largely through lover-beloved forms that depend on an empowered poetic speaker as lover and a comparatively disempowered beloved. In *The Transmutation of Love and Avant-Garde Poetics* I ask why sexual love flourishes in avant-garde poetry. I answer this question by exploring how key modern and contemporary poets change the form of love poetry to a projective love and libidinized field poetics. They engage love as immanent and transform it through a writing that acts on itself.

The poets discussed in this book have sometimes been included in poetry evaluations seeking to identify avant-garde poetry. Yet they also have been dismissed for their romanticism, traditionalism, and language use. Since I am suggesting that their avant-garde practice inheres in their transmutation of love, the rather generalized critique of their romanticism needs to be revised and, with respect to their traditionalism, their active engagement with figures and languages that derive their significance from epochs of cultural evolution needs to be addressed in ways that do not simply label their use of these as antiquated. In creating their libidinized fields from a diverse set of mythical and historical figures they do not simply insert these figures from an earlier time but reengage them. Additionally, these poets sometimes have been dismissed for what is regarded as an inconsistent attention to and understanding of the materiality of language. Indeed, while their engagement with language sometimes manifests as an attention to the material aspects of language—as a heightened and disruptive foregrounding of the aural or visual elements of language—they engage language foremost as a medium but one that possesses material properties. These poets relate to language as mediating their experiences in relation to their "real" historical time and as a potentially transforming and transformative medium. For them, language is both symbolic and material, conduit and object.

I initiate this inquiry by considering Pound's and Duncan's changed love poetry to convey the radical and far-reaching aspects of these poetics. For both Pound and Duncan, as with the other poets considered in this book, their changed love writing is important not only because it provides a different way of writing love for modern times, but because it is directly productive of their most important and inventive poetry. *Canto IV*, published in 1919, is Pound's first poetry in which he fully realizes a projective love and libidinized field poetics, and it led him to to a rapid revision of *Three Cantos* and the creation of new cantos, resulting in the publication of *A Draft of XVI Cantos* by 1925 (Bush 301–3). Duncan's "Often I Am Permitted to Return to a Meadow," citing as its source "the First Beloved," is the initial poem in *The Opening of the Field*, his first volume to realize these poetics. Although in subsequent chapters I engage each of these key poems in relationship to Pound's and Duncan's overall evolving poetry, I begin with these to explore these poetics and their implications for poetry. Both poets came to reject the poetic speaker as a self-dramatizing lover and engaged a poetics described by Duncan as working "with all parts of the poem as *polysemous*, taking each thing of the composition as generative of meaning" (*Bending the Bow* ix).

I then discuss how I am drawing some of my primary concepts from Olson's "Projective Verse" while modifying them. While there is much debate regarding Olson's originality in relationship to Pound and Williams, I argue that Pound's and H.D.'s projective love writing precedes and enables Olson. In abstracting and generalizing the projective and composition by field poetics apart from Olson's specific theorizing of these concepts, I suggest a much longer and more involved development of the projective and composition by field poetics per se. I ask and answer, in part: How important is projective love to a projective poetics, or what does love have to do with projectivism? How pervasive is a more broadly understood projective and field poetics, including a libidinized field poetics, in avant-garde and innovative poetry of different types? In the afterword, I address the relationships between projective love and projective poetics more generally; here, I consider projective love and libidinized field poetics through Olson's apt terminology in "Projective Verse" and explore Olson's useful descriptions beyond his specific engagements.

I then address several theoretical considerations that *The Transmutation of Love and Avant-Garde Poetics* challenges. To understand these authors' poetics, it is most useful to understand the poet as a medium and language itself as a medium. While much description of avant-garde activity has circled around the poet as an agent acting on a material language, in this book, I stress that the poet is as much acted on by language as acting. Moreover, it is precisely in the poet's engagement with the figures and languages of the past that a shift in the entrenched languages of love can occur. While in critical discussions of several of the poets covered in this book the concept of the poet as medium or a description of the poet's orientation to language as mediumistic arises, these descriptions almost always fall outside of specific claims for avant-gardism. Both nominations are often judged as anathema to a poetry that would make itself new. For these poets it was their changed relationship to signifying systems brought on by their being in love that was critical for their transmutation of love and the innovative poetry and poetics that followed.

As early as 1911, Pound in "The Fault of It" notes that despite their compelling quality, lover-beloved poems do not sufficiently "touch us." The poetic speaker recalls writing poems:

Saying: a lovely voice is such and such;
Saying: that lady's eyes were sad last week,
Wherein the world's whole joy is born and dies;

But he repudiates this form:

Ask us no more of all the things ye heard;
We may not speak of them, they touch us nearly. (*Ezra Pound's Poetry and Prose* I: 43)

The poetic speaker rejects poetry that he is moved by because it "touch[es] us nearly," or not enough. In titling his poem "The Fault of It," Pound draws attention to the inadequacy of love poetry for "we" of this time and suggests that this insufficiency creates a "fault," a chasm separating him from the past, to which there is no return. One of the "faults" that Pound may be intimating through his title is the hierarchical relationships in traditional love poetry in which an empowered poetic speaker constitutes his speech in relationship to a comparatively disempowered beloved.

In the decade after he wrote "The Fault of It," Pound discovered a new way to write love in his *Cantos*. The radical difference between his conveyance of love in the early love poetry and in *The Cantos* is evident. In "La Donzella Beata" from Pound's *Hilda's Book*, the poetic speaker celebrates the "transport" that the maid provides him, but he also uses this sublime beloved as a foil to constitute his poetic speech. Addressing his beloved as "Soul," the poetic speaker also refers to the object of this poetic quest as "thing," so beyond any set of sublime vocabularies is this divine entity, now rendered earthly:

Soul
Caught in the rose hued
                    mesh

.   .   .   .

Stooped you again to bear
This thing for me
And be rare light
For me, gold white
In the shadowy path
                    I tread?

But although Pound initiates this poem by placing attention on the poetic speaker's transporting love for his beloved, after this lover addresses her as "Soul," he is left wondering whether she is after all the "bold" maid he seeks:

Surely a bolder maid art thou

Than one in tearful
            fearful longing
That would wait   Lily-
            cinctured
Star-diademmed at the gate
Of high heaven crying
            that I should come
To thee[1]

This poetic speaker, despite his attestation that his beloved is his "Soul," reveals the underlying rhetorical dynamics of traditional love poetry, which enable him to move without pause between adulation and condemnation. Yet, however circumscribed this poem is by its lover-beloved dynamics, it is worth noting that the transport of love to which the poem attests may well give the actual writing in this poem pitch and precision. In the last lines, beginning with "Lily-cinctured," the subtle relationships between the poem's semantics and its visual and aural relations, particularly between its consonance and assonance, presage Pound of *The Cantos*.

In *The Cantos*, erotic transport is not engaged through a poetic speaker as lover, but rather is presented directly, through an expanded set of references.

This writing does not depict the drama of the poetic lover seeking a beloved, but rather conveys a moving speech. In *Canto IV*, an unidentified poetic speaker rallies multiple associations that impart the state of being in love:

> Thus the light rains, thus pours, *e lo soleills plovil*
> That liquid and rushing crystal
> > beneath the knees of the gods.
> Ply over ply, thin glitter of water;
> Brook film bearing white petals.
> The pine at Takasago
> > grows with the pine of Isé!
> The water whirls up the bright pale sand in the spring's mouth
> "Behold the Tree of the Visages!"
> Forked branch-tips, flaming as if with lotus.
> > Ply over ply
> The shallow eddying fluid,
> > beneath the knees of the gods. (*The Cantos* 15)

By foregoing a poetic speaker as an egoistic lover, Pound extends his libidinal energies to a much wider range of references. Pound portrays eros as light turning into crystal, a trope drawn from multiple sources and likely connected to Pound's insistence on actual perceptions. Stephen Hinds notes that in Latin elegiac poetry the presence of the beloved is conveyed through liquid light and crystallized vision (Hinds 125). Kevin Oderman comments on Pound's transitioning light in relationship to erotic depictions throughout *The Cantos*: "The liquidity of light which the lover sees around or before the body of the beloved is figured in many ways, perhaps principally in the verbs—it flows, falls, and pours. And just as [a figure] seems capable of metamorphosing into aura, and flame into light, the liquid light seems to become—again by implicit progression—'crystal'" (120–21).[2] Crystallization is also Stendhal's preferred metaphor for evoking the transformative effects of being in love.

In this passage, as throughout Pound's *Cantos*, the semantics and materialities of language are brought into interactive relationships in ways too multiple and subliminal, finally, to delineate fully. Throughout the passage there is a play between long and short *i*'s, suggestive perhaps of alternating states of desire and satisfaction. "Takasago" and "Isé" are references to pine trees in a Noh drama that symbolize a couple growing old together, demarcated not by a lessening of desire, but by a doubled "pine." "Beneath the knees of the gods" suggests a bodily vulnerability and therefore also tenderness. The phrase "ply over ply" calls up the multiple pleats of a folding skirt or fan, or the qualities of water creasing on itself. The phrase "*e lo soleills plovil*," taken from the troubadour poet Arnaut Daniel and translated earlier by Pound as "the rain falls from the sun," given its multiple *l*'s, creates a visual sense of rain or of a downward striking motion (Terrell 33).

In his early love poems, Robert Duncan manifests a suffering caused not only by frustrated desire but also arguably by the form of love poetry itself. In engaging a love poetry that had been developed primarily through heterosexual relations, his poetic speaker frequently experiences himself as isolated and his same-sex beloved as both overly present and absent. In the following, Duncan's poetic speaker pronounces on his own "monotone":

> O with what pain I watch in my vision
> my proud and reluctant animal self
> where he sings in his lonely monotone; (*Collected Early* 92)

Within this economy the beloved is both a "hoax" and a "drowning place":

> Your image is the daylight hoax
> on which my soul & body wrecks.
> The absence of your body is
> the drowning place, the deep abyss. (55)

Indeed, the possibilities for relationship are everywhere and nowhere:

> Any stranger is dangerous, holding perhaps
> the locks of self, who may release a flood. (32)

While at that time Duncan inscribes this wrenching pain as if it were entirely self-originated, he was writing through poetic traditions that do not adequately speak him as a lover seeking a same-sex beloved. The failure of love here, while depicted as created by the self's own needs and dramas, was also constituted by the inadequacy of the form of traditional love poetry itself: its patriarchal and heterosexual stances and rhetorics could not provide Duncan a precise or enriched way of speaking a same-sex love.

While in Duncan's early poetry he came up against the limitations of a self and a way of writing that isolated him, in his groundbreaking *The Opening of the Field* he discovered rather different economies. Although in his early poems, his poetic speakers are locked into egoistic stances, now the "I" is one entity of several and falls through his poetry. In the first poem of *The Opening of the Field*,

"Often I Am Permitted to Return to a Meadow," the poetic speaker finds transport through a "First Beloved" accompanied by a "Lady":

> Wherefrom fall all architectures I am
> I say are likenesses of the First Beloved
> whose flowers are flames lit to the Lady.
>
> She it is Queen Under The Hill
> whose hosts are disturbances of words within words
> that is a field folded. (7)

In contrast to Duncan's early poetic speaker, who is all too cognizant of singing in "lonely monotone," this poetic speaker shifts between a double "I am /
I say"—an entity falling through the poem's "made place" that "is mine" and
"not mine" (7). This relationship is enacted through the poem's inverted syntax
in which the "I" is as much predicate as subject: from "the First Beloved" "fall
all architectures I am." Duncan's First Beloved is source and object, and as such
recalls the First Beloved in Diotima's speech in Plato's *Symposium*, who serves
as the origin of all "beautiful" practices. Proprioceptive relations are engaged,
as capable as the "hosts" of the "Queen Under The Hill" of moving and disturbing words. While just how the "it . . . Queen" relates to the First Beloved is unclear, they are connected by flowers turning into flames. On the one hand, the
"it . . . Queen" may allude to a love writing in which female muses figure as first
beloveds; on the other hand, this figure may be calling up a queer queen, with
Duncan engaging both possibilities to at once link this figure with homosexuality and keep at bay any easy sense of the fey. "She it" is nameable finally only
as a kind of stutter and points to the gender and sexual aporias through which
Duncan composes this changed love poetry. For Duncan, as Kathleen Fraser describes, the page itself is a "graphically energetic site in which to manifest one's
physical alignment with the arrival of language in the mind" (*Translating* 186).

While in *Canto IV* Pound avoids the first person altogether, Duncan in "Often
I Am Permitted" engages it. However, for neither poet is the poetic speaker an
egoistic, self-dramatizing lover but rather a conveyor of love. Most useful to my
analysis from Olson's "Projective Verse" is his emphasis on the dispensation of
the poet as one in which he or she attempts to get "rid of the lyrical interference
of the individual as ego" and on his discussion of a writing practice in which
"ONE PERCEPTION MUST IMMEDIATELY AND DIRECTLY LEAD TO A FUR-
THER PERCEPTION" (*Selected Writings* 24, 17). This then puts the poet, in Ol-

son's words, "in the open" and within a writing practice in which they can "go by no track other than the one the poem under hand declares for itself." This engagement involves the poet in "the kinetics of the thing": "the syllable, the line, as well as the image, the sound, the sense . . . must be taken up as participants in the kinetic of the poem just as solidly as we are accustomed to take what we call the objects of reality" (16, 20). In such a practice the poet is not only the agent of the poem but also is its medium, and language is both material and medium.

In developing this terminology, I am entering into specific debates around Olson and asking a different set of questions. On the one hand, I am recuperating a rather different sense of Olson's formulations than the Olson dismissed by subsequent generations as being primarily speech-based, and on the other hand, I am suggesting that his poetry has an important origin in Pound's and H.D.'s love writing, among other influences.[3] While Olson urged the importance of speech and breath, he also engaged language as a medium with material properties in his adventurous page compositions and his objectifying of language. Moreover, for Olson, "speech" is a complex term, existing as a set of relations between bodily production and a material language and between language as symbol and as object. Olson's articulation of the projective is useful because it conceptualizes an inceptive language act. Stressing exactly this point, Mackey quotes from Olson's "Human Universe": "The distinction . . . is between language as the act of the instant and language as the act of thought about the instant" (*Discrepant* 122).

In claiming that projective love and libidinized field poetics are directly enabling for a more widely practiced projective and composition by field poetics that extends into the twenty-first century, I seek to draw attention to how these poetics are based in a changed legacy of love poetry. Not by any means is all projective verse projective love poetry. However, as I develop further in the afterword, projective writing as a libidinal and associative delivery emerged in relationship to a changed love writing. So important is the subject of love to poetry that for decades modernism itself was identified with poems that pronounced the failure of love: T. S. Eliot's "The Love Song of J. Alfred Prufrock" and *The Waste Land* (*Collected Poems*) and Pound's pristine *Mauberley*: "Of Eros, a retrospect. // Mouths biting empty air" (*Personae* 198). Yet the difficulty in these early poems that both Eliot and Pound created with respect to their inability to write an immanent and convincing love has been largely ignored for the conflicted ennui of their poetic speakers. Moreover, their very different responses to this dilemma also have been ignored. Eliot wrote less and less poetry, pronouncing in *Four Quartets*: "Words strain. . . will not stay in place / Will not stay still" (7–8; "Burnt Norton," ll. 150, 154–55). Pound discovered a projective love and libidinized field poetics that remains instructive for avant-garde verse to the present time, although he turned his propulsive stream to a blinkered support of Italian fascism. Moreover, his vital love writing in the early *Cantos* was often reduced in the later *Cantos* because of his adherence to repeating ideograms and dicta. However, if Pound's projective love and libidinized field poetics led him to a troubling fascism, for the other poets here, the discovery of this changed way of writing love enabled an enhanced participation in a democratic society and its beliefs in equality.

While Olson's terms provide important articulations for theorizing a projective love and libidinized field poetics, as well as a projective and composition by field poetics, they are also bound and limited by his particular predilections and use of them. Although arguably Olson's statement that perception leads to a further perception implies not only projection but also introjection, Olson placed little emphasis on the latter. Yet, it is precisely through a combined projection and introjection that relations between the symbolic, visual, and aural manifestations of language combine in unpredictable ways and that these poems attain their charged meanings. While Olson stressed that these poetics were to be "INSTANTER," the poets examined in this book write at rather different speeds. Far more important than Olson's emphasis on "IMMEDIATELY" is how an initial projection "LEADS DIRECTLY" and becomes a basis for a subsequent projection (*Selected Writings* 17). Whether fast or slow, this projective practice allows the poet to create his or her poetic response through the impetus of an initiating projection and its introjection in an amplifying and concatenating signification. Indeed, while throughout his writings, Olson emphasized an almost compulsive push, he also articulated different dispensations. In Olson's statement that the poet must listen to what the poem is telling him, to "his hearing" as well as "his breath," he presumed a process of projection and introjection in which the poem's symbolic and material properties can be remixed. Or as Olson cited and commented about projective verse: "Each of these lines is a progressing of both the meaning and the breathing forward, and then a backing up" (*Selected Writings* 23).

While some might confuse projectivist with expressivist poetics, there are important differences. Expressivist poetics conceive of emotional expression as emanating directly from the poetic speaker, whereas projective poetics presume a gap between the poet and his or her utterance. Simply put, projective poetics allow for a poetry writing that is libidinally connected to the poet while simultaneously moving beyond poetic forms that are dependent on a recognizable psychological subject and set of references. Thus, while we can certainly trace objectionable forms of authority and representation in projective poetry, the poetics nonetheless have the capacity to free up energies from preconceived meanings, and thereby to shift emotional realities. Projective poetics enable writers to engage—without professing—received ideas, forms, and representations through a writing whose value resides in the movements and transformations of the writing itself. Bypassing a poetry structured through lovers and beloveds, a projective writing of love has the capacity to engage love as immanent and to alter it through a writing that acts on itself. Projective poets may thus call on love without professing it, writing love in a time of sexuality.

While one might argue that the projective began in Whitman and Shelley, and somewhat differently in Rimbaud and Mallarmé, it is only in twentieth- and twenty-first-century poetics that it yielded a writing in which the poet in producing a propulsive set of languages and objects became intensely interactive with his or her own production. Although in the nineteenth century, poets such as Whitman and Shelley engaged in a kind of cataloging of ongoing associations, they did not relate to language as a symbol or object to the same extent as did the poets covered in this book, nor was their "open field" as "open" as these poets'.[4] And while Rimbaud and to a greater extent Mallarmé projected language as such, they did not transmogrify words. Indeed, despite Shelley's at times almost poststructuralist ideas about language in "Defense of Poetry," his postulate that "the mind in creation is as a fading coal" suggests a different economy of composition than the poets here for whom poetry writing is stimulated by the act of writing itself (503–4). In a projective poetics as practiced in the twentieth century and now in the twenty-first, writing itself inspires writing. Although in some instances, the projection of complex figures provides the primary modality for this writing, often language itself is the focus, a potential object in the compositional process, such that its symbolic and material properties are remixed in the "INSTANTER" "heat" or the "cool observation" of the author's ongoing poetic production.[5] Introjected figures and language itself have the capacity of intervening in a poet's habitual emotional and thought processes as the poets cathect these through their changed social and historical orientations. Indeed, while most of these poets work between these modalities, H.D.'s work is much defined through her introjection of mythic figures, whereas Fraser's late work interacts most assiduously with her projections onto the compositional space of the page as well as language itself.

The concept of language as a medium directly aids an understanding of the synergistic relations between being in love and writing love, which have engaged love poets throughout the centuries. But whereas traditional love poets are primarily engaged by language's symbolic meanings, the poets examined in this book are responsive to the entire spectrum of language as a visual, aural, and symbolic medium. In perhaps his most famous sonnet to Laura, Petrarch associates the sounding of her name with the poetic laurels that he seeks to win and reveals how a heightened love writing may break words into syllables that tell of immortality:

And so, to "LAUd" and to "REvere" the word
Itself instructs whenever someone calls you,
O lady worthy of all praise and honour,

Unless, perhaps, Apollo be incensed
That "morTAL" tongue be so presumptuous
To speak of his eternally green boughs. (24)

While this poem certainly signals, as many have maintained, Petrarch's self-love—while professedly seeking love, he is also after poetic laurels—this poetic speaker creates his poetry through a language that, acting on him, reveals a secondary substrate of syllabic meaning. Although love poets of the past were sensitive to the mediumistic effects of the languages of love, for the most part they marshaled their love energies by binding these to a poetic speaker as lover. The poets discussed in this book, however, unleash these verbal energies and their references in a libidinized field poetics.

Giorgio Agamben in *The End of the Poem* turned to the Italian love poetry of *dolce stil nuovo* as a corrective to current theories of language in which the enthusiasm for the signifier could bring with it a reductive engagement with language. Addressing what he regards as a problematic "theology of the signifier," Agamben is preoccupied with the moment of speech itself, with an inceptive speech in which event and utterance are inseparable—or what he calls the "primordial experience of the event of language" (55). He engages love poetry to locate a speech in which "what is lived and what is poeticized . . . [are] truly only what is made in speech" (81). Focusing on *dolce stil nuovo* poetry and its relationship to an emergent vernacular language, Agamben comments that love writing is a kind of "shamanism" by which the poet experiences "the indissoluble unity of lived experience and what is poeticized" (94).[6] As a primary example of this speech, he refers to Dante's statement that he writes as "Love dictates" (94). In such speech, Agamben emphasizes, "poetry and life are united . . . in a medium. This medium is language" (93). He quotes Mallarmé to suggest something of the nature of this event of language: "Words rise up unaided. . . . Our mind . . . sees words not in their usual order, but in projection (like the walls of a cave), so long as that mobility which is their principle lives on, that part of speech which is not spoken" (46).

The cultural critic Steve Shaviro has noted with considerable ambivalence how the refusal to distinguish language from an empirical realm creates "a radical mutation in the space of our understanding" (186). Shaviro is not drawing attention to the commonplace presumption that language constructs reality, but rather is looking at a dispensation in the subject him- or herself in which language is inseparable from reference—a means of neither expression nor construction—but itself constitutive of reality. In making this point, Shaviro draws on Foucault's comments in *The Order of Things* regarding the double aspect of language as a cultural transcendent that preexists changing social configurations and as a mediator of what Marxists might call "the real conditions" of our existence: "Man is a strange empirical transcendental doublet since he is a being such that knowledge will be attained in him of what renders all knowledge possible" (Foucault, *Order of Things* 318–22). The very refusal to separate language from empirical existence is likely at play in poetic experiences of "dictation" as well as an "outside."[7] Indeed, this coalescing between language and reference likely creates poets' experiences of the synergies between being in love and writing love. That is, if being in love leads to writing love poetry, and if writing love poetry intensifies this love, then love and the languages of love are experienced as one and the same.

Pound, Duncan, and Mackey all find the concept of language as a medium most useful in understanding and conveying their poetics. In his essay "Vorticism," Pound initially claims that there are poets of "conceiving" and "receiving," and then he delineates two types of artists: "the artist who moves through his art, to whom it is truly a 'medium' or means of expression; and [. . .] the mediumistic artist, the one who can only exist in his art, who is passive to impulse, who approaches more or less nearly to the 'sensitive' or to the somnambulistic medium." On the heels of this assertion, Pound corrects himself, stating that there are not two kinds of artists, but rather different "faculties" within artists, singling out being sensitive to the "somnambulistic medium" as a "most useful part of the artist's equipment" (*Ezra Pound's Poetry and Prose* 2: 14). For Mackey, it is precisely Duncan's engaging of "the medium qua medium" that draws him to Duncan, noting his "sense of susceptibility, of being subject-to," which is also a useful description of Mackey's own writing (*Discrepant* 98–99). Mackey insists on the symbolic nature of language in an environment in which the materiality of language is just surfacing as the commanding intellectual and poetic paradigm of this era. In his much-anthologized essay "Sound and Sentiment, Sound and Symbol," first published in *Callaloo* and included in Charles Bernstein's *The Politics of Poetic Form*, Mackey links "orphism" with "orphanism" and argues by way of analogy that language like music is symbolic by virtue of the fact that it does not exist solely as a set of material sounds. As a meaningful set of arranged sounds that connect us to the "invisible," both music and poetry as material manifestations are cut off from what they express, a condition that intensifies their "speaking" of a lost or failed love (*Discrepant* 231–34).

Among the poets discussed in this book, Robert Duncan pushed furthest just what it might mean to conceive of language as a medium. For Duncan, writing "bring[s] a foreign element into action." He explains: "The weaving or the painting or the writing is 'subjective.' . . . The 'subject matter' is 'objective,' is some thing or event . . . we reach out to capture to draw into a texture with ourselves. In the medium, our work and this thing becomes mixed, changed then. A ground appears as a new condition of what we are doing" (*The H.D. Book* 237). By projecting and introjecting figures, the poet changes the "ground" that is him- or herself and potentially the "ground" of his or her cultural and social reality. In *The Truth of Life and Myth*, Duncan draws out the implications of this merger between subjective and objective, suggesting a link between poetry, shamanism, and psychosis, along with other outlier states of being: "When a man's life becomes totally so informed that every bird and leaf speaks to him and every happening has meaning, he is considered to be *psychotic*. The shaman and the inspired poet, who take the universe to be alive, are brothers germane of the mystic and the paranoiac. We at once seek a meaningful life and dread *psychosis*, 'the principle of life'" (*Truth* 7). In linking "psychosis" with "the principle of life," Duncan conveys how language as naming can cause reference itself to shift. And by calling "psychosis" "the principle of life," Duncan conveys the extreme mobility between word and reference that a creative response can enable—with the fate of whether the poet is a genius or a schizophrenic hanging on the thin thread of whether the shift in reality he or she presents is one others are willing to engage.

To enlist the concept of avant-garde in relationship to the transmutation of love may be a perversity. Its militaristic and futuristic orientations have led to the jettisoning of this concept by many critics. Yet, avant-garde remains the most recognizable term to signal an art that is deliberate in its efforts to intervene in its historical conditions by altering both the form and the content of art—or, more broadly, its "how" and "what." Indeed, the "how" of art is a capacious term, designating *how* it is produced, *how* it is disseminated, and *how* it is received. While different avant-gardes have concentrated their work on rather different hows, this avant-garde specifically addresses how art is produced *through* sexual love in response to changing dispensations of sexual love in the culture at large. By discovering a different way to write love—shifting their erotic energies away from a poetic speaker as lover and onto their poems' others and languages—the poets create a changed love.

In Jochen Schulte-Sasse's "Foreward: Theory of Modernism versus Theory of the Avant-Garde" in Bürger's *Theory of the Avant-Garde*, Schulte-Sasse modifies Bürger's idea that an avant-garde must change society directly by shifting Bürger's emphasis on social existence to "social practice." Schulte-Sasse names the potential rupture that submerged, unarticulated experiences can have on hegemonic social formations as key for avant-garde activity. He locates the possibility of this intervention in the presumption that there "exist[s] a *material* organization of social reality external to language and imprinted on our psyche (and physical being), written into our existence via the mechanisms of material as well as cultural reproduction" (xxvii). Utilizing Walter Benjamin's analysis of how the surrealist poets, writing through "intoxication" (whether induced by ecstatic states, alcohol, or drugs), were able to relate to "objects" differently because of how "intoxication sharpens the senses," Schulte-Sasse suggests that this very alteration of the apprehension of the "concrete" can lead to a change in social forms and languages. Drawing attention to Benjamin's sense of surrealism's revolutionary potential, Schulte-Sasse maintains that the prevailing evaluation of surrealism as having value only as an immediate excitement of the senses is far too limited. Schulte-Sasse partially analyzes and quotes from Benjamin's essay "Surrealism: The Last Snapshot of the European Intelligentsia": "The intense experience of intoxication sharpens the sense for those 'materialistic inspirations'—a term meaning nothing other than the sudden transformation of sensuous-material experiences into forms of awareness. Avant-garde works capable of such inspirations 'bring the immense forces of "atmosphere" concealed in these [concrete] things [of our life world] to the point of explosion'" (xlv).

Schulte-Sasse brings to the forefront Benjamin's famous question in "One-Way Street": "What form do you suppose a life would take that was determined at a decisive moment precisely by the street song last on everyone's lips?" He analyzes the significance of this question: Benjamin "opposes the smothering of the concrete by an abstract pretending itself to be concrete," so that the bodily response necessary for a revolutionary response becomes "innervated" (xlv). Similarly, for the poets examined in this book, the writing through love, being in love, can be seen not only to make way for erotic intensity but to alter hegemonic forms, especially as they concern sex, sexuality, and love making. Indeed, if the surrealists sought to be "intoxicated," the modernist poets aimed to be "in love," as in the *cras amet* verse that serves as an admonishing refrain for both H.D. and Pound: "Let those love now who never loved before; let those who always loved, now love all the more" (H.D. *Paint* 11–12). The surrealists intended to write a different poetry through changed relationships to objects; the poets here sought to make it new by unbinding sexual love from dyadic lover-beloved and heteronormative patriarchal economies.

One of the commonalities shared by all poetry in the twentieth century that has been accorded avant-garde status is that it promotes a present-tense composition, or an inceptive speech. Indeed, poetry that makes much of how it is a present-tense formation—despite differences between how this present composition is understood and practiced—is often recognized as avant-garde because it finds the act of composing in the present necessary to the recasting, or reconstruction, of representation and of language itself. The futurists, the Dadaists, the vorticists, the surrealists, the New Americans, the Beats, the New York School, the L=A=N=G=U=A=G=E poets, Flarf, and Conceptual Writing—all engage in different practices of what it means to write in the present, having to do with how the poetic speaker and the act of poetry writing are conceived as well as what aspects of contemporary culture are engaged. The poets in *The Transmutation of Love and Avant-Garde Poetics* can be distinguished from other avant-garde poets by their refusal, for the most part, of discrete or self-reflexive subjectivities and of chance-driven procedures, and their use of what is often referred to as impersonal poetic speakers, or what in more contemporary parlance is called posthuman subjectivities. By refusing the definitive subjectivity of even an uncertain or "loosened" subject as well as the nonsubjectivity of chance-driven procedures, these authors compose a poetry that is motivated by libidinal desires, in which perception leads directly to perception, and language to further language. They do not write *about* life but *of* life. They make their own often passionate or emotional energies defining for their projective verse or, as Olson put it, "A poem is energy transferred from where the poet got it [. . .] by way of the poem itself to, all the way over to, the reader" (*Selected Writings* 16).

By writing love through states of limerence during historical epochs of radical social change, these poets are able to cathect their poems' others and languages differently. Their present-tense commitment to poetry, to not writing "about" a world that is separate from their artistic expression but creating an inspired writing inseparable from their perception, emotion, and cognition, is their avant-garde practice—a practice that is set against an instrumentality of politics, ethics, or sense-making as preceding the poetic act itself. These poets make their own intense responses, their own sexual love for others, determining for their poetic composition—and these responses have the capacity to shift representation because they originate in sexual desire and being enamored.

2

Being in Love and Writing Love

There is no act, just as there is no sexual act, outside of love, for it is in the constituent violence of its field that the subject's structure is shaken, drives and ideals included.

—Julia Kristeva, *Tales of Love*

Although poets frequently have attested to the synergistic relationship between being in love and writing love, little theoretical attention has been given to this subject. In this chapter I explore theories that provide understanding of the generative powers of sexual love and that correct for its dismissal and for misapprehensions that have arisen around key sexual love theories. Much critical and theoretical analysis of love poetry in the last several decades has been concerned with the so-called self-love of love poetry and its gender and sexual hierarchies. That analysis has put much attention on the epistemology of the desiring subject and less focus on the phenomenon of sexual love and, consequently, has tended to shore up dichotomies between sexual desire and sexual love.

While there are important differences in the ways that love poetry has been written over the centuries, no more so than among the poets studied here, there are many commonalities. Sexual love is experienced as a sustained desire for a single beloved that is often so overwhelming that the passion and feeling for this other overpower sexual desire itself. This love invades or floods the subject with an infusion of otherness that supplants the subject's usual egoistic moorings and changes his or her orientation toward otherness itself. As Kristeva states, "In love, 'I' has been an *other*" (4). Or, as Duncan writes, "There is a love in which we are outcast and vagabond from what we are that we call 'falling in love'" (*The H.D. Book* 578). In this state, the subject is transported outside of or beyond him- or herself and wishes to convey this transmutation in writing. Earlier love poets rebind these energies to a poetic speaker as lover, but the poets covered by this book unleash these energies in a projective love and libidinized field poetics.

In the twentieth and twenty-first centuries, numerous dichotomies between sex and love form, including between entire areas of study and most notably between object relations and Lacanian theories. For object relation theorists, an overly intense sexual desire for a specific beloved bespeaks an inadequate response to this other and to otherness itself. In *The Bonds of Love*, Jessica Benjamin, ostensibly setting out to address both sexual desire and object love, ends up subordinating the former to moralizing statements about the best way to relate to others.[1] For Lacan, intense sexual love, while motivated by a "real" desire, is caught up in illusory formations. Lacan locates sexual desire and soulful love, respectively, in his bifurcated symbolic and imaginary realms, and he describes courtly love as "an altogether refined way of making up for the absence of sexual relation by pretending that it is we who put an obstacle to it" (*Feminine* 141). Although Lacan notes that "it is in the dialectic of the demand for love and the test of desire that development is ordered," he maintains that it is precisely what the love object does not possess, what he or she can never give the lover, that the lover seeks (*Ecrits* 289).

Although object relations theories have had some play in literary analysis, Lacan and sex theorists who validate sex apart from love have been far more influential. Indeed, literary critics, finding much compatibility in analyses that focus exclusively on desire and on language and not on the body and love, simply ignore the dispensation of the subject who experiences "being in love" as a physical, emotional, *and* language phenomenon. An excellent example of the far-ranging influence of Lacanian theory is *Ovid's Poetics of Illusion* in which Philip Hardie analyzes Ovid's writing as motivated entirely by a supplementary desire. Asserting that poets use language to overcome the loss of an illusory presence, Hardie insists on a desire that is linked to absence. He calls directly on Lacan in creating his theory: "For Lacan, the human subject is born out of division and alienation . . . and driven on by desire of the other in the impossible search for the recovery of a lost state of wholeness, a delusional pursuit whose search is in the order of the imaginary." Hardie contends that the names of beloveds in classical love lyrics are taken from earlier love poetry and have no relation to actual beloveds. Love writing itself is a response to "absent" "puellae" (31–34). Hardie finds Ovid's initial love writing compounded in *Metamorphoses* in which "the full presence of the object of desire is again and again eluded" (30).

But Lacan and other theorists of desire and sex who would reject love or ignore it as an insufficiently motivating phenomenon raise basic questions: Why do lovers seek specific beloveds? Why do they persist against all odds when the pursuit of love causes them untold pain? These theories suggest that Leonardo da Vinci did not know what he was talking about when he claimed, "great love springs from great knowledge of the beloved object" (qtd. in Freud 449). And that Stendhal's evocatively described process of "crystallization" is mere illusion. While the attack on love has brought out some defenders, most notably Barthes in *A Lover's Discourse*, in which he engages multiple, sometimes conflicting, dis-

courses of love, eros, and sex, Barthes also sustains a strong Lacanian orientation. Rather than the beloved, the lover repeatedly seeks an "Image-repertoire"
(4). More recently, Cristina Nehring in *A Vindication of Love* directly contests the
presumption that love creates at best an illusory projection onto a beloved and
claims that being in love may be "the only state of mind in which one is entirely
and uncompromisingly open to another person" (18).

I initiate an inquiry into the generativity of sexual love with Plato because of
how in the *Phaedrus* and the *Symposium* he engages the ways that erotic energies
based in love for a beloved, or a First Beloved, have special properties of extension. Plato's ideas contrast with recent theories of sublimation, with which they
are often confused, since they entail neither Freud's concept of sublimation as a
"rerouting" of the sexual instinct nor, as is commonly thought, the suppression
of sexual desire. I find, as Anne Carson has analyzed, Plato's emphasis on "the
moment of *mania* when Eros enters the lover" as leading to transfixing change
and erotic extension to be far more suggestive than critiques that assume that
what Plato is really after is either a transcendence of the body or a metaphysics
of presence (Carson 153).

I then turn to Freud's distinction between ego libido and object libido and
how these different orientations affect the subject. For Freud, the state of being in love is one in which object cathexis leads to a lessening of egoistic impulses. Freud not only maintained that being in love is "the highest phase" of
object libido, but he also delineated how diverse subjectivities form in relationship to different kinds of object cathexes (547). Freud's concepts of "mourning"
and "melancholia" are most useful in a criticism addressing unrequited or lost
love. Parallel concepts of the "enchantment" and "mania" of a requited or hopeful love, extrapolating from Freud's few remarks on the state of being in love,
can also be fleshed out and are particularly illuminating for the poets considered by this book. Although Freudian theory has been most instrumental in initiating dichotomous understandings of love and sex, Freud's theoretical writings
do not consistently sustain this division. In Freud, there is considerable engagement with sexual love, but much slippage occurs in his naming of sex and love
since often in his nomination of one he also intends the other. Further, in Freudian theory investigations into sexual desire and object relations are deeply intertwined. Freud differentiates ego libido and object libido in his essay "On Narcissism," an inquiry that has been utilized by theorists and critics who would
consign love poetry to being little more than a form of self-love. Yet in doing
so, they interpret him reductively, paying no attention to Freud's concept of primary narcissism as basic to all subject constitution. Although Freud's concepts
of object cathexis and object libido have been utilized in diverse theoretical en-

deavors, particularly in queer analyses of object choice, they have been little consulted in analyses of love poetry.[2]

I conclude the chapter by considering the "turn to language" in the latter part of the twentieth century in relationship to Freudian and Lacanian theories, arguing for the usefulness of Freud's complex sense of diverse dispensations of language over Lacan's split between imaginary and symbolic modes. I find Freud's inquiry into the relationship between subject constitution and language expression valuable precisely because of the ways he registers vicissitudes in language use—a sense of language echoed in Lacan's distinctions between "full" and "empty" speech. I query the similarities and differences between the poets' process-based projective love writing and Freud's and Lacan's process-based psychoanalysis. Both practices place considerable value in the temporal unfolding of the subject's invested speech and in associational relations. Yet despite these broad similarities, there are important differences. Freud and Lacan maintain the value of their scientific, analytic approaches over the compromised virtues of an art based in "pleasure" and "ensoulment" and engage the process of psychoanalysis with exclusive attention to the "cure" of an individual subject. The poets examined in *The Transmutation of Love and Avant-Garde Poetics* alter symbolic meanings through the inventive movement of their writing. It is precisely because these authors form their poetry through sexual love that they have the capacity to shift the formation of love—a creative capacity to alter meaning itself that neither Freudian nor Lacanian psychoanalysis claims. The poets' amplifying and concatenating works create tensile connections and subtle alterations as they write love, through object cathexis.

Erotic Extensions

Although commenters on Plato's erotic theories sometimes conflate them with Freud's theories of sublimation, there are important differences. For Plato, an enamored subject transmutes this enamoring into other things, including "beautiful" practices and "speech-making." For Freud, sublimation, as he sometimes defined it and as Leo Bersani developed it, is a rerouting of sexual desire into intellectual and artistic activities that do not have a sexual aim (Freud 452). However, as Bersani has analyzed at some length, Freud urged one set of ideas regarding sublimation but was contradictory in his application of them.[3] In the essay "Leonardo da Vinci and a Memory of His Childhood," Freud insists on his rerouting theory of sexual energies apart from any repression or love interest, but then takes as his example da Vinci's *Mona Lisa*, which he suggests is a great work of art not only because of how da Vinci's sublimated sexual energies led to its creation but because of how da Vinci's displaced love for his mother directly informed the painting. For love poets, Plato's theories of eros are directly explanatory in contrast to Freud's concept of sublimation as a rerouting of sexual desire, since Plato understands love energies themselves as prone to extension (443–80).

Two of Plato's most famous dialogues on love, the *Phaedrus* and Diotima's speech in the *Symposium*, address how love for a beloved leads to an extension of erotic energies. In the *Phaedrus*, Plato demonstrates how making speeches *about* love, when love itself is not respected, leads to a base composition, whereas a writing *through* love that pays respect to eros and draws inspiration from a present beloved is worthy of its subject. Throughout the dialogue, Socrates playfully remarks that it is Phaedrus's presence that has inspired him to such a lofty discourse. Diotima in the *Symposium* provides two different models of eros, one that recounts love's movement as a phenomenon of the present, shuttling between "Resource" and "Poverty," and one that tells of its continuance over time, of love as initiated through a "first beloved" and the extension of this love into "beautiful" practices.

In the *Phaedrus*, Socrates proclaims that "the greatest goods come to us through madness that is given as a divine gift" and that "more perfect and more valuable [is] the madness that comes from a god than the sanity that is of human origin" (102; 244a, 244d). Socrates describes four types of madness, elevating the madnesses of the muses and of "Love" as the highest types: "A third kind of possession and madness comes from the Muses. It seizes a gentle, inexperienced soul and awakens within it a Bacchanalian enthusiasm for lyrical songs and other kinds of poetry." He further enjoins, "If anyone comes to the halls of poetry without the madness of the Muses, convinced that technique alone will make him a good poet, both the poetry of this man who is in possession of his senses and the man himself will fall short of perfection and be eclipsed by the poetry of those who are mad" (103; 245a). Plato's fourth kind of madness is of love: "love is not sent from the gods for the benefit of the lover and the beloved. We must prove the opposite, that this sort of madness is given by the gods for the greatest possible good fortune" (103; 245b). Later in the dialogue, Socrates lists different kinds of madness and places on his highest rung those "devoted to the Muses and the affairs of love" while placing on a lower rung the "poet or someone else involved in the imitative arts" (106; 248d–e). Plato seems to separate out two different kinds of inspired responses—an emanation that is imitative and one that is directly inspired by love and the muses. While, for instance, this valuation might place poetry higher than novel writing insofar as the latter has a greater basis in mimesis, it would also put projective love writing above traditional lover-beloved forms since the latter are comparatively more mimetic.

The *Phaedrus* is both an inquiry into love and an inquiry into exposition, claiming that both are best realized as present-tense undertakings. It inveighs against a prescribed argument and elevates oral dialogue. Indeed, what Socrates laments in a rhetorically driven speech and in written discourse is a loss of the present—a present that for Socrates in this dialogue is animated by a respect for the divinity of Eros and by an attraction to Phaedrus. In a discussion of this dialogue in *Eros the Bittersweet*, Anne Carson stresses that a defining aspect of Plato's eros is that it happens in the present: "the moment of *mania* when Eros enters the lover, is for Socrates the single most important moment to confront and grasp. 'Now' is a gift of the gods and an access onto reality. To address yourself to the moment while Eros glances into your life and to grasp what is happening in your soul at that moment is to begin to understand how to live." She further comments, "Eros' mode of take over is an education: it can teach you the real nature of what is inside you. Once you glimpse that, you can begin to become it" (153). She elaborates that this is "a glimpse of the immortal 'beginning' that is a soul," where "'then' disappears" (157, 158). As such this "now" has the capacity of "prolonging itself over a whole life" (153). Carson summarizes, "Socrates conceives of wisdom as something alive, a 'living breathing word.'" It is from within this economy that Socrates warns, "you keep your mind to yourself at the cost of closing out the gods" (155).

The dramatic situation of the *Phaedrus* amplifies these ideas. Throughout the dialogue, Socrates claims that it is Phaedrus who has moved him to create his fanciful and inspired speech, commenting that the very rhythms of his speech change when Phaedrus is near. Initially listening to and then delivering a mock speech of his own against love, Socrates interjects that he has received a warning that he has offended the god of love: "Just as I was about to cross the stream my familiar daimonic sign came to me. . . . I seem then to hear a voice forbidding me to leave before I purify myself, as I have committed an offense against the divine." Socrates contends, "If Love is a god or something divine, as he surely is, he couldn't be evil, but both speeches just now spoke of him as though he were such." Socrates describes how the poet Stesichorus was struck blind because of an invective against Helen, but through his *Palinode*, his recantation, "recovered his sight." Socrates announces that before suffering any punishment from speaking "ill of Love," he will render his own recantation (100–101; 242c–243a).

Plato's *Phaedrus* is the philosophical treatise through which Derrida in *Dissemination* advances his critique of the "metaphysics of presence," in which he upholds the materiality of writing in Western culture as having been suppressed and debased. While Derrida criticizes the "phallologocentric" author of the *Phaedrus*, he does not address Socrates's claim in that dialogue that his own philosophical discourse on love succeeds when made in the throes of love rather than when driven by rhetorical argument. While, for Derrida, Plato's rejection of what

Derrida conceives as a material writing is most limiting, Anne Carson suggests that the advent of writing during Plato's time was likely experienced as an impoverishment. Carson emphasizes that Plato's main problem with writing in the *Phaedrus* is the "fix[ing] of words permanently outside the stream of time" (130). She analyzes how reading the written word reorients perceptions and restricts the senses: "As an individual reads and writes, he gradually learns to close or inhibit the input of his senses, to inhibit or control the responses of his body, so as to train energy and thought upon the written words. He resists the environment outside him by distinguishing and controlling the one inside him" (44). For the twentieth-century poets examined in this book, the sense of language's materiality is rather different than Plato's response to the written word as explained by Carson—a historic difference completely ignored by Derrida. For these poets, language's materialities have the potential of disrupting a transparent and repressive reading process. That the poets examined in this book give considerable articulation in their compositions to the aural and visual materialities of language reveals a strong desire to break through a conventional literacy that would give prominence to language's stabilized, fixed meanings apart from a changing present. For these poets, a mediumistic language whose morphemes and phonemes become pronounced is an effect of eros, not its suppression. Indeed, such a language, while an implicit argument against a stabilized "metaphysics," enlists the presencing of a present to disrupt it.

In Diotima's speech in the *Symposium*, Socrates offers two seemingly different models of love or eros to "describe Love and his character, and then his works" (39; 201d). The first provides a sense of love's "character" as shuttling endlessly between various kinds of "Poverty" and "Resource," such as badness and goodness, ugliness and beauty, mortality and immortality (41–42; 203c–204b). In this description, love's presence as a continuous immanence and intervening conveyer is emphasized. In the second model, which attends to love's "works," Socrates offers the famous staircase vision, in which love for one beautiful body leads to love of multiple beautiful bodies and ultimately to an eternal beauty. Midway up this staircase are multiple endeavors now infused with love: "from beautiful bodies to beautiful practical endeavors, from practical endeavors to beautiful examples of understanding" (48–49; 211c–211e). On the surface, it may seem difficult to draw together these two models of love, to combine "an intermediary that will never be abandoned" with this path of ascension.[4] But if we interpret the first as a kind of immanence and the second as transcendence, they are brought much closer together, especially if transcendence, rather than being defined as a form of repressive sublimation, is understood to mark an "exceptional difference" from normative experience, a kind of radiant presence.[5]

In a discussion of the *Symposium* in "Sorcerer Love," Luce Irigaray draws attention to what she regards as its problematic split—between love as a conveyer and love as telos—but then retracts this evaluation. She notes how Diotima's definition of love as a conveyer is demonic in that it sustains a "permanent passage between mortal and immortal." And, conversely, she analyzes Diotima's staircase vision as promoting a concept of love as involved in a telos that transcends the mere mortal state of being in love. For Irigaray, Diotima's initial definition of love as a mediator makes way for the possibility of enchantment between lover and beloved, whereas the staircase vision ultimately repudiates mortal love. Irigaray contrasts these two visions of love, the one an endless "state of becoming" and the other "the search for endless time, imperishable glory" (21, 28). In initially rejecting the second part of Diotima's speech and not inquiring into how the two models may relate to each other, Irigaray does not consider how both are models of sexual love as a kind of extension. However, after making her case against the second model of eros, Irigaray makes way for just this possibility: "Perhaps Diotima is still saying the same thing. But in the second part, her method runs the risk of being reduced to the metaphysics that is getting set up." Irigaray postulates that Diotima may in fact be contemplating "that which confounds the opposition between immanence and transcendence. As an always already sensible horizon on the basis of which everything would appear. But one would have to go back over everything to discover it in its enchantment" (33). Irigaray thus suggests that both models may make way for erotic continuance and extension: "to fall in love, to become divine or immortal, is to enter into an 'intermediary current'" (29–30).

Object Cathexis

Freud's theories of object cathexis are most revealing for understanding how being in love may create special dispensations in the poet. In his essay "On Narcissism" he says that "not until there is object-cathexis is it possible to discriminate sexual energy—the libido—from an energy of the ego-instincts." And he notes, "The highest phase of development of which object-libido is capable is seen in the state of being in love, when the subject seems to give up his own personality in favour of an object-cathexis" (547). Freud theorizes an "antithesis between ego-libido and object-libido. The more the one is employed, the more the other becomes depleted" (547). In love, lovers suffer a profound loss of ego libido to object libido, leading to the familiar tropes of the lover who feels himself to be "nothing" in relationship to his beloved or a "slave" to his beloved. While Freud claims that men, in particular, are prone to engaging in this "overvaluation" of their love objects, he also notes that women can be similarly disposed. (Freud's analysis of women's love inclinations generally tend to ignore women as erotic agents and to underestimate the intensity of their responses, as has been discussed elsewhere.) While in unrequited love relations "not being loved lowers the self regarding feelings," being loved raises them (561). Although in both requited and unrequited love considerable ego libido shifts to object libido, in requited love some of the object libido can return to the ego libido. Freud postulates that "a real happy love corresponds to the primal condition in which object-libido and ego-libido cannot be distinguished" (561).

Drawing on distinctions Freud makes in "On Narcissism" and other writings, Elizabeth Grosz comments on how Freud developed concepts of a "realistic ego" and a "narcissistic ego": "Where the realistic ego stands out over and above the two combatants (reality and the id), the narcissistic ego cannot readily be separated from its own internal processes (e.g., the flow of libido) or from external objects." She elaborates: "the narcissistic ego is an entirely fluid, mobile, amorphous series of identifications, internalization of images/perceptions invested with libidinal cathexes" (28–29). In a projective love writing, the poet drawing on object libido writes from what Grosz describes here as the field of "the narcissistic ego." Importantly, for Freud, narcissism is not a narrowly construed self-love, but is basic to all subject constitution and is the "libidinal complement" to "the instinct for self-preservation" (Freud 546).

In differentiating ego libido from object libido, Freud postulates that object libido is necessary lest the subject become ill. Freud notes that the "damming-up of libido" is inherently unpleasurable, and healthy people seek to remedy this state. Freud summarizes, "A strong egoism is a protection against falling ill, but in the last resort we must begin to love in order not to fall ill, and we are bound to fall ill, if in consequence of frustration, we are unable to love" (552–53). Indeed, Freud suggests that artistic creation as an extension of libidinal energies is at least a partial remedy to these dammed energies, connecting sublimation itself, at least in this essay, to object libido. He cites the poet Heinrich Heine, whose verse is translated and paraphrased in *The Freud Reader* as "illness was no doubt the final cause of the whole urge to create. By creating, I could recover; by creating, I became healthy" (553).

While Freud in "Mourning and Melancholia" defines object cathexis in relationship to lost or unrequited love, he only minimally investigates successful or hopeful cathexes, or the state of being in love. Freud showed limited interest in the state of being in love and linked it, at times, with states of insanity (385). In "Mourning and Melancholia," Freud presents mourning as a process of lessening one's attachment to an object over time, so that one can attach to another object. Through repeated approaches to the object, through remembering him or her, the subject gradually frees libidinal energies from their cathexis in this other. In melancholia, the process of detachment from an object does not occur, and instead the subject turns the beloved into an "ideal" to which he or she must abject themselves. This object now becomes a critical standard for self-reproach because the subject does not deem himself as living up to, or as worthy of, his ideal. In identifying his ego with the abandoned object, "the shadow of the object [falls] upon the ego," and the latter is now judged as if it were a lack, for which only the rejecting ideal can compensate. Freud summarizes, "in this way an object-loss was transformed into an ego-loss and the conflict between the ego and the loved person into a cleavage between the critical activity of the ego and the ego as altered by identification" (584–89). In states of melancholia, the egoistic lover is propelled outside of himself, often filling this void with an ever more entrenched ego ideal.

From Freud's analysis of grief and melancholia, it is possible to see how the experience of an unrequited or unavailable love could lead to a writing in which the poetic speaker through positioning himself as the lover enhances his capacity to write poetry. In the case in which object loss is responded to in ways similar to those of mourning, the poet's love writing could initially sustain or even intensify feelings of love, but eventually those feelings would lessen as the poet comes to transfer energies devoted to his beloved back to himself, or changes object libido back into ego libido. In the case of love writing that engages melancholic modes, the lover in failed pursuit of his love object is locked into an eternal return of his beloved, as the poetic speaker in seemingly self-limiting or self-destructive acts shores up a self-pronouncing superego. In both cases, an initial love writing would lead to more love writing as the poet increases his love by repeatedly seeking a beloved while simultaneously experiencing a diminishment of his ego libido from this failed love quest. Writing successful poems, the poet replenishes his ego; yet, in doing so, he reinitiates the cause for his loss of "self-regarding feelings" and therefore increases the need to write poetry—easing the wounds of love as he reconstitutes them. When the lover's loss of the love object resembles mourning, this sense of loss eventually lessens, and the poet forgoes writing further love poems, at least to this particular beloved. In the situation in which the poet's response is melancholic, he is locked into his poetic production through alternating gains and losses, triggered by an aggrandized superego contending with a diminished ego. Freud notes that melancholia is characterized by "an insistent communicativeness which finds satisfaction in self-exposure"—which may be the melancholic's way of getting out of himself (585).

In *The Gendering of Melancholia*, Juliana Schiesari notes how Petrarch in his perpetual seeking for a dead Laura is exemplary of a melancholic artist. Schiesari paraphrases Freud: "The melancholic [might be] someone who suffers from unrequited love but who then finds satisfaction by abusing part of the self as if that part of the self were the disappointing object" (47). Schiesari claims that Freud's analysis of melancholia is dependent on a literary tradition that accords the male melancholic artist a special access to "truth," which is not available to the merely mourning, or depressive, female artist and which as a gendered, privileged "affect" continues to give the male writer "a privileged position within literary, philosophical, and artistic canons" (11). For Schiesari, this affect is gendered because of men's and women's different relationships to signifying economies, such that men's melancholia is valued precisely because it is uncompromising and women's mourning is disregarded because it is transient. While Schiesari analyzes this cultural status, I suggest that women (and other writers marginalized through race or sexuality) cannot take on melancholic stances in love poetry with the same unspoken power as that of white male love poets because of how this affect depends on the possibilities of positioning oneself as an entitled poetic lover. While all the male poets considered in this book at least engage the possibilities of taking on the stance of the melancholic lover, they move beyond it. Indeed, none of these poets, with the exception of Pound, can constitute themselves as entitled lovers in quite the same socially or culturally empowered way as do white male heterosexual lovers, however much they may experience abiding loss in their love relations.

While Freud's theories of unsuccessful love—of mourning and melancholia—are useful for analyzing love poetry, Freud is far less specific about the effects of a hopeful or successful love. If in the writing of unrequited love, the lover's position becomes pronounced, with the superego sometimes getting in on the act, requited love may well encourage a weakening of the lover's position as isolated and bounded. Indeed, in a requited love, or one felt to have the potential to be successful, the lover simply finds more satisfaction or reward in object libido. The persistent trope of unity between lovers may find considerable exegesis in this relationship, shifting in its significance in different kinds of love relations. On the one hand, in Freud's version of "a real happy love" that "corresponds to the primal condition in which object-libido and ego-libido cannot be distinguished," the illusion of fusion between the lovers may be due to the balance or unification of these two libidos in one subject (561). Another version of unity, which would be more intense, would occur when the balance between these two libidos moves over to object libido. In this instance, the lover might imagine himself to be one with his beloved because he has largely forgone his ego libido inclinations—intuiting that some mystical marriage has occurred beyond or outside himself—and thus attributes the experience of ecstasy to the beloved rather than to his own egoistic forbearance.

Were Freud to have analyzed this experience of present or hopeful love more fully, he might have made distinctions between enchantment and mania, similar to those he made between mourning and melancholia. In enchantment, which might be akin to Freud's "real happy love," the subject places his affection on a love object without negating his ego libido or egoistic self. In mania, ego libido and ego instincts may be largely relinquished for object libido. The subject forgoes any sense of reality, or motility, apart from his intense love for a beloved. In mania, the subject is outside or beside himself—described positively in states of ecstasy or jouissance and negatively in psychosis or other kinds of disassociation. Robert Duncan, who describes falling in love as becoming "outcast" from himself, understands how poetry writing can border on psychosis. Duncan would seem to share with Plato, Freud, and others the sense of a linkage between poetry, madness, and love, noting both the positive and negative aspects of these—the ability to discover meaningful connection *and* to enter into psychotic disassociation.

The Turn to Language

One of the most defining intellectual developments of the twentieth century was the turn to language. Lacan claimed that his theory was entirely drawn from Freud with the only difference being his efforts to relate Freudian conceptions to language itself. However, he also introduced as key to his conceptual thinking a split between imaginary and symbolic modes, claiming that the former are illusory and that the latter are the only reality-based registering of desire. For Lacan, love is an operation of the imaginary, or of mirroring relations, and desire is based in the symbolic, or in language. While love for an other stimulates desire, desire itself is derived from what the subject constitutively lacks, a set of ideas developed by Lacan through his concept of the *objet petit a*. For Lacan, the subject needs to correct for his illusory identifications by locating his desire in language. The subject then will find that his "real" desire aligns with the symbolic schema of language. While Lacan entertained the idea of jouissance as linked to an impossible real outside of language, a kind of mania or freewheeling nonidentification, his analytical and theoretical endeavors stressed the need to create a "full speech" of desire as registered in language, casting off an "empty speech" of illusory formations or, alternatively, of repressed desire.

For Freud, the subject's relationship to language is multiple, a vehicle for analytic understandings, narcissistic investments, and material interventions. "Interpositions" of "word-presentations" into "thought processes" may manifest as "things" as well as meanings. Freud claims that "when a hypercathexis of the process of thinking takes place, thoughts are actually perceived—as if they came from without—and consequently held to be true" (634). Thus the unconscious gives rise to "word presentations," and these presentations can create perceptions that seem so definite to the perceiver that they are seen as things. In "On Narcissism," Freud describes how in the mental life of "children and primitive peoples" a combined "ego-libido" and "object-libido" creates a "thaumaturgic" relationship to language: "In the latter we find characteristics which, if they occurred singly, might be put down to megalomania: an over-estimation of the power of their wishes and mental acts, the 'omnipotence of thoughts,' a belief in the thaumaturgic force of words, and a technique for dealing with the external world—'magic' which appears to be a logical application of these grandiose premises" (547). Although Freud disparages this "magical thinking" by ascribing it to populations he perceives as limited in their mental acts, that is, "primitive peoples" and "children," poetry as magical thinking, or as a set of magnetic associations, was noted as early as Plato, causing the curious to turn to the study of the etymological roots and the sounds of words for the ways these might produce a web of hyperassociations. At the beginning of the twentieth century, the Russian movement called Zaum made much of these relations. Marjorie Perloff links Zaum's "super-sense" with Pound's often quoted statement that "poetry is language charged with meaning to the utmost possible degree" (*21st-Century Modernism* 126). But she does not query how this "super-sense" is produced, rather validating poets' intelligent and deliberate wordsmithing. However, given Pound's and other poets' most complex effects, in which semantic, aural, and visual elements are drawn together in surprising and meaningful ways, one can assume that something in addition to their conscious writerly acumen, their diligent craft, has helped to create this poetry—if only their eros.

While Lacan's ideas about language are schematized into imaginary and symbolic realms, his distinction between "empty" and "full" speech in "The Function and Field of Speech and Language in Psychoanalysis" is revealing. Indeed, his insistence on an invested speech of desire does much to convey the necessity of a noninstrumental use of language. Through a "full speech" of desire, the living subject activates meanings that apart from this activation remain inert. Lacan delineates three different ways that "empty speech" occurs. In the first, "the subject . . . is spoken rather than speaking," and he draws on "symbols of the unconscious in petrified forms" (*Ecrits* 69). In this instance, the subject has no relation of desire to the symbolic languages that he employs and is simply miming communication. Then, there is the subject who "loses his meaning in the objectification of discourses" (70). While in the first case, the subject simply has no engagement with a meaningful set of signifiers, in this instance, the subject's disciplining in a "scientific civilization" has created habits in which he or she voids the *je*/I that can act for the *moi*/me of an egoistic passivity (90), or what Ron Silliman has called, in a different context, the dangers of the "neutral" voice. Indeed, for Lacan in 1953, when he first wrote this essay, the pervasiveness of a "neutral," objectifying voice in the realm of psychoanalysis was most upsetting: "I consider it to be an urgent task to disengage from concepts that are being deadened by routine use the meaning that they regain both from reexamination of their history, and from a reflexion on their subjective foundations" (33).

In the third example of "empty speech," the subject does have a relationship to his "symbols," but the signified is repressed from consciousness. Lacan elaborates on the numinous and magnetic qualities of these "hermetic symbols": "hieroglyphics of hysteria, blazons of phobia, labyrinths of the *Zwangsneurose*—charms of impotence, enigmas of inhibition, oracles of anxiety—talking arms of character, seals of self-punishment, disguises of perversion" (69–70). While these signifiers are clearly charged with desire, they constitute imaginary identifications. Lacan's calling this particular kind of speech "empty" cuts deeply into the field of poetry writing, not to mention the broader fields of literature and art. Yet, there is nothing in Lacan's analysis to say why a speech void of these identifications is any less illusory than a speech that courts them. Indeed, these hermetic symbols do not fix desire in the same way as does analytic discourse, allowing more exploratory relations of desire to be created—relations that in forming through identifications with "objects," "others," and language may take on not only the numen of love but its extensions.

For Lacan, Freud, and the love poets examined in this book, projective formations and associational thinking are important techniques. Freud's and Lacan's "talking cures" and the poets' projective poetics have in common their valuing of the production of conscious and unconscious language as a propulsive and self-generating stream. Indeed, for both psychoanalysts and poets these shared methodologies indicate how a speaking in the present may carry more significance than purposive efforts at meaning making. Both emphasize the importance of an individual subject's creation of his or her own speech, and both refuse a controlling egoistic speaker who would still the exigencies and urgencies of this speech through limited sense-making operations. Yet while all, to some extent, depend on the "free" movement of a subject's mind activated by desire, there are important differences. Lacan stressed the hard work of "free association," which needs the corrective intervention by an analyst to avoid any streaming of the unconscious or conscious that would merely replicate the subject's delusions (*Ecrits* 40). Freud, on the other hand, emphasized the active intervention of an analyst not only as a collaborating interpreter of this "free association" but also as a direct participant in its scripts. He thus found "transference" to be a most useful tool in inculcating a subject's desire or ability to speak. Not surprisingly, Lacan and Freud markedly disagreed on the subject of transference since, for Lacan, the therapist's primary role is to supplant the subject's propensity for illusion making. Freud, on the other hand, found ego libido, object libido, and subject formation to be inextricably linked and aimed to activate all of them, if sometimes through the potentially dangerous modality of transference, to help the subject move beyond his or her fixed significations.

Yet, both Freud and Lacan, often touting art, were quick to point out what they regarded as the limitations of artistic endeavors with respect to their own science. Lacan was dismissive of most literature and art ventures, placing them in the imaginary realm. As he saw it, they are involved in a regimen of ensoul-ment, not of truth. For Freud, artists, who have gone some distance in revealing psychological truths, are constrained by the need to make art pleasurable. Con-sequently, his own science was of utmost importance given the need to present less pleasant truths. In "Contributions to the Psychology of Love," he notes that writers have contributed much to our understanding of some aspects of love, but their depictions are restricted by their need to "evoke intellectual and aesthetic pleasure as well as certain effects on the emotions." He further remarks, "For this reason, they cannot reproduce the stuff of reality unchanged but must . . . tone down the whole" (387). Similarly in "Creative Writers and Day-Dreaming," he suggests that writers make what is unacceptable to their audiences acceptable by "softening" it. Curiously, he begins this piece with a definition of creative writ-ing as resembling child's play because of how child's play is involved in reality testing and reality production. Freud writes, "Might we not say that every child at play behaves like a creative writer, in that he creates a world of his own, or rather he re-arranges the things of this world in a new way which pleases him?" The child takes "his play very seriously and he expends large amounts of emo-tion on it" and "likes to link his imagined objects and situations to the tangible and visible things of the real world" (437). But when Freud focuses exclusively on creative writing itself, he drops from his discussion how art as well as child's play may be involved in reality testing, spending the rest of the essay describing how art is akin to fantasying. Completely missing is any carry-through whatso-ever on how the creative writer, like the child, is preoccupied with "reality" and how the play of creative writing is a rearrangment of the things of this world.

For projective love poets, worthy or serious art does not emerge as mere fan-tasying or fictitious language, but is connected to the rigors of actual desire and love. Although Lacan would surely contest the "truth" of projective writing in and of itself, he does enlist a sense of temporality very close to that implied by projective verse: "I identify myself in language but only by losing myself in it like an object. What is realized in my history is not the past definite of what was, since it is no more, or even the present perfect of what has been in what I am, but the future anterior of what I shall have been for what I am in the pro-cess of becoming" (Ecrits 86). Yet for Lacan, the subject must speak this desire apart from love for a specific entity. While Lacan stated that subjects are motivated by their desire for the other, the other is only an imaginary other, which they must get beyond. In contrast, for Freud, even the analyst can be usefully made into a love object, with the subject being able to speak their desire because of this transference.

Projective love writing places its credence, or ethos, with perception propelling perception in an ongoing process of poetic composition. It is precisely through a projective love writing that the poets studied in this book can construct their desire and their love—and their relationship to the languages on which they depend. The poets forgo the demands of holistic image making, characteristic of Lacan's imaginary, without making conscious analysis their only access to their "real" desire. If the need for art to induce pleasure is defining for art (however oblique or perverse this pleasure), then the making of pleasurable objects or languages may finally be more constructive, more creative, of love than what emerges through a corrective analysis, politics, or ethics devoid of love.

Imagism as Projective Love

You must remember that writing poetry requires a clarity . . . a
clairvoyance almost.

—H.D., Letter to John Cournos

The Imagist poetry and poetics of Pound and H.D. are a nascent projective love
and libidinized field poetics that they develop more fully in their subsequent
works. In their Imagist poems, Pound and H.D. initiated a writing in which an
egoistic poetic speaker no longer serves as the primary locus of the poem and
in which one perception leads directly to the next, one language phrase to another, in rather short poems. All of H.D.'s initial Imagist poems were written
in relation to her early lovers, and almost all of H.D.'s and Pound's poems published in the 1914 *Des Imagistes,* as edited by Pound, are based in sexual love.
As several critics have analyzed, H.D.'s 1912 poems (published in *Poetry* in 1913)
provided Pound with an example of a new way to write that he came to understand and practice only gradually. For H.D. they led to her 1916 volume of poetry, *Sea Garden,* but she did not extend these poetics into epic poems until relatively late in life.

Although Imagism is often described through Pound's pithy statement "An
'Image' is that which presents an intellectual and emotional complex in an instant in time," the "instant in time" is misleading insofar as it is understood to
characterize an Imagist poem rather than its apprehension. Both Hugh Kenner and Cyrena Pondrom have insisted on the importance of Imagism as a poetics of juxtaposition and change. Kenner, initially referring to Imagism as an
"enigmatic stone," later corrected this misstatement: Imagism is a writing of
"darting change" in which "perception succeeds perception like the frames of
a film" (Kenner, *The Pound Era* 7, 367). Although Kenner did not cite Olson in
the *The Pound Era,* his phrasing is markedly close to Olson's "ONE PERCEP-
TION MUST IMMEDIATELY AND DIRECTLY LEAD TO A FURTHER PER-
CEPTION." Cyrena Pondrom, separating H.D.'s earliest Imagist poems from
Pound's poems published contemporaneously under his Imagist agenda, notes
how H.D.'s poems, unlike Pound's, refuse a controlling perspective or themati-

zation of meaning—electing instead to use "juxtaposed images [that] epitomize the 'objectivity' which came to be identified as a hallmark of modernism." Pondrom argues that even though Pound prior to his discovery of "H.D. Imagiste" may have engaged ideas that he enlists in statements about Imagism, he did not envision how they applied to actual poems (85, 88, 95).

Although both Kenner and Pondrom have provided valuable understandings of Pound's and H.D.'s Imagist poetics, both fail to address how the motivating force for this writing was erotic. In 1912, when H.D. wrote her initial Imagist poems, there was much upheaval in her love life.[1] Her off-and-on-again romance with Pound had just ended because of his announcement that he was engaged to Dorothy Shakespear, and H.D. had become engaged to Richard Aldington. Also in 1912, she had definitively broken up with Frances Gregg, a lover whom she shared briefly with Pound. Barbara Guest writes of H.D.'s relationship with Gregg, "the first girl love was an excitement that eclipsed any other." As she was nearing fifty, H.D. wrote to a friend that she was still "living down" her relationship with Gregg and that "love terrible with banners only emerges or materializes once or twice in a life-time" (Guest, *Herself* 23, 228).

Imagism is often seen as coextensive with the creation of literary modernism. And while much criticism has concentrated on the competitive relations among Imagism's practitioners, Imagism significantly emerges through erotic relations.[2] H.D. describes how Pound "discovered" Imagism through her poems while sitting in the reading room of the British Museum with her and Aldington: "'But Dryad . . . this is poetry.' He slashed with a pencil. Cut this out, shorten this line. 'Hermes of the Ways' is a good title. I'll send this to Harriet Monroe of *Poetry*. Have you a copy? Yes? Then we can send this, or I'll type it when I get back. Will this do? And he scrawled 'H.D. Imagiste' at the bottom of the page" (*End* 18). While feminist scholars have criticized Pound's appropriation not only of H.D.'s work but of her very identity, what has been little explored, or not at all, is how Pound discovered and theorized Imagism through erotic poems written by a woman inspired by both same-sex and different-sex lovers.[3] H.D. created many of her Imagist poems as translations and adaptations from verse collected by J. K. Mackail in *Select Epigrams from the Greek Anthology*—a volume that provided H.D. with examples of men and women of diverse sexual orientations saying their love with unabashed aplomb. The epigrams, which often begin with poetic speakers who objectify themselves through a self-nomination, as in "I, Homonoea" or "I, Hermes," provide a different example of erotic expression. Through referring to themselves in the third person, these poetic speakers create a sense of themselves as one entity among other entities and as the vehicle of the utterance, rather than as a self-empowered poetic speaker who constitutes his or her poetic speech through the use of others as foils or mirrors.

Scant attention has been paid to Paton's *Greek Anthology* as a source for Imagism or, for that matter, for H.D.'s early writings in *Sea Garden*, for which it is a most significant source.[4] The epigrammatic qualities of the short poems from *The Greek Anthology* gave H.D. models of poetic speakers who establish their erotic authority through the definiteness of their utterances, rather than as lovers who create their speech in dynamic opposition to their beloveds. In *H.D. and Hellenism* Eileen Gregory notes how Greek epigrams offered H.D. an important alternative to nineteenth-century lyricism, although Gregory does not comment on their erotic subjects: "One of the chief advantages of [the] dedicatory epigrams of *The Greek Anthology* for her purposes is precisely their distance from the overdetermined lyric spaces of the late nineteenth century: their strangeness—strange gods, customs, creatures; their ordinariness, littleness, unloveliness. What is also important is the absence of the naturalizing context of exfoliated forms like ode or elegy. These dedications are contextless but distinct gestures of speech within estranged landscapes" (171). This love economy is markedly close to that denoted by Giorgio Agamben in *The End of the Poem* as constituted by "desubjectivized" "ones" (94). Through this terminology, Agamben draws attention to the ways the *dolce stil nuovo* poets spoke apart from egoistic orientations, experiencing, in Dante's case, the writing of love as "dictation." In *The Coming Community*, Agamben comments on love further: "Love is never directed toward this or that property of the loved one (being blond, being small, being tender, being lame), but neither does it neglect the properties in favor of an insipid generality (universal love): The lover wants the loved one *with all of its predicates*, its being such as it is. The lover desires the *as* only insofar as it is *such* . . ." (1: 2). While the "direct sayings" of Imagism frequently have been enlisted to support a clear, economical writing style, H.D.'s Imagist poems were motivated by her attention to her beloveds "*as such.*"

It is likely that Pound took some of his Imagist ideas, and even wordings, from Mackail's introduction to *Select Epigrams*. Mackail remarks on the Greek epigrams' "lapidary precision" and how the poems do "not desire to make a point." He notes how the epigrams avoid "repetition of idea not necessary to the full expression of thought" and reject "verbosity which affects the style throughout and weakens the force and directness of the epigram" (2, 5). In addition to commending the poems' written styles, Mackail also praises their erotic dimensions. He begins *Select Epigrams* with the Greek love poet Meleager's "Garland," in which Meleager honors with different flowers the writings of many women love poets. Mackail draws considerable attention to Meleager's love writing, commenting, "Many of his turns of thought, many even of his actual expressions, have the closest parallel in poets of the thirteenth and fourteenth century who had never even read a line of his work or heard his name. As in them the religion of love . . . is a theology; no subtlety, no fluctuation of fancy or passion is left unregistered" (36).

Part of Pound's excitement about H.D.'s "Hermes of the Ways" may have been not only that he recognized something new in H.D.'s writing that he had yet to attain, but that he felt it was directed to him. In "Compassionate Friendship," written relatively late in her life, H.D. identifies Pound as the first of her seven male initiators, describing him as "Hermes, actor, charlatan, magician" (18). In "Hermes of the Ways," the poetic speaker declares:

I know him
Of the triple path-ways,
Hermes,
Who awaiteth.[5]

In describing Hermes as waiting, H.D. is characterizing Pound's ongoing relationship to her at this time, her sole connection in London to her Philadelphia home after Frances Gregg's departure.

Here, H.D. utilizes two epigrams from *Select Epigrams*, taking the title from an unknown author while deriving much of the poem from a work by the Greek female poet Anyte de Tegea. As an ur-text of the much-anthologized, much-discussed "Hermes of the Ways," Anyte's poem is startling in its familiarity and singularity: "I, Hermes, stand here by the windy orchard in the cross-ways nigh the grey seashore, giving rest on the way to wearied men; and the fountain wells forth cold, stainless water" (Mackail 207). In taking on the nomination of "I, Hermes," Anyte creates a poetic speaker who exists not only as a first-person "I" but as this thing or entity called "Hermes." And while H.D. changes her poem to "I know him . . . / Hermes," she replicates the Greek epigram's objectifying manner of presentation. Much of her poem utilizes a descriptive writing, moving between multiple figurations of transmuting objects. "Hermes of the Ways" begins:

The hard sand breaks,
and the grains of it
are clear as wine.

In the second section, H.D. registers impoverishment, struggle, and transmutation:

Small is
this white stream,
flowing below ground
from the poplar-shaded hill,
but the water is sweet.

. . . .

The boughs of the trees
are twisted
by many bafflings

In these passages, H.D., engaging transmogrifying processes through which one thing becomes something else, may well be drawing on erotic texts she read with Pound, including work in which eros and the occult are linked.[6] While the poetic speaker's address to Hermes is not a love proclamation per se, it conveys a passionate relationship to Hermes as a figure of transformation:

Hermes, Hermes,
the great sea foamed,
gnashed its teeth about me;
but you have waited,
where sea-grass tangles with
shore-grass.

Imagisme

Pound created sometimes revealing, sometimes inchoate descriptions of Imagism in multiple essays at this time, saying at one point that he could only describe it "autobiographically."[7] Although critics have sometimes divided Pound's Imagist stage from his vorticist stage, Pound connected them, noting that vorticism was another name for Imagism that allowed him to extend his concept to multiple art forms. In two essays, "Imagisme" and "Vorticism," he listed his three now-famous principles:

1. Direct treatment of the "thing," whether subjective or objective.
2. To use absolutely no word that does not contribute to the presentation.
3. As regarding rhythm: to compose in sequence of the musical phrase, not in sequence of a metronome.[8]

While criticism on Imagism has gravitated toward the clarity of Pound's principles along with specific statements in his "A Few Don'ts by an Imagiste," Pound stressed that his dos and don'ts were intended for a beginner. In that document Pound noted that he was deliberately withholding the "Doctrine of the Image" since "it did not concern the public, and would provoke useless discussion" (*Ezra Pound's Poetry and Prose* 1: 119). In other writings of this time, Pound connected image formation with eros. He singled out Dante's *Paradiso* as exemplary of "the most wonderful *image*," contrasting it with Browning's *Sordello* as one of "the finest *masks*" (*Ezra Pound's Poetry and Prose* 1: 279). And he claimed that Beatrice was behind all of Dante's writings since "this lover stands ever in unintermittent imagination of this lady (co-amantis)."[9] In "The Serious Artist," he notes that "the readiness of the image is indeed one of the surest proofs that the mind is upborne upon the emotional surge" (*Ezra Pound's Poetry and Prose* 1: 200).

Although Pound came to develop a set of abstract principles and rules for Imagist writing, in his initial commendation of H.D.'s poems, urging Harriet Monroe to publish them in *Poetry*, he alludes to the erotic aspects of H.D.'s verse: "The subject is classic . . . it's straight talk. As straight as the Greek" (*Selected Letters* 11). And he cites Sappho, Catullus, and Villon as the principal models for H.D.—all writers of erotic verse (*Ezra Pound's Poetry and Prose* 1: 119). While Pound uses the word "straight" to signify how the poems are written, it is quite clear, contrary to some recent commentary, that Pound understood H.D.'s predilection for women lovers. When H.D.'s Imagist poems appeared in the January 1913 issue of *Poetry*, they were published under the title "Verses, Translations, and Reflections from the *Anthology*," referring to Mackail's *Select Epigrams from the Greek Anthology*. Commenting on Imagism in the following issue of *Poetry*, Pound notes that the new writing exists most significantly as a discovery of a group of authors in contact with each other—and as a new, unprecedented creation, it could not be encapsulated through a definition but rather was recognized by its practitioners as a superior way to write poetry. Pound was only able, or willing, to indicate this new writing's broadest dimensions—as existing between Yeats's "subjectivism" and Ford Maddox Ford's "objectivism" (*Poetry* 1.4: 125–26).

Critical attention to Pound's principles and rules has led some scholars to conclusions about how Imagism does not adhere to its own tenets; some complain that it "tells" as well as "shows" and that it employs excess words. Meanwhile, in *The Pound Era*, Kenner insists on a radical division between Pound's "hygienic rules" of Imagism and his "Doctrine of the Image" (186). However, both judgments fail to see that Pound created his Imagist rules for the purpose of poetic production and not for critical evaluation. The rules for this writing practice insist on a "direct treatment" of the "thing," specifying that this "thing" can be either "subjective or objective." As such, they reject an introspective writing, what Pound refers to as a "viewy" poetic speaker, but not a subjective response (*Ezra Pound's Poetry and Prose* 1: 121). In their injunction to "use absolutely no word that does not contribute to the presentation," they encourage the poet to close all gaps between intellect, emotion, and composition. No words are to be added to the composition that do not arise from the necessity of the presentation itself—at its time of inscription. As Pound puts it, "The image is itself the speech. The image is the word beyond formulated language" (*Ezra Pound's Poetry and Prose* 1: 278, 280).

Although Pound's "instant in time" has led to misunderstandings of Imagist poetry, Pound through this definition was likely referring to the kind of apprehension he sought, and not the resulting product. Most revealing about the connection between Imagism as love writing and Pound's often abstract explorations of poetics is his statement that Imagism "record[s] the precise instant when a thing outward and objective transforms itself, or darts into a thing inward and subjective" (*Ezra Pound's Poetry and Prose* 1: 281). In this formulation of outer becoming inner, Pound describes a process akin to "falling in love" or "love at first sight." Indeed, this quick movement, this internalization of what is external, depends on states of intense perception and emotion, through which an object or "thing" is newly constituted in the poet's "conceiving" and "receiving" mind (2: 14). In this moment of transposition, projection and introjection are indistinguishable.

Pound attributed Imagism in part to the *dolce stil nuovo* love poet Cavalcanti (*Pound's Cavalcanti* 214). Pound's 1910 essay on Cavalcanti contains first urstatements of Imagism. Of Cavalcanti, Pound remarks, "It is only when the emotions illumine the perceptive powers that we see the reality." Pound praises Cavalcanti's poetry as a "true delineation" precisely because of his ability to "stand aside" and let intense "feeling" "surg[e]" across some thing or being with whom [he is] no longer identified" (*Pound's Cavalcanti* 12). By considering statements from this essay in relationship to Pound's yet to emerge Imagist doctrines, it is possible to see how Pound's seemingly "hygienic" rules and his "Doctrine of the Image" interrelate. Pound formulates: "The perception of the intellect is given in the word, that of the emotions in the cadence," and "it is only, then, in perfect rhythm joined to the perfect word that the two-fold vision can be recorded" (*Pound's Cavalcanti* 18). These statements focus on the same elements of writing as do Pound's three principles, but, in suggesting how these elements synergistically combine, Pound reveals how they are connected to vision and eventually to his veiled "Doctrine of the Image." In linking perception, intellect, and emotion with the apprehension of the word, Pound creates conditions by which words will not serve as preexisting "counters"[10] but as potentially mediumistic vehicles beyond "formulated language."

Des Imagistes

In looking closely at H.D.'s and Pound's poems in *Des Imagistes* (1914), which he edited, we can see how H.D.'s poems were inspired by her early lovers and how Pound was struggling to attain qualities already realized in H.D.'s poetry. All of H.D.'s poems first published in *Poetry* (1913) under the signature "H.D. Imagiste" are included in *Des Imagistes*, whereas none of Pound's poems published in *Poetry* under the auspices of his Imagist agenda were included, bearing out the contention that H.D.'s writing was instrumental for Pound's "discovery" of Imagism and that his understanding of its implications increased over time.[11] In their poems both Pound and H.D. negated or lessened the power of individuated poetic speakers as lovers and created an inspired or libidinal verse through juxtaposed "presentations." Both poets utilized other erotic texts in creating their work, with H.D. drawing heavily on Mackail's *Select Epigrams* and Pound engaging Chinese sources well in advance of encountering Fenollosa's papers.

While H.D.'s practice of creating her fiction through the use of people she knew is well recognized, this practice was also instrumental for her poetry writing. Both "Sitalkas" and "Priapus" are written to gods of fecundity and draw on H.D.'s and Aldington's shared travel experiences in southern Italy, where foliage, flowers, and landscapes suggested an eros that Aldington, especially, elected to obscure.[12] "Sitalkas," the first of H.D.'s poems in *Des Imagistes*, does not use the first person but refers rather to "us." Sitalkas is a little-mentioned god, whom H.D. differentiates from a "cool god" and a "high god," likely referring to diverse figurations of Apollo, "Who touches us not." Possibly recalling Pound's poem "The Fault of It," which includes the phrase "touches us nearly," H.D. may be signaling that she is electing a different métier for her love writing, based on an anonymous or little-known god. This god is even "More beautiful" than Argestes, a northwest wind, whose "scattering" of the "broken leaves" suggests that he moves above the "seeded grass" where "we" reside. "Thou" is defined entirely by what he is—"More . . . than"—and what he is not, an oscillating presence and absence:

> Thou art come at length
> More beautiful
> Than any cool god
> In a chamber under
> Lycia's far coast,
> Than any high god
> Who touches us not
> Here in the seeded grass.
> Aye than Argestes
> Scattering the broken leaves. (*Des Imagistes* 20)

The poem's metonymy between displaced figures creates a kinetic movement, a "seeding," created in part by the delicate aural relations of the poem: "the intricate rhyming pattern of assonance and consonance (for example, *e*, *a*, and *s* in "here in the seeded grass / Aye than Argestes)" (Gregory, *H.D. and Hellenism*

235). "Sitalkas" is most powerful in the movement between figures, and the poem seems to hold us in the liminal time and space "when a thing outward and objective transforms itself, or darts into a thing inward and subjective."

In "Priapus," later called "Orchard," based on an epigram by Zonas in Mackail's *Select Epigrams*, the poetic speaker brings offerings to the god of fecundity. After an appeal to this god, "alone unbeautiful," asking him "to spare us from loveliness," H.D. concludes with a rich inventory of fecund fruits, themselves a kind of metonymic displacement:

> The fallen hazel-nuts,
> Stripped late of their green sheaths,
> The grapes, red-purple,
> Their berries
> Dripping with wine,
> Pomegranates already broken,
> And shrunken fig,
> And quinces untouched,
> I bring thee as offering. (24–25)

In *Select Epigrams*, Mackail categorizes epigrams under various subheadings, with one category being "Dedication," an action that can entail the displacement of emotion onto things. In later retitling the poem "Orchard," H.D. may have wished to avoid the blatant sexuality of the Priapus figure—especially since Pound in his poem "The Faun" (his nickname for Aldington) made fun of what he perceived as H.D.'s and Aldington's idyllic romance.[13]

"Epigram" and "Acon"—the two poems published with "Hermes of the Ways" in *Poetry* in 1913—are about erotic loss and mourning and were likely inspired by Frances Gregg, given their respective references to the swallow and to the hyacinth, complex literary allusions H.D. used in her writings about Gregg in other works.[14] While "Epigram" is an adaptation from an anonymous poem in *Select Epigrams*, "Acon" is derived from the the sixteenth-century neo-Latin writer Giovanni Battista Amalteo and was remembered late in life by H.D. as taken from a "Renaissance Latin anthology that Ezra gave me in the very early days. I think he suggested that I translate it. It was beautiful and easy Latin" (Gregory, *H.D. and Hellenism* 235). In "Epigram," H.D. alters the poetic speaker of her Greek text from "I, Homonoea," who bemoans her own death, into a third-person description in which the people Homonoea left behind, particularly the woman Atimetus, respond to her loss. Mackail's translation reads: "I Homonoea, who was far clearer-voiced than the Sirens, I who was more golden than the Cyprian herself at revellings [sic] and feasts, I the chattering bright swallow lie here, leaving tears to Atimetus, to whom I was dear from girlhood; but unforeseen fate scattered all that great affection" (165). H.D.'s adaptation of this poem reads:

> The golden one is gone from the banquets;
> She, beloved of Atimetus
> The swallow, the bright Homonoea:
> Gone the dear chatterer. (30)

While in the Greek text the sense of excessive loss is brought forth because Homonoea "was more golden than the Cyprian" (Aphrodite), in H.D.'s version the sense of loss is conveyed by the succinctness of the poem—and the silence that follows "Gone the dear chatterer." The Greek epigram must have suggested much to H.D. about her relationship with Gregg, including the sense that with Gregg's leaving England an "unforeseen fate scattered all that great affection" and the loss of the "revellings and feasts" of their shared literary and social realms in Philadelphia and London. H.D. dropped "Epigram" from her subsequent collections of poems, perhaps because while this poem has no "I," its grieving lover subordinates the depiction of her beloved to the implied poetic speaker's own sense of anguish. In many ways, the Greek epigram remains a superior modernist or Imagist rendering.

In the longer "Acon," the burden of the poem moves away from an angst that focuses attention on the lover, shifting the gaze to the beloved and the things with which she is associated. In the first part of the poem, a first-person speaker elects to bear flowers to "She, Hyella, / whom no god pities." The speaker does not lament Hyella's unexplained demise directly, but conveys her feelings through dedicated objects:

> I choose spray of dittany,
> Cyperum frail of flower,
> Buds of myrrh,
> All-healing herbs,
> Close pressed in calathes. (26)

In the second section of the poem, the first-person poetic speaker no longer appears and instead "Dryads" and "Nereids" perform acts of mercy, including "bear[ing] ripe fruits from Arcadia, / and Assyrian wine." (H.D. may well be referring to herself as "Dryad"—a name that both H.D. and Pound adopted for her during their relationship and that she continued to use in many of her subsequent intimate relations.) The loss of Hyella is acute, but H.D. stays attentive to Hyella: "The light of her face falls from its flower, / As a hyacinth." H.D.

conveys this loss through the delicate, highly economical, shifting relations between "face," "flower," "light," and "falling" and the comparison of Hyella to a
"Hidden" "hyacinth," which perishes "upon burnt grass" (*Des Imagistes* 26–27).
The implicit mourning of this poem is brought forth through the allusions to
the hyacinth, recalling Apollo's accidental killing of his beloved Hyacinthus and
his consequent inconsolable grief.

Of the six poems by Pound published in the *Des Imagistes* anthology, only
one, "The Return," is not based on overtly erotic relations or texts. Four of the
poems are derived from translations from Chinese, including Herbert A. Giles's
A History of Chinese Literature (Ruthven 31). Indeed, the rather different kinds
of poetic speakers in these poems suggest that Pound was still struggling to
locate his subjectivity in a writing that is located in the "thing itself." Pound's
first poem in *Des Imagistes*, "Doria," makes an interesting comparison to H.D.'s
"Sitalkas," since both poems are likely addressed to their respective fiancé(e)s,
Aldington and Shakespear.[15] "Doria," in addressing a feminine beloved, reveals
how Pound is attempting to strike a stance in which his poetic speaker's empowerment will come directly from the objects or others of the poem. Indeed,
while H.D. is aided in establishing her Imagist poetics by her position of outsider to centuries of lover-beloved poems written within masculinist heterosexual
economies, Pound is swaddled in such a tradition and must find ways of moving away from it without forgoing a libidinal economy.

In "Doria," Pound engages the dichotomized relations between a lover and
beloved, while simultaneously attempting to undo them. In beginning the poem
with "Be in me as the eternal moods / of the black wind, and not / As transient
things are," Pound seeks a state in which the presence of the beloved persists
in his poetic speaker—one that is life altering rather than transitory. Yet, seem-
ing to sense the one-sidedness of this request, the implicit dominion over the
beloved that his command initiates, he immediately seeks to make himself her
object of desire: "Have me in the strong loneliness / of sunless cliffs / And of
grey waters." In asking, then, that this lover not only "Be in me" but "Have me,"
the poem would seem to be after a mutual inhabitation, if not an intrasubjec-
tive extension. At once celebratory and melancholic, the poetic speaker's desires
slip from a present to a hoped-for future to a projected past: "Let the gods speak
softly of us / In the days hereafter, / The shadowy flowers of Orcus / Remember Thee" (*Des Imagistes* 41). These enjambed lines constitute a change from
the commands of the first lines of the poem by creating a set of metonymic relations. The reference to Orcus calls up larger underworld forces, focusing the
poem not only through eros but through occult practices and understandings.
While the poem is melancholic because of the loss or demise of a specific beloved, the melancholia of its poetic speaker extends and sustains the presence
of the beloved—or the state of love itself. The poem hovers around but does

not enact an economy in which "a thing outward and objective transforms it-self, or darts into a thing inward and subjective." Rather it presents the drama of a speaker trying to attain this possibility. Indeed, while the melancholia of this poem might suggest a loss of an earlier lover, perhaps H.D. or one of the "mystery women" from Pound's past, Pound's disappointment in his relationship with Shakespear is thought to be its main subtext (Ruthven 62).

The Chinese poems that inspired four of these works provided Pound with examples of writing in which erotic relations were often stated indirectly, through things.[16] If, in order to write her love, H.D. needed to discover models of autonomous poetic speakers who could provide alternatives to the preceding centuries of self-dramatizing poetic lovers, Pound was in need of lessons on how to focus his poems on "objects," on "others." While Pound's final three poems strike a mournful or melancholic tone at the loss of a specific beloved, the first of the four, "After Ch'u Yuan," manifests an ineptness with the poetic speaker's position in the poem. "After Ch'u Yuan" is a rather bald piece of sexual fantasy, almost a picaresque tale, albeit a short one, of maidens gathering grapes for the leopards that pull their cars. The speaker at first seems to wish to subordinate himself to this vision—"I will get me to the wood"—and he describes an erotic scene of maidens and leopards, but by the end he has become one of the actors in the scene: "I will come out of the new thicket / and accost the procession of maidens" (*Des Imagistes* 43). Of all the poems in *Des Imagistes*, this one seems furthest from Pound's prescription for Imagism: capturing the precise moment when something objective becomes something subjective.

Pound's other three poems based on the Chinese translations have no first-person poetic speaker. "Liu Ch'e," which begins with a mournful description of loss, abruptly changes point of view, concluding with a troubling gendered reference:

The rustling of the silk is discontinued,
Dust drifts over the courtyard,
There is no sound of footfall, and the leaves
Scurry into heaps and lie still,
And she the rejoicer of the heart is beneath them:

A wet leaf that clings to the threshold. (*Des Imagistes* 44)

Although the first part of the poem seems to honor the loss of a particular beloved, the final sentence portrays a potentially pathetic feminine "clinging," especially since the fine, light array, the delicate traces of the first section, precipitate into this limp leaf.

"Fan-Piece, for Her Imperial Lord" is by contrast a far more poised poem in which lover-beloved relations and subject-object bifurcations coalesce into a writing that does seem to exemplify how a "thing objective" can "dart into" a "thing subjective":

> O fan of white silk,
>> clear as frost on the grass-blade,
> You also are laid aside. (45)

While this poem is brief, it moves between multiple frames of reference. The title, "Fan-Piece, for Her Imperial Lord," is a double entendre; the "fan-piece" might be the mistress herself, a mere thing to be used and discarded at a whim by her lord, or the "fan-piece" might refer to the poem itself—a "piece" of writing to be displayed on a "fan," written by a female poet to her lord, reminding him that he can be "laid aside." Indeed, the refusal of a single point of view, of a stabilized poetic speaker determining his or her relationship to an objectified other, initiated a field poetics that Pound developed to a far greater extent in *The Cantos*.

In shifting erotic energies away from the poetic speaker as lover and onto their poems' others and languages, Pound and H.D. initiated the projective love and libidinized field poetics that they would develop to a far greater extent in their subsequent work. By writing a poetry of "the direct treatment of the 'thing,' whether subjective or objective," Pound and H.D. created a poetry in which the poet is no longer primarily an expressive agent who uses language, but is a "conceiver" and "receiver" of a projected language that acts on them. The injunction to "use absolutely no word that does not contribute to the presentation" encourages the poet not to parse her words, but rather to close all gaps between perception, intellect, and emotion as she composes. H.D., late in life, queried the assessment of her early poems: "I grew tired of hearing these poems referred to as crystalline. Was there no other way of assessing them?" She then modified this statement: "For what is crystal, or any gem but the concentrate[d] essence of the matrix, with the energy either of over-intense heat or over-intense cold that projects it." H.D. concluded that the "matrix" of her early poems had never been revealed ("Delia" 184).

II

Love Poesis

4

"Circe's This Craft"

EZRA POUND'S BEGINNINGS

As the man matures, as his mind becomes a heavier and heavier
machine, it requires constantly a greater voltage or emotional energy to
set it in motion.

—Ezra Pound, "The Serious Artist"

Through Imagism Pound first began to discover a projective love and libidinized field poetics, but he did not fully realize these poetics until *The Cantos*.
The change from Pound's early poetry to his *Cantos* is most remarkable and
has prompted considerable critical speculation. One of the accounts much repeated with respect to Pound's poetic development is that he needed to cast off
his early love poetry to develop his modernist idiom. In this book I provide a
rather different understanding of Pound's trajectory. To write *The Cantos*, Pound
needed to address sexual love as a personal experience and a symbolic legacy in
ways that fully acknowledged its powers and amplified its animating energies.[1]

In his Imagist poems, Pound began to change his poetry from one in which
poetic speakers serve as the dramatic center to a writing in which attention is
focused on his poetry's others and languages. Yet he did not fully engage these
possibilities until *The Cantos*. In *The Cantos*, egoistic poetic speakers are negated
for what is typically called Pound's "impersonalism" or, as defined here, his projective love writing and libidinized field poetics. To write his *Cantos*, Pound must
shift libidinal energies away from a poetic speaker who seeks or quests after
others to a writing inspired directly by these others and the languages that convey them. Jean Rabate validates Pound's *Cantos*: "Language . . . can take on its
full function when it is seen as the locus from which the poet can speak as the
Other of the System" (10). Importantly, this is not a language that is controlled
by the poet, but a language that speaks through him. Although Rabate is drawing on Lacanian analysis that, as already discussed, has its limitations, he draws
useful attention to how language inhabits Pound.

In "Blood for the Ghosts" Hugh Kenner claims that Pound's possession of
other voices in *The Cantos* came from his studied and internalized sense of
their rhythms and sonorities as developed in his early poems. According to Kenner, Pound drew from his psyche, his "column of air," these previously learned

sounds. But, if Pound in writing his *Cantos* was drawing on a repertoire of internalized sounds, he was also writing them out of a rather different kind of possession—of love and love writing. To write *The Cantos* Pound reengaged the erotic dispensations of his earliest poems and came to understand love as a powerful but morally ambiguous force. Pound's early love poetry vacillates between states of melancholia and enchantment—orientations that Pound instantiated in two long poems, *Hugh Selwyn Mauberley* and *Homage to Sextus Propertius*, which he created after his disappointing *Three Cantos* (his ur-cantos) and before writing *The Cantos* proper. In *Mauberley* Pound assumes a melancholic speech and debunks "Of Eros, a retrospect. // Mouths biting empty air." In *Propertius* he explores enchantment and extols love: "My genius is no more than a girl" (*Personae* 198, 213). In *Canto IV*, which led him to revise and jettison most of his previous *Three Cantos*, Pound moved beyond the dualities of melancholia and enchantment and away from professing obeisance to and profaning love. He came to realize that love is neither good nor evil, but it is entirely powerful. Much like Socrates in the *Phaedrus*, to write love in a nonreductive manner, Pound had to acknowledge the powers of love. By activating his full knowledge and experience of love, Pound was able to move beyond his ur-cantos as a "rag-bag to stuff all its thoughts in" (Bush 53).

Canto IV is the first canto that Pound composed that stayed relatively unchanged in his *Draft of XXX Cantos*, and it was the beginning of a way of writing that would enable him to create his *Cantos* proper. Crucial to Pound's changed writing was a reassessment of the importance of metamorphosis. In 1918, at the same time that he was working on *Mauberley*, *Propertius*, and *Canto IV*, Pound published remarks on Ovid's *Metamorphoses*: "The undeniable tradition of metamorphoses teaches us that things do not always remain the same. They become other things by swift and unanalysable processes" (*Literary Essays* 431). In *Canto IV* he took on a writing in which perception leads directly to further perception and which manifests "the precise instant when a thing outward and objective transforms itself, or darts into a thing inward and subjective." He drew together the opposed dispositions of enchantment and melancholia and initiated an ecstatic writing of unprecedented "schizopoetics."

Although through Imagism Pound first began to discover the possibilities of poetic speech apart from individualized poetic speakers, most of the poems in the 1915–1918 period were written with limited poetic speakers. His much-touted *Cathay* poems derive their clear-sightedness from nostalgic poetic speakers who cast their longing eyes upon a visualized and objectified world apart from them. In *Three Cantos*, published in 1916–1917, Pound engaged a verbose, self-parodying poetic speaker, who is entirely skeptical about love when he does not revile it. In *Mauberley* and *Propertius*, Pound began to locate an impersonal speech, albeit one dependent at least in part on the personae through which these poems are written. Pound extended the scope of this poetic speaker in *Mauberley* but remains very skeptical about love. In *Sextus Propertius*, Propertius extols love and validates a lineage of love writing from ancient Greece to Italy. In *Canto IV* and subsequent cantos, Pound combined these disparate dispositions. His so-called impersonal speech became an ecstatic delivery in which his poetic speaker is libidinally connected to what he says, but also exists apart from it.

Pound's love poems of enchantment and melancholia are much evidenced in *Hilda's Book* and his many translations of Cavalcanti from this early period. In *Hilda's Book*, Pound explored the possibilities of enchantment in relationship to a beloved whom he portrayed as loving him. In his Cavalcanti translations, love was often portrayed as a masculine Amor who rendered the poetic speaker speechless, a speechlessness that resulted sometimes in the poetic speaker's death at the hands of a cruel domina or in his salvation by a distant and beneficent beloved. In the Cavalcanti poems, Pound learned not only of a lover taken out of himself through powerful surges of emotion, but also about recording that experience as if it were not written by the poetic speaker. In other words, if in *Hilda's Book*, Pound's poetic speaker waxes eloquent about the joys and beauties of his beloved, in the Cavalcanti poems Pound removes his egoistic self from the center of his poems. It is this very hollowing out, this dispossessed possession, that produces Pound at his most Lacanian: the poetic speaker seeks love but exists apart from any possibility of its attainment. To write *The Cantos*, Pound had to learn how to access not only his desire, but his love. He had to draw together his melancholia with his enchantment. He did so by extending his melancholic disposition in *Mauberley* and reorienting himself to the possibilities of love's enchantment in *Sextus Propertius*—an enchantment that in this poem reaches toward erotic mania. Whereas the melancholic stances of his Cavalcanti translations and of *Mauberley* enabled Pound to explore a poetic delivery apart from a limited, egoistic control, the enchanted relations in *Hilda's Book* and *Propertius* encouraged a cathexis in others and in language.

Homage to Sextus Propertius was particularly important for Pound's writing of *The Cantos*, for it not only enabled him to reengage the possibilities of writing through love, but it did so through an impersonal poetic speaker. In that work, he revalued love and developed a comedic vision. Pound staged the comic failings of his hero, Propertius, and love itself while extolling love as surpassing everything else. Pound, unlike many of his critics, gave *Sextus Propertius* a primary place in his opus, placing it after *Mauberley* as the final poem of his much-revised, carefully selected 1926 *Personae*. Indeed, in *Sextus Propertius*, Pound first engaged in a practice that he called "logopoeia"—"the dance of the intellect among words"— which directly enabled the agile "dance" of *The Cantos* (*Literary Essays* 25).

Several critics have attempted to trace Pound's love philosophies and mythos in *The Cantos*. These formations are important not because they can be pinned down as a set of stable ideas about eros, but because of the poetry Pound wrote through them. Far more important than any codified beliefs is their subtle morphing in his poetry. Two of Pound's most repeated love investigations (namely, the complex of beliefs that might loosely be grouped together as Neoplatonism and the conviction that there is a lineage of occulted love that began in ancient Greece and continued to the present of his own writing—a belief summarized by Pound as "a light shines from Eleusis") actively underwent restatement and mutation throughout his writing. As his biographer David Moody succinctly summarizes, these love beliefs were "being practiced, not expounded." In *The Cantos*, Pound created "love" as an "impersonal" force, a set of moving signifiers, inseparable from a signified. Or, as Cavalcanti wrote and Pound translated, "None can imagine love / that knows not love" (*Pound's Cavalcanti* 175).

Throughout his early writing and into the 1920s, Pound was actively engaged in developing an understanding and practice that would address the manifold aspects of poetry writing as an aural, visual, and semantic medium. But while early on he sought to find ways of aligning diverse aspects of poetry, he came to see them as possessing powers of their own that could be brought out variously in different poems. By 1918, when he was writing *Sextus Propertius*, he had developed three concepts for different kinds of poetry, or different elements in poetry: melapoeia, phanapoeia (which he also referred to as Imagism), and logopoeia. Initiating the concept of logopoeia in his observations of Mina Loy's and Marianne Moore's poetry, he related phanapoeia to "phantasmagoria."[2] In writing *The Cantos*, he at different times enabled each of these three aspects of poetry to have a kind of agency, so that any one or a combination of these features could have prominence and thereby disrupt sure-footed meanings or provide subliminal currents. Pound in activating these properties of poetry allowed them to alter the poetry he produced, not only through what Kristeva would refer to as the "semiotic" of his bodily unconscious, but directly as an intervention in meaning making itself.

"Hearts Crimson"

Pound's early love poetry used two different modalities. The first included poems of a lover's partially requited love for a beloved who is of the same, or nearly the same, status as the lover—poems of intersubjective enchantment. Examples of these may be found in *Hilda's Book*, poems Pound wrote to H.D. in 1905–1906, which he gave to her in a small handmade book. The second were Pound's translations of the love poems of Guido Cavalcanti, in which a lover pursues a domina of a superior social or spiritual caste and abjects himself sometimes to her, sometimes to a masculine Amor she inspires. If the former enabled Pound to explore a cathexis with others and language itself, the latter produced a melancholic subjectivity, usefully described through Freudian concepts of melancholia and Lacanian "lack."

In *Hilda's Book*, the experience of enchantment predominates. Indeed, while these poems were produced through an economy in which the poetic speaker as lover constitutes his subjectivity in relationship to his beloved as objectified other, this dichotomy is at times surpassed. To better appreciate the qualities of these poems, it is important to observe them as they were first typed by Pound— with many short, irregularly indented lines and with some poems taking up several pages. This presentation brings out the poems' tender and ethereal qualities, which are negated, in part, in their only extant publication (in an appendix to H.D.'s *End to Torment*) through regularized lineation and pagination. In the book's first poem, "La Donzella Beata," which I discussed in chapter 1, the poetic speaker constitutes himself rhetorically in opposition to his beloved while celebrating the "transport" that the "bold" maid inspires. In the poem immediately following, "The Wings," lover and beloved are bare traces on the scene as the effects of their interaction are experienced through such transient motions as "whirring," "lapping," and "flutter[ing]":

A wondrous holiness hath
      touched me
And I have felt the whirring
      of its wings
Above me , Lifting me above
      all terrene things
As her fingers fluttered
      into mine
    Its wings whirring
   above me as it passed
A lapping wind among the pines
. . . .
Half shadowed of a hidden
      moon
A wind that presseth close
      and kisseth not
But whirreth , soft as light
Of twilit streams in hidden
      ways (3–4)

Here, the pronounced aural and visual aspects of the poem (with its many double consonants) are an indication of Pound's sensitivity to language's multiple registers. While critics have dismissed poems such as these as simply replicative of Yeats's *Celtic Twilight*, Pound manifests a rather different relationship to language's material properties—giving them comparatively more play, more agency, than Yeats did.

In the poem "Domina," the poetic speaker playfully presents the superiority of his beloved as attributable to her height: "My Lady is tall and fair to see / She swayeth as a poplar tree / When the wind bloweth / merrily." While this poem translates the hierarchical relationship between lover and domina from medieval poetry into a modern idiom—this lady's superiority comes from her physical height—it largely sustains the medieval dynamics. However, in the following "Per Saecula," the lady's eyes and the speaker's desire are indistinguishable, leading to their shared "reaping":

> Where
> through your tangled
> hair
> Have I seen the eyes of my
> desire bear
> Hearts crimson unto my
> hearts heart? As mown
> Grain of the gold brown
> harvest from seed sown
> Bountifully amid springs
> emeralds fair
> So is our reaping now (19)

Drawing most likely on the Demeter myth and its attendant Eleusinian rituals, Pound creates a correspondence, or merger, between lover and beloved through replicative concepts and sounds—as in "Hearts crimson unto my / hearts heart" and the multiple open *o* sounds of the concluding lines. In several places in *Hilda's Book*, Pound elected to print short, epigrammatic verses in capital letters, inscribing an intensity of feeling for his beloved with an emphatic delivery of language—methods he will employ in *The Cantos*:

ONE WHOSE SOUL WAS
SO FULL OF ROSE
LEAVES STEEPED IN

GOLDEN WINE THAT THERE
WAS NO ROOM THERE IN
FOR ANY VILLEINY – (24)

The poems in *Hilda's Book* contrast in striking ways with Pound's translations of Cavalcanti (first published in 1910). In Pound's 1920 collection of poems, *Umbra*, the preface reads, "all that he wants to keep in print," with more than one-fourth being translations, most of which are from Cavalcanti. Through Cavalcanti, Pound explored a subjectivity in which the egoistic self is negated through the wounding or death-inflicting blows of Amor. While it is often through the domina's or the lady's eyes that Amor delivers his arrows and wounds, the lady through her beneficence can ameliorate these deathly blows or through her indifference subject the speaker to further death.

Pound notes that the domina, who at times is depicted as possessing "masculine" eyes, may be a substitute for her lord. Thus, some of the extreme deathliness of these poems might be explained as the collapse of the rhetorical triangle described by DuPlessis in "Corpses of Poesy" as constitutive of much poetry—made up of a male lover, a male audience, and a female beloved—since the entire cast in the Cavalcanti poems is now male or masculine (17). In these poems, the beloved is at times no more than a conduit, not even an exchange object, for Cavalcanti's masculine Amor. Pound translates Sonnet XXVI: "Knowest well that I'm Amor / And that I leave you this my portraiture / And bear away from thee thine every thought" (*Pound's Cavalcanti* 99).

In Sonnets I–III, included in Pound's *Umbra*, Amor, in addition to exiling the poetic speaker to death or speechlessness, has the power to constitute a new poetic speaker. Sonnet I initially addresses the beloved as "You," but this "You" becomes a mere vehicle for an Amor that leaves the speaker in "agony" and that "slasheth in his going with such might / That all my smothered senses turn to flight" (23). Pound conveys the drama of how Love shoots his dart from the beloved's "noble eyes":

See, he hath hurled his dart, where from my pain
First shot's resultant! And in flanked amaze
See how my afrighted soul recoileth from
That sinister side where the heart lies slain. (23)

This love dart is so penetrating that the "soul recoileth" from the "slain" "heart." Yet it is precisely as a result of this death-dealing blow that the poetic speaker celebrates his new voice, experienced as if delivered by an entity separate from himself:

New is the face that's set in seigniory,
And new the voice that maketh loud my grief. (23)

Severed from his egoistic self, the poetic speaker possesses a new speech, made over in "seigniory"—an implacable voice that "maketh loud" his grief. "Seigniory" is the power, rank, or estate of a feudal lord; "seignorage" refers to the minting of coins, as well as to the difference between the face value of a coin and the bullion used to back it. From a Freudian perspective, this melancholic subject has relegated all of his subjectivity to his superego, a hollowed out semblance of his former self, which has been all but negated by Amor. From a Lacanian perspective, the speaker freed of his illusory love for a beloved is newly minted in and through a paternal symbolic order that is the only "real" through which desire can register. As such, he assumes his place in the cast of men who have legal and moneyed rights, a privileged subject within this order.

In Sonnet II, the poetic speaker recovers from his "fright" through the "Lady's" grace:

The instant that she deigned to bend her eyes
Toward me, a spirit from high heaven rode
And chose my thought the place of his abode
With such deep parlance of love's verities
That all Love's powers did my sight accost
As though I'd won unto his heart's mid-most. (27)

While the "powers" of Love "accost" the speaker's sight, presumably rendering him blind, they enable his entrance into a "deep parlance of love's verities" and into Love's "heart's mid-most." In Sonnet I, the poetic speaker finds his speech apart from his love for a particular beloved; in Sonnet II, he finds a "deep parlance" in the company of his beloved. These two sonnets well convey the insights and limitations of Lacan's symbolic and imaginary binary since different kinds of speech are availed by the different relationships to a masculine Amor and a feminine beloved. While Freud's analysis of language production would validate the second sonnet as "real" enough speech, Lacanian theory would castigate this speech as an imaginary identification.

In all of Cavalcanti's poems, relationships between the enunciation and enounced are complex, as the poetic speaker tells of various states of abnegation and negation—of existing through a divided self or outside of himself. An important lesson Pound learned from Cavalcanti was the creation of an impersonal speech connected to a libidinal economy that depends on a poetic speaker assuming an outsider relationship to the experiences of which he speaks. Pound, often the assured egoist in his public life, may have found through Cavalcanti's poems a way to get out of or beyond himself, thereby discovering a linguistic readiness that surfaces through negation of an egoistic self. Through Cavalcanti, Pound took on a subjectivity that forwent enchantment and identification, opting instead for melancholy and disalignment, as Rabate describes: "An absence of reciprocity, a disalignment, a fundamental disparity, all brand the speaking subject with the seal of desire" (15).

"There Is No High-Road to the Muses"

In his early poems Pound affirmed the powers of love, but in the period following his initial Imagist discoveries and immediately preceding his *Cantos* proper, he frequently castigated love in visceral ways. He praised love in such poems as "Phanapoeia" and "Langue d'Oc," with by far the most significant affirmation of love, *Homage to Sextus Propertius*. Both *Sextus Propertius* and *Mauberley*, composed after Pound published *Three Cantos*, jettisoned Pound's self-identified, parodic poetic speaker of the preceding cantos for comparatively more impersonal presentations. But while *Mauberley* debunked eros, *Sextus Propertius* extolled love. In these two ambitious long poems, Pound vacillated between melancholic and enchanted poetic speakers and engaged satiric and comedic visions. In *The Cantos*, he combined these opposing orientations.

Three Cantos contains prolonged meditations on the speaker's dissatisfactions with writing his long poem as well as several cynical accounts of love. Initially modeling his poetic speaker after Browning's *Sordello*, Pound comments on his choice: "the modern world / Needs such a rag-bag to stuff all its thoughts in" (53). Yet he also notes that *Sordello* "had some basis, had some set belief," whereas his poetic speaker does not. Pound's speaker asks, "what were the use / Of setting up figures and breathing life upon them / Were 't not *our* life, your life, my life, extended" (54). He queries, "What have I of this life, / Or even of Guido," referring to Cavalcanti (59). He tells several short narratives of youthful love that resulted in failed love, often through marriage. In addressing Catullus's love for Lesbia, he suggests that Catullus merely "Wrote out his crib from Sappho" (61). While, as Pound tells it, Sappho's "crib" initially leaves Catullus nearly speechless with his love, over time his love dwindles into a dissipated, dishonorable love. Noting this was "the way of love, *flamma dimanant*," the speaker concludes this sequence with how Catullus's Lesbia

Is now the drab of every lousy Roman
So much for him who puts his trust in woman
So the murk opens. (62)

76 / Chapter 4

What troubles Pound here is not only his presumption of the failure of love, but also perhaps the publicness of Catullus's "public woman"—a publicness due both to her position in Latin culture as a prostitute or courtesan and to Catullus's public telling of his consummated love.[3]

In *Hugh Selwyn Mauberley*, much admired for its writing technique, the foppish Mauberley meditates on the inconsequence of his art, which he connects to a failure of eros itself. At the beginning, the poetic speaker declares, "His true Penelope was Flaubert," and he notes that, with respect to Circe, he is drawn not to her, but to the "elegance of [her] hair." He condemns the world's indifference to sexual chasteness, noting that "Dowson found harlots cheaper than hotels." And at a time when Lady Valentine inhabits a "stuffed-satin drawing room," "the sale of half-hose has / Long superseded the cultivation / Of pierian roses." In "Yeux Glauques," Pound pronounces on the weakness of his Victorian predecessors, including Swinburne and Rossetti, noting their creation of a "thin," "still-born" "Rubaiyat." Both their writing and the eyes of their female figures are "thin like brookwater / with a vacant gaze." Of Eros, the poem concludes, "Mouths biting empty air." The retrospective aspects of the poem and the relatively fixed position of Pound's poetic speakers give Pound, as in his *Cathay* poems, considerable control. Yet it is a control that isolates elements and satirizes human failings, stilling power and passion (*Personae* 185–202).

Homage to Sextus Propertius, written after Pound's ur-cantos and contemporaneous with the composition of *Hugh Selwyn Mauberley*, constitutes a radical change in Pound's increasing skepticism about love.[4] In paying homage to Propertius, Pound singled out a writer who insisted on the writing of love over empire and whose love writing was based not in a "delayed" but in a consummated love. According to his biographer Humphrey Carpenter, 1917 was the year that Pound lost his virginity, and as he brags in a poem written at the time, "He was thrown into a sea of six women" (332). Pound eventually affirmed this changed orientation in unequivocal terms in *Canto XXXV*: "Sacrum, sacrum, inluminatio coitu" (*The Cantos* 180).

Sextus Propertius offers a vision of life that is essentially comedic, not only extolling the virtues of love, but also offering up a hero who possesses laughable foibles. Pound critics have paid limited attention to *Propertius*, either lambasting it for its malapropisms or debating how intentional some of Pound's mistranslations were. Critics who have commended this poem have tended to characterize its perspective as ironic, suggesting that the poem's logopoeia is intended to communicate a satirical view on love. Yet, while there is undoubtedly humor and irony in *Sextus Propertius*, it also conveys an unbridled enthusiasm for love and love writing. Its intentional, and perhaps sometimes unintentional, logopoeia is in service of an irony that while providing critique also opens up a play of meanings. What Pound seems to want to bypass in this poem and in *The Cantos* is a faithfulness to the boundedness of much of anything—including things seen in an object world and referenced through preexisting language formations. *Homage to Sextus Propertius* initiated a projective love writing, or a writing in which one perception leads to another perception. At times approaching a maniacal enthusiasm, the poem provides glimpses of—if it does not entirely enact—an ecstatic eros.

Sextus Propertius as the concluding poem of Pound's *Personae* presents a major change in Pound's love philosophy—both repudiating his previous allegiance to medieval "delay" as a way of intensifying eros and honoring consummated love, which he had previously dismissed. A likely 1918 compositional date makes this poem contemporaneous with Pound's affair with Iseult Gonne (Moody 349). If so, the part of Propertius's *Elegies* about Propertius's altercation with his friend over Cynthia would have been most resonant for Pound, who vied with W. B. Yeats for Gonne's affection. However, Pound's repeated line in this poem, "My genius is no more than a girl," may not only be a reference to the "much too young" Iseult Gonne, but may refer to other "young girls" who inspired Pound's poetry, including the archetypal Kore and an earlier Iseult, whom he called "Is-Hilda" (213).

Pound's enthusiasm for this poem is likely related to the enthusiasm he had while writing it. While Pound, as did Propertius, cordons off a writing of love from a writing of empire, exonerating "small talk" over "a large-mouthed product," Pound also wishes to link these different literary genres, declaring this poem to be a predecessor to a much larger poem: "clear the street, O ye Greeks, / For a much larger *Iliad* is in the course of construction" (223). Pound's poem provides a number of comedic vantages on Propertius's love affair with Cynthia, including Propertius's fear of traveling over dangerous roads at night and thereby his failure to initially arrive at Cynthia's bedside as she requested; a messenger's report of Cynthia's behavior when Propertius does not arrive that verifies her fidelity; and altercations with his friend over their shared interest in Cynthia. In doing so, its tone sometimes vacillates between the ribald and the serious and is unable to combine them.

Sextus Propertius is very different from *Hugh Selwyn Mauberley* in its headlong rush, brought on in part by the poet's propensity for catalogs and lists, which enable Pound to string together diverse entities through often subliminal connections and leaps. The poem engages a sense of love as divinity and as bathos, rejecting the "Fool who would set a term to love's madness" (216). While at times this writing approaches Pound's projective love writing in *The Cantos*, at other times it devolves into a romp. When the gods of love appear, they take on divine and burlesque roles. Proclaiming dismay that their victim "thinks that we are not gods," the gods act like scoundrels and street thugs, and accost the feckless lover: "Get him plumb in the middle? / Shove along there, shove along!" (220). Elsewhere, Pound's vocabulary takes on a weightier cast: "I had seen in the shade, recumbent on cushioned Helicon, / The water dripping from Bellerophon's horse" (207). This passage alludes to the myth that when Pegasus stomped on Mount Helicon the waters of the Hippocrene began to flow; that water was thought to possess the power to inspire poetry in those who drank it (Ruthven 96). When Pegasus appears much later in the poem, Pound conveys a sense of love descending upon the horse and, presumably, the rider with all the force of which Propertius writes, "Then my resolute disdainful eyes were cast down, and my head was trampled underfoot by—Love" (1.1.3–4; Kennedy 48):

> Though you heave into the air upon the gilded Pegasean back,
> Though you had the leathery sandals of Perseus
> To lift you up through split air,
> The high tracks of Hermes would not afford you shelter.
>
> Amor stands upon you, Love drives upon lovers,
>   a heavy mass on free necks. (221)

Pound literalizes the "trampling" of Propertius's "head" as the force of Pegasus himself driven on by Love. Conjuring the sensations of flight and of oppressive weight, Pound conveys some of the seriousness that love commands in *Propertius*, although he initiates this sequence with a profane warning to any bystanders: "Escape! There is O Idiot, no escape." While in *The Cantos* Pound utilizes humor and invective, Pound integrates his vocabulary and moods in individual cantos and passages to a much greater extent than he does in this poem. It is as if it has just occurred to him that language can move in poetry, and he forces it to gallop.

In *Sextus Propertius*, Pound affirms an interrelation between being in love and writing poetry, writing about this relation through the subjunctive:

> Yet you ask on what account I write so many love-lyrics
> And whence this soft book comes into my mouth.
> . . . .
> If she with ivory fingers drive a tune through the lyre,
>   We look at the process.
> How easy the moving fingers; if hair is mussed on her forehead,
> If she goes in a gleam of Cos, in a slither of dyed stuff,
> There is a volume in the matter; if her eyelids sink into sleep,
> There are new jobs for the author (212–13)

What has changed for Pound from his early love writing is that the "I as lover" is now "my homage to Propertius as lover"—both being authors who convey love.

Pound presents Propertius's Cynthia in lines much quoted, as translated from Propertius:

> And Cynthia was alone in her bed.
> I was stupefied.
> I had never seen her looking so beautiful (221)

Kenner suggests that Pound wants the reader to read "stupefied" as a negative judgment on love (*The Pound Era* 285). Yet Kenner fails to note how this famous line is often translated as signifying foremost an experience of awe at Cynthia's beauty. If Pound intended for love to be stupefying in the ways that Kenner proposes, Pound also wished to have it other ways—suggesting that the lover's awe at the beauty of his beloved stupefies in all senses of the word. By this multiple use of the word "stupefy," Pound elects logopoeia, a "dance of words," putting in abeyance any sharp-witted satiric impulses that would recommend one meaning over the other. Kenner's refusal to see positive love and awe in this passage is indicative of how love itself as a motivating and transforming force is regularly suppressed in literary criticism. And while critics who opt for a psychoanalytic approach have expended much attention on angst-driven writing, they have largely ignored the other side of this complex, namely the ways that sexual love produces creative energies.

Sextus Propertius begins and ends by calling up a lineage of love poets and their beloveds. The poem starts in Greece, calling on Propertius's influential predecessors Callimachus and Philetas. (Callimachus was primarily known as a poet-scholar, and Philetas was a love poet who directly influenced Propertius and Ovid.)[5] Beginning his poem with these figures, Pound indicates that there is a lineage of love writing that traveled from Greece into Italy, which he will later summarize in *The Cantos* as "a light shines from Eleusis." The "I" of the poem declares that he is bringing the "Grecian orgies into Italy" and that "there is no high-road to the muses" (205). While K. K. Ruthven comments that Pound's rendering of "*orgia*" (mysteries) has degenerated into the modern "orgies," more likely Pound was pressing, or at least entertaining, the opposite point, that "orgies" and "mysteries" are inseparable. After a final tribute to the lineage of love poets and their beloveds who preceded Propertius, the poem ends:

> The waters of Styx poured over the wound:
> And now Propertius of Cynthia, taking his stand among these.
> (*Personae* 224)

Pound's "translation" puts added emphasis on Propertius's "wounds" of love by concluding with the same term (in *Elegies*, the reference to "wounds" occurs much earlier in the poem). Through this line he suggests that the only remedy to a wounding love is to allow oneself to be laved by the "pour[ing]" waters of Styx. However, in general, *Sextus Propertius* largely conveys a comedic vision of love and makes few references to the deathliness and wounds of love—aspects that are integrated into a more complex vision of love in *The Cantos*. Any deathliness that invades this poem can only be attributed to Pound's robust refusal of his prior melancholic poetic speakers: Pound's speaker now rushes headlong in the ways of love.

"Circe's This Craft"

At about the same time that Pound was composing *Hugh Selwyn Mauberley* and *Sextus Propertius*, he was also initiating work on *Canto IV*—the first canto to realize a way of writing that would set a direction for all of his future cantos. In *Canto IV* (1919), Pound discovers how to extend his Imagist "direct treatment of the 'thing,' whether subjective or objective." He is no longer compelled to generalize about love as good or evil, as beneficial or detrimental, but rather presents its tales and effects through a montage of associations. In this canto, Pound brings together his divergent dispositions of enchantment and melancholia in a writing in which an ecstatic poetic speaker—a speaker who stands apart from his egoistic or managerial self yet remains libidinally connected to his writing—presents rather than describes. *Canto IV* is replete with multiple processions and metamorphoses, with these serving simultaneously as subject matter and writing modality. Language and reference coalesce, and the object sought by love corresponds with the very language in which this canto is written.

One only need contrast Pound's writing in "Phanapoeia," created around this same time, to appreciate his success in conveying eros in this canto. In "Phanapoeia," Pound attempts to convey the pervasive intensity of sexual love, yet his depictions tend toward comical caricature:

> The swirl of light follows me through the square,
> The smoke of incense
> Mounts from the four horns of my bed-posts. (169)

Although Pound wishes to communicate the ephemeral character of this experience, his crisp denotative language precipitates solids: "The whirling tissue of light / is woven and grows solid beneath us" (170). In contrast in *Canto IV*, Pound leads his projective writing with a procession in which a beauteous configuration of ethereal figures, including a "Choros nympharum" and a breaking dawn, is conveyed through an associative writing of glimpsed reflections and heard sounds. This enchanting movement is preceded and followed by references to an eros linked with death and destruction:

Palace in smoky light,
Troy but a heap of smouldering boundary stones,
ANAXIFORMINGES! Aurunculeia!
Hear me. Cadmus of Golden Prows!
The silver mirrors catch the bright stones and flare,
Dawn, to our waking, drifts in the green cool light;
Dew-haze blurs, in the grass, pale ankles moving.
Beat, beat, whirr, thud, in the soft turf
            under the apple trees,
Choros nympharum, goat-foot, with the pale foot alternate;
Crescent of blue-shot waters, green-gold in the shallows,
A black cock crows in the sea foam (13)

Pound at the very outset of this canto engages a writing in which poetry's visual and aural relations have considerable power. The most immediate reference for the procession may be a marriage procession, since Aurunculeia is a bride praised in Catullus's *Epithalamium*. There are also several references to lyres through "ANAXIFORMINGES," which Terrell links to Pindar and Cadmus, who as the founder of Thebes was associated with the lyre (11). Pound thus provides an alternative to the Wordsworth he condemns in *Three Cantos* for his declaration that "the lyre should animate but not mislead the pen" (57). Pound depicts a Wordsworth who "bleeteth" presumably because of his election of an introspective poetry written amid a pastoral tranquility. At the end of his lovely sequence on the nymphs, Pound adds, "A black cock crows in the sea foam," thereby inserting a sinister figure at the very arrival of dawn. The figure of the black cock usurps Aphrodite's traditional place—her emergence from the sea—or possibly intimates that the black cock is copulating with her in a miasma of sea foam.

Pound's superior way of writing in this canto, of conveying this procession, is made evident by contrasting it with his failed early Imagist poem "After Ch'u Yuan," in which a poetic speaker stakes his territory and then boils over in anticipation: "I will come out of the new thicket / and accost the procession of maidens." In *Canto IV*, Pound creates a "procession" in which the subject matter itself suggests the need for an associative writing. The procession may refer to the May Day celebrations in which Pound and H.D. participated in Philadelphia or the processions associated with the Eleusinian mysteries. Later in this canto the refrains of Sappho and of Catullus's *Epithalamium* are repeated, followed by a reference to the breaking of the hymen: "Hymenaeus Io! / Hymen, Io Hymenaee! Aurunculeia!"

In *The Genesis of Ezra Pound's Cantos*, Bush traces how Pound made a breakthrough in *Canto IV* and then revised *Cantos I–III*. Bush maintains that Pound, learning from the prose masters of his time, namely Flaubert, James, and Joyce, "began to see that poetry did not need the actual presence of verbs so much as a syntax that could incorporate their action and relate it to the other actions" (179). Bush contrasts *Three Cantos* and *Canto IV*: "*Three Cantos* describes externals. . . . *Canto IV* records 'a seeing' . . . in the instant those events are being registered . . . rendering the sequence and impact of perception upon consciousness" (203–4). Although, as Bush contends, Pound likely learned much from these modern prose masters, Bush simply does not engage how the subject matter of this poem and its method of writing coalesce in its processions and metamorphoses. Nor does Bush address how this breakthrough canto is immersed in the subject of sexual love and addresses both sexual initiation and sexual betrayal, at a time when Pound was starting an adulterous relationship in the wake of what for him was a disappointing marriage to Dorothy Shakespear. One of Pound's failed early efforts to turn *Three Cantos* into *The Cantos* he was seeking to write involved editing his initial writing into much shorter, abbreviated poems, presumably to give them the quickened energies of his Imagist verse.

After beginning *Canto IV* with a moving cortege, Pound is pressed to imagine a different kind of procession or process: metamorphosis. Indeed, if procession depends on a temporal succession, metamorphosis engages physical transformation. Immediately after the soft footwork of his initial procession, Pound rapidly invokes myths of metamorphosis, of love and trauma—the stories of Philomela, Ityn, Cabestan, Actæon, and Vidal. As he conveys these tales, Pound turns their emotional plots into a phenomenal present, creating sensate perceptions of the hearts of these myths made overly familiar through repeated tellings. In a writing of glimpses, rather than pictures, Pound creates a sublime beauty that links love and terror as a deceptive familiarity turns into an envisioned defamiliarity. Pound combines two different myths of people who unwittingly cannibalize their loved ones—Tereus and his son, and Lady Seramonda and Cabestan—and focuses attention on just what the forever aftertaste of these eating experiences would entail:

> "All the while, the while, swallows crying:
>
> Ityn!
>
> "It is Cabestan's heart in the dish."
> "It is Cabestan's heart in the dish?"
> "No other taste shall change this." (13)

In these sensate renderings meant to pierce or, in Barthes's terminology, to serve as a "punctum" of the myths, Pound creates an absolute present for the retold tales. Turning to the Actæon myth, Pound brings out the sexual allure of Artemis through the phenomenal glitter of sunlight, leaves, and roof tiles, associating the roof with fish scales:

> 'Tis. 'Tis. Ytis!
>   Actæon . . .
>   and a valley,
> The valley is thick with leaves, with leaves, the trees,
> The sunlight glitters, glitters a-top,
> Like a fish-scale roof (14)

The sequence of the myths of metamorphoses concludes by drawing together the multiple pools of water associated with Persephone, Artemis, and Salmacis, a water nymph, as Cygnus as "cygnet" moves on.

> Stumbling, stumbling along in the wood,
> Muttering, muttering Ovid:
>   "Pergusa . . . pool . . . pool . . .Gargaphia,
> "Pool . . . pool of Salmacis."
>   The empty armour shakes as the cygnet moves. (15)

Although the immediate reference for the "stumbling" character is the troubadour "Old Vidal," whose fate replicates that of Actæon, this stumbling may also be referring to Pound's search for another measure, a different modality, that will sustain his poem and enable him to move on. The son of the sea gods Neptune and Thetis, Cygnus escapes Achilles's death-dealing blows by turning into a swan. Achilles, who thinks he has crushed Cygnus, finds only empty armor. Thus, Cygnus, as "cygnet," a young swan, "moves" on. The word "cygnet" must have intrigued Pound, given that it is a homonym of "signet," an official seal. Finding through myths of metamorphosis not only subject matter but a model of how to write his cantos, as figures morph into other figures, Pound may well have felt that he had discovered a "cygnet"/signet. Immediately following this declaration of victory, the poem moves into the ecstatic sequence discussed in chapter 1 in which through a series of metamorphosing allusions and sounds, the love poet Daniel's quoted *e lo soleills plovil* transforms into "The liquid and rushing crystal / beneath the knees of the gods. / Ply over ply, thin glitter of water" and into an "eddying fluid" (15).

In *Canto IV*, Pound no longer contains love within moralizing judgments of good and bad. Now he simply conveys love as powerful in its capacity to incite desirable and horrific effects. In this canto, Pound presents rather than describes moments of transportation and bliss, trauma and love. Indeed, while the device of metamorphosis allows Pound to instantiate a movement between diverse figurations, it also enables him to explore a transformative love. Through the trope and writing modality of metamorphosis, Pound conceptually and temporally extends his Imagist practice of "the precise instant when a thing outward and objective transforms itself" into a series of metamorphosing moments. It is probably no accident that Pound's much-touted pre-Imagist "Actæon," based on a myth of metamorphosis, is one of his few early poems to manifest a projective writing. Indeed, as many commentators have noted, "Actæon" is a superior example of an Imagist poem compared to many of the poems that Pound created under his Imagist banner.

To suggest that *Canto IV* led to all of Pound's subsequent cantos is a large claim. Yet the suggestion here is that the simultaneous engagement with traumatic and enchanting sexual love through a writing process that at once registers and alters them using a processual and metamorphosing métier *did* enable Pound to create his subsequent cantos. This method of writing enabled Pound to draw together his enchanted and melancholic dispositions and his celebration of and disgust with love. After writing *Canto IV*, Pound continued writing *Cantos VI–VIII*, publishing them in short succession. By the time he published *A Draft of XVI Cantos* in 1925, he had decided to use only a small, revised portion of *Three Cantos* as *Canto I* and had turned *Canto VIII* into *Canto II*.

I conclude this chapter by considering *Cantos I* and *II* as Pound's concerted response to how to begin *The Cantos* in light of his subsequent discoveries. In configuring the final order of his *Cantos*, Pound initiated two rather different movements in *Canto I* and *Canto II*. In *Canto I* there is a journey to the underworld, and in *Canto II* there is an entrance into a fecund sea. In other words, there is a journey through melancholia and into enchantment, from Hades into erotic mania, a pattern that repeats elsewhere in *The Cantos* and replicates Freud's theory of how ego libido becomes object libido through object cathexis as well as Eleusinian rituals and other acts of mystery cults in which self-denial leads to a desubjectivized flourishing.

Pound states in *Canto I* that "Circe's this craft," thereby naming Circe's enchanting sexual powers as indispensable to his "craft." And while "craft" refers to the relationship between sexual attraction and poetic technique, "craft" should also be understood as a moving boat. In *Canto I*, Pound's omniscient poetic speaker, as Odysseus, must bury Elpenor, who has died of his own drunken excess on Circe's island and has not yet been buried. No longer possessed of a satiric attitude toward a hapless youth, as in *Mauberley*, Pound's poetic speaker seeks to give Elpenor a proper burial. Indeed, to the extent that Mauberley is modeled on a youthful Pound, *The Cantos* enacts a deliberate revision of this autobiography. Through the canto, the sense of descent and an untoward movement into darkness are marked from the outset, as proprioceptive energies prevail: "And then went down to the ship, / Set keel to breakers, forth on the godly sea," and more mysteriously, "The ocean flowing backward, came we then to the place" (3). In having Circe, Aphrodite, and Persephone all present in this canto, Pound refuses moral distinctions frequently engaged to contrast three kinds of sexual love: lust, amour, and occulted eros.

In *Canto II*, the rapidity and agility of Pound's metamorphosing métier increase as the aural, visual, and semantic registers of the poem attain surprising combinations. Entirely absent from this canto is any moralizing judgment that would bifurcate a lustful from a sublime love. At the outset of the canto, Pound presents a composite figure of sexual enticement. Beginning with an image of seals sporting in the "cliff-wash," Pound continues:

> Sleek head, daughter of Lir,
> eyes of Picasso
> Under black fur-hood, lithe daughter of Ocean (6)

As elsewhere in Pound, the relations between the aural, visual, and semantic elements of this verse are complex and work at different levels of depth and surface as well as association and disassociation. While the figure of a seal moves through these lines, "Lir" (an archaic spelling of King Lear) tips into the reference to Picasso, both *i*'s—eyes—unsettling the surface to make way for the yoked association of Lir and Picasso, based on the material relations of language and an intimated sexuality connected to the seal. While other metamorphosing passages of this canto are less intertwined, the relations between elements are often complex since Pound's perception leading to further perception is derived from a human bedrock of "unanalysable processes." The sound relations in particular aid in the delivery of the canto's multiple metamorphoses—from rope to vine, from captive to feral animals, and from men to porpoises and fish:

> And where was gunwale, there now was vine-trunk
> And tenthril where cordage had been,
> grape-leaves on the rowlocks (8)
> . . . .
> Lynx-purr, and heathery smell of beasts,
> where tar smell had been,
> Sniff and pad-foot of beasts,
> eye-glitter out of black air. (8)

. . . .
Black snout of a porpoise
     where Lycabs had been,
Fish-scales on the oarsmen. (9)

Particularly important for all three passages is the writing of glimpsed presences, rather than sustained depictions; in the first two excerpts the *th* and other soft sounds buffer the metamorphosing moment.

The predominant myth that informs *Canto II* may be of the capture of Dionysus by seafaring men, although there are also references to Circe's transformations and to Tyro's rape by Poseidon, who took on a disguise and assumed the rightful place of her sought-after lover, the divine river Enipeus (Terrell 6). The Dionysian plot is taken from a Homeric hymn, in which Dionysus escapes being tied up with ropes because the cordage turns to vines, and he himself metamorphoses into a lion. The canto enters into its Dionysus episodes very much in medias res, thereby avoiding a dramatic plot. Pound also elects to present unaccounted-for moments in the myths themselves. For example, Pentheus is shown as not yet having made his fateful decision to reject the worshipping of Dionysus when he is torn to bits by the maenads, but in the company of those who would advise him differently. Important to many of the myths of Dionysus is the Dionysian mask, which at once symbolizes identity, its transformation, and its splintering. As Pound in this canto furthers his subject matter and writing method of metamorphosing elements, his engagement with Dionysus, who represents the possibility of ecstatic states, a standing outside of oneself, compounds his explorations. Indeed, this canto's excess of transforming languages and episodes are an ecstatic disseminating of the more limited ecstatic moments in *Canto IV*.

Pound's decision in *Cantos I* and *II* to engage a movement from Hades to fecundity carries through on his autobiographical and occult narrative—the burial of the hapless Elpenor as a replacement for the melancholic Mauberly—and his election of a metamorphosing enchantment or mania.[6] Pound finds a way to write his long poem through transforming both his understanding of love and its writing. While much has been written on Pound's depiction of love in his cantos, there are moments in which Pound's projective writing produces erotic energy and moments in which it does not. Richard Sieburth in his introduction to Pound's *Pisan Cantos* draws attention to Pound's "wooden writing" through his predetermined tropes: "[The] moments of goddess-induced transcendence may be the least convincing passages in *The Pisan Cantos* less because of their Parnassian classical garb [. . .] than because they somehow feel too programmatic, emerging as they do from Pound's preconceived plan for his *Paradiso* in the Italian drafts of early 1945" (xvii). In *Ezra Pound and the Erotic Medium* Oderman provides a valuable account of Pound's replicating erotic tropes throughout his cantos, although he does not examine them for the ways that they convey erotic energy or do not.

While Pound's exploration of love was hardly finished at this relatively early stage, he had found his way through the writing of love to a projective and libidinized field poetics that would continue to instruct him for the remainder of his career. Although Pound and his readers may question just what kind of vision or order Pound achieved through this lifelong endeavor, he did open up the ways that love and sex are presented rather than entrenching restrictive self-other and lover-beloved economies. Assessments of Pound are much troubled by his fascist politics and his many racist and sexist pronouncements. However, his creation of a different writing of love that fully engaged him has remained telling for subsequent generations. The love writing of all the other poets examined in *The Transmutation of Love and Avant-Garde Poetics* enabled their progressive and often radical politics. That Pound's love writing found accord with fascist politics reveals the blinded, not to mention the blinkered, aspects of love itself.

"Love Is Writing"

The Advent of H.D.

> He succeeded (when he became most impassioned) by ceasing to
> become personal.
> —H.D., "Notes on Euripides, Pausanius, and Greek Lyric Poets"

To claim that both Pound's and H.D.'s formal innovations are implicated in the transmutation of love is not to suggest that their projects are the same. Pound, inheriting centuries of love poetry in which male poets constituted their subjectivity in relationship to a female beloved, a female other, more quickly than H.D. shifted the subject-object duality on which this writing depends into a projective love and libidinized field poetics of epic dimensions. H.D., discovering a largely erased tradition of female poets as lovers, wrote a long love poem, *Sea Garden* (1916), but did not extend this writing into epic poetry until *Trilogy* and *Helen in Egypt*, both produced relatively late in her life. Yet, while it took Pound more than a decade to discover how to engage fully the discoveries he made through his Imagist explorations, H.D. quickly extended these poetics in *Sea Garden*, which carries the strains of lover-beloved poetry while voiding the place of the situated poetic speaker as a self-dramatizing lover.

Although H.D. realized a sustained love writing well in advance of Pound's *Cantos*, shortly after publishing *Sea Garden*, she turned her major efforts to prose fictions. In a letter to John Cournos, H.D. tells of changing from a "poetic art" to writing a "novel": "I must explain to you that the novel is not intended as a work of art—at least not as it stands. . . . Well, I do not put my personal self into my poems. But my personal self has got between me and my real self, my real artist personality. And to clear the ground, I have tried to write things down. . . . You must remember that writing poetry requires a clarity, a clairvoyance almost" (H.D., "Art and Ardor in World War One" 147–48). Decades later, H.D. commented that if she had known how to bridge her poetry and prose, she would likely not have written either.[1] H.D.'s quandary between prose and poetry suggests the doubleness of her quest: to negate her egoistic self and to alter the terms of her subjectivity or of representation. H.D.'s prose fictions and narrative poems provided her a forum in which she could reconstitute the terms, or representations, of her existence far more overtly—a set of rich investigations in which "this" is often reconstrued as "that." In her poetry writing, H.D. sought a writing of the present, a clairvoyance in which "this" is "this." Throughout her life, H.D. did much to critique and revise what she came to call the "sex-gender" system, and she also sought the possibilities of a present-tense love writing.

Pound's ability to carry his Imagist discoveries into an epic poem more quickly is due to the fact that, despite his refusal of a masculine lover as a poetic speaker, he could still engage the field of patriarchal heterosexual representation from an empowered place within it. H.D. had to revise the "sex-gender system" far more radically to extend the poetic authority of her initial love poetry. Unlike Pound, H.D. consistently asserted and never questioned the importance of love for her writing, but she did not possess the representational means (which did not exist) to extend her initial love writing into an epic poetry. Pound's initial poetic quest with the love lyric was marked by struggles with selves and negated selves, personae and impersonality. H.D.'s writing from the beginning bypassed the self as a centered poetic speaker. While H.D. never completely deleted the personal "I," it was only one of many configurations or dispensations in her poetry. While both poets came to write epics that engaged a projective love and libidinized field poetics, H.D. retained the introjective moments of these poetics to a far greater degree. As Robert Kelly remarks, "H.D. more than any poet I know was faithful to [her feelings'] sensate and particular arisings" (34).

In *Psyche Reborn*, Susan Stanford Friedman, noting similarities between H.D.'s earliest poetry in *Sea Garden* and her poetry in *Trilogy*, looked for reasons for H.D.'s recovery of her poetic powers in her successful analysis with Freud. H.D.'s ability to return in later life to a poetics she had initiated earlier poses many psychological questions beyond the purview of this book. However, necessary to this renewed love writing in these long poems were the alternative understandings and models for addressing sexual love she created in the intervening decades in her prose fiction.[2] In both *Trilogy* and *Helen in Egypt*, H.D. engaged the demands of projective poetry in which one perception leads directly to the next. And while in *Trilogy* and *Helen in Egypt*, H.D. employed narrative frames to a much greater extent than in the other poetry considered here, the writing itself is in line with the Imagist injunction that it record "the precise instant when a thing outward and objective . . . darts into a thing inward and subjective." As H.D. writes in *Helen in Egypt*, "She herself is the writing" (22).

If, for Pound, an important device for his initial projective love writing was the concept and enactment of metamorphosis, for H.D. theophany and related beliefs that allowed for the presence of the human in the god and the god in the human were directly enabling. H.D. writes in *Notes on Thought and Vision*, "it was *de rigueur* for an Olympian not to appear to a mortal directly" but "as a tree or river spirit" (38). Gregory maintains that H.D. was acquainted with and drew on the cult of Dionysus, which she describes utilizing Jane Harrison's *Prolegomena to the Study of the Greek Religion*: the "cardinal, the essentially dramatic, conviction of the religion of Dionysus is that the worshipper cannot only worship but can become, can *be*, the god" (*H.D. and Hellenism* 122). The various beliefs and rituals associated with theophany, including the notion of the demonic itself, provided H.D. with a rich field of culturally resonant languages and practices by which to explore cathexes with her beloveds. In imagining her beloveds as godly, or as having the presence of a god in them, H.D. was able to amplify her feelings for her beloveds.[3] Moreover, as a mortal addressing a "god," a common practice for both female and male Greek citizens, H.D. could engage a sense of her beloved as having power while not disempowering herself, or at least no more so than a male subject bowing before his gods. She thus was able to evade the limiting decorums of centuries of heterosexual love writing based on hierarchical, gendered relations. In addressing her beloveds as deities, and by invoking rather than objectifying them, H.D. avoided the problematic decorum for a female writer of overpowering her beloved through treating him or her as *her* love object.

Perhaps more than any poet in this book, H.D. has been criticized for her love poetry and the love relations of which she wrote. One of the reasons for at least some of the discomfiture, especially at a time when feminist critics in revising the literary canon are attempting to correct for misogynist misappraisals, is the extent to which H.D. wrote out of failed or lost love relations. Yet men love poets are rarely criticized for what might be judged as unwarranted love responses, but are often celebrated for their very excesses. Moreover, while H.D. found impetus for her love writing through experiences of loss, her poetry almost always evoked the presence and power of love. Many of the poems in *Sea Garden* were written out of love loss with respect to all three of H.D.'s most significant early lovers, Pound, Aldington, and Gregg, but for the most part *Sea Garden* explored the powers of love rather than mourning its loss. While H.D. drew on a failed relationship with the field marshal Hugh Dowding in writing *Helen in Egypt*, she projected their relationship onto the figures of Helen and Achilles, who meet up after the Trojan War and pursue their ongoing love struggle.

From the outset, H.D. maintained the importance of the experience of love for her writing. In letters written to John Cournos in 1916–1918, H.D. reveals a well-developed conviction that "being in love" is necessary for writing inspired verse. In these letters, H.D. insists that whatever personal difficulties love presents, all requited and unrequited lovers pursue their love to cultivate their capacity to write—their "daemon" (H.D., "Art and Ardor in World War One" 125). Of herself, she writes, "The hurt I suffered has freed my song—this is most precious to me" (134). And "I seem to be a spirit now—something that burns and flames away and wants to write. R. [Richard Aldington] has made me this" (134). So definite was H.D. about these ideas that she wanted to help Aldington free himself of the brutality of war and gain access to his writing, by helping him to meet up with the woman of his affair, however painful to herself. She writes, "If being torn by unanswered passion is going to make a great poet we must not let *any* personal consideration come between R and his work" (134). Although she was entirely clear in these letters that she did not return Cournos's passion for her, she advised him, "If love of me—absolute and terrible and hopeless love— is going to help you to write—then love me. Do not let *ought* and *ought not*, this evil spirit torment you. With the Daemon, there is no conscience" (125).

In her manifesto, *Notes on Thought and Vision*, H.D. declares, "There is no great art period without great lovers," and "we must be 'in love' before we can understand the mysteries of vision" (21, 22). In that work, she explored the relationship between mind and love, insisting that for vision to occur these two must be brought into alignment: "I have said that the over-mind is a lens. I should say more exactly that the lover-mind and the over-mind are two lenses. When these lenses are properly adjusted, focused, they bring the world of vision into consciousness. The two work separately, perceive separately, yet make one picture" (23).[4] For H.D. the first step in the Eleusinian mysteries "has to do with sex" and she insists that "body" is the source of "spirit," whether that "spirit" be expressed as "physical love" or as that "which we refer to in common speech as spirit." She concludes that the "body . . . like a lump of coal fulfills its highest function when it is being consumed." She notes that when "coal burns" or "when the body is consumed with love," they "give off heat." And, "taken a step further, coal may be used to make gas, an essence, a concentrated ethereal form of coal." While, for Pound at this stage of his career, sex energy must go in one direction or another—reproductive "heat" or educational "light"—for H.D. the body "in love," regardless of its expression, is "all spirit . . . in different forms." And she emphasizes, "we cannot have spirit without body . . . the body of individual men and women" (*Notes on Thought* 47, 48).

Critical commentary on H.D.'s love relations has divided between an abjured "romantic thralldom" and an honored "intersubjectivity." In an early and influential essay, Rachel Blau DuPlessis coined the term "romantic thralldom," defining it as "an all-encompassing, totally defining love between unequals. . . . Such love is possessive, and while those enthralled feel it completes and even transforms them, they are also enslaved. The eroticism of romantic love, born of this unequal relationship between the sexes, may depend for its satisfaction upon dominance and submission" ("Romantic Thralldom" 406). DuPlessis further comments, "H.D. was especially vulnerable to the power of what she termed the "*héros fatal*,"a man who she saw as her spiritual similar, an artist, a healer, a psychic. Again and again, this figure whom she conspired to create betrayed her; again and again, she was reduced to fragments from which her identity had once more to be painfully constructed" ("Thralldom" 406–7). In *Erotic Reckonings*, Thomas Simmons utilizes DuPlessis's definition, distinguishing H.D.'s bad love relations of enthrallment from her good relations of intersubjectivity. Drawing much of his study from Jessica Benjamin's *Bonds of Love*, Simmons remarks: "The one mode . . . places her at the mercy of men who demean her. The other mode . . . [as a] reciprocity that affirms each knower's identity leads her toward a lesbianism that assuages" (57).

Yet, relations of intersubjectivity, as they are generally conceived, validate a negotiated relationship between two individuated lovers and as such tend to occlude the transfixing experience of "being in love" that compels H.D.[5] Moreover, in basing understanding on the individual personalities of two lovers, intersubjective philosophies still the exchange between self and other, subject and object, which is defining for sexual love. While the recognition of lovers' individualities may be an important aspect of a love relation over time, one that H.D. certainly recognized, intersubjective love does not get at the demonic energies and visionary seeings that H.D. saw as defining of love. H.D. was not only the writer who experiences, but also the writer who elects as her poetics "to sing love, / love must first shatter us." Hers is a poetics that not only permits transportation through love, but pursues it, as in the *cras amet* refrain she repeats throughout her novel *Paint It Today* (written in 1921 but not published until 1992): "Let those who never loved before, love now; let those who always loved, love now the more" (11–12).

In dividing H.D.'s "good" love relations from the "bad" ones, critics have not recognized H.D.'s major accomplishment of putting *her* love into writing. H.D. distinguishes between various kinds of love, valuing each differently. For H.D., passionate love and companionable intimacy are not mutually exclusive, but different stages of love. She writes in an early essay on Euripides: "It is to a bird, they call . . . a small familiar loving spirit, one whose voice calls them home, back to the woods, veiling the elements and fire and strength of the earth, the kind woods tender as a lover's arms after the fire and elemental power of love is over" ("Notes on Euripides, Pausanius, and Greek Lyric Poets" 14). In her essay on Meleager in this same grouping, H.D. praises this bisexual poet for "exonerat[ing] those who had 'loved much'" (8). In a later assessment of her entire career, "H.D. by Delia Alton," H.D. engages rather different vocabularies for eros, including "romance," "love," "rapture," and "desire," finally designating the whole ball of wax with an indefinite referent: "It means everything to her, she must not let go her hold on romance or on writing" (211).

In separating H.D.'s lesbian lovers from her heterosexual lovers, critics have tended to ignore the powerful and painful erotic struggles with her female lovers, particularly Frances Gregg. Much of the analysis of H.D.'s lesbian relations has been based on her roman à clef works, which are modeled somewhat loosely on bildungsroman and künstlerroman narratives that have as their telos the protagonist's realization of herself as an individual self or artist who has found her place in the world. Not surprisingly, in these prose works H.D.'s same-sex lovers enable her to achieve a sense of self that her male lovers do not. Yet, H.D.'s poetry does not indicate a clear preference for male or female beloveds, and she often uses pronouns in ambiguous ways. If establishing a sense of self or artistry is the culmination of works based on the genre expectations of bildungsroman or künstlerroman, love poetry finds its raison d'être in the strength of its impassioned address. In H.D.'s novel *Asphodel*, Hermione (the H.D. character) remarks to Fayne Rabb (the Frances Gregg character): "Will anyone ever say I love you Fayne as I say it? I don't want to be (as they say crudely) a boy. Nor do I want to be a girl. . . . None of that seems really . . . to matter. I see you. I feel you. My pulse runs swiftly" (100).

I do not mean to suggest that the gender identity of H.D.'s object choice is a matter of indifference, but rather to emphasize *how* she says her love may be more important for her poetry than the gender identity of specific beloveds. In her prose writing and her narrative poems, H.D. directly engages representational figures or symbolic forms that are problematic for her as a woman and as a bisexual writer; in her lyric poetry, intense sayings often occlude social positionalities and identities and, if they do not exactly transcend these, they do evade them. A defining characteristic of almost all of H.D.'s early love relationships is that she formed them with writers or aspiring writers. Far more important for her writing than intersubjective relations between lovers was how she and her lovers created shared imaginings. H.D. credited Meleager's love writing to his meeting up with a specific beloved, "his Heliodora" ("Notes on Euripides, Pausanius, and Greek Lyric Poets" 3). Late in life, she commented that through writing it is possible to retain a "vow" of a relationship that is "materially 'ditched,'" since "nothing is ever lost or can be, of . . . 'a spirit love'" (*End* 58). While some may find this remark overly romantic, or desperate, for H.D. it was a fact of her writing life.

In the novel *Paint It Today* what Midget (the H.D. character) finds most exciting in her relationship with Josepha (the Gregg character) is that they "see things" together. After their breakup, Josepha taunts Midget with the lack of reality of their "seeings": "Do you remember that night we spent in Liverpool before the boat left? I didn't really see those ghost pigeons on the window ledge. You thought I saw them. How could they have possibly been there? Why did you always believe in all the lies I told you?" (50). In Midget's return letter she upholds their shared imaginings and poetry, as if these were inseparable: "You used to know what poetry is? . . . Were those the wild birds you say, the blue blue-birds or, as you said, blue sparrows? Wasn't it sparrows that drew the chariot of the goddess?" (55). Midget castigates what she perceives to be Josepha's betrayal by insisting that those things they exchanged, whether imaginary or real, are irrevocable: "Do you remember the very first hyacinths were out that day your train left? Your arms were full of them and your eyes hated me above them and you seemed to say, 'You see there are other people, you see there are other hyacinths than the ones you bring me.' Yes, you tell lies, Josepha. There were never other hyacinths" (55). Midget may be obliquely referring to the homoerotic aspects of their relationship through references to "hyacinths," but she is also insisting that their love and what was produced through it is singular, and therefore cannot be duplicated—nor can it be duplicitous.

Sea Garden

In *Sea Garden*, H.D. extended the poetics she first discovered in her Imagist poems to an entire volume of poetry. While many of the individual pieces evince a poetics of direct presentation, of one perception leading to a further perception, the movement from poem to poem also entails something of this relation. *Sea Garden* might be seen as a deconstruction of traditional love poems into poems of pursuit and of icon. *Sea Garden* is significantly defined by its poems of iconic sea flowers—"Sea Rose," "Sea Lily," "Sea Poppies," "Sea Violet," and "Sea Iris"—and poems of pursuit: "The Helmsman," "Mid-Day," "Pursuit," "Huntress," "Loss," and "The Cliff Temple." In the sea flower poems, the poetic speaker does not figure except as the voice of the poem. The pursuit poems, often written from the perspective of an unidentified "we," carry the sense of a lover's desire for submission or enthrallment to a beloved. In the sea flower poems, a flower hardens into an iconic virtuality; in the pursuit poems, a path or action disappears into a sublime transparency. Indeed, the tensions in traditional love poetry between an active lover and a passive beloved are transmuted in *Sea Garden* into poems that render love as an excess of mobility or stasis.

H.D. begins *Sea Garden* with an iconic flower poem followed by a poem of pursuit, "Sea Rose" and "The Helmsman." The rose is the flower H.D. associates with Sappho, and she quotes Meleager as characterizing the rose as a "lover-loving." The sea rose and the other iconic flowers in this volume are described in partially negative terms, which paradoxically seem to ennoble them. "Sea Rose" proceeds through metonymic displacements that explore contiguous relations:

> more precious
> than a wet rose

single on a stem—
you are caught in the drift.

Stunted, with small leaf,
you are flung on the sand,
you are lifted
in the crisp sand
that drives in the wind. (*Collected Poems* 5)

H.D.'s insistence in this poem, as throughout her work, on "drift" is enacted by the lists of phrases. The replicated *st* sounds create a brief stutter or stoppage to the poem's predominantly quick pace, which comes to an end in its slowed-down final lines:

Can the spice-rose
drip such acrid fragrance
hardened in a leaf? (5)

The emphasis on the open sound of "spice-rose" contrasts with "acrid fragrance," and the "drift" of the poem eventuates in a "drip." Although H.D.'s emphasis on sharp delineation and hardness in "Sea Rose" and in other iconic flower poems in this volume has caused some critics to see these poems as limited by a masculine modernist poetics, these qualities are engaged to redefine a feminine beloved. H.D. may be creating an implicit critique of the carpe diem motif to which she was exposed in Theocritus, read together by H.D. and Gregg, in which a maiden defends her refusal "to seize the day" and to make herself available: "The grapes turn to raisins, not wholly will the dry rose perish" (Lang 148). Further, this rose may be dry because, like Sappho, she may be "burnt" by passion (H.D. *Notes* 64).

The movement forward in "Sea Rose" depends on metonymic relations, and "The Helmsman" engages in a similar listing of paratactic phrases. In "The Helmsman," an unidentified "we" escape into inland woods, but are brought back abruptly to the helmsman and the sea. The experience of the woods is rendered through a same that replicates same, or a same that divides from same, in what seems to be simultaneously envisioned as an internal and an external scene:

We forgot—we worshipped,
we parted green from green,
we sought further thickets,
we dipped our ankles
through leaf-mould and earth,
and wood and wood-bank enchanted us—

and the feel of the clefts in the bark,
and the slope between tree and tree—
and a slender path strung field to field
and wood to wood
and hill to hill
and the forest after it. (6)

Although the poem expends most of its energy describing an inland pastoral landscape visited by supernatural energies, the helmsman is presented as possessing greater power. In the conclusion of the poem the "we" are delivered to the ascending motion of a boat at sea and to the same fear with which the poem began:

But now, our boat climbs—hesitates—drops—
climbs—hesitates—crawls back—
climbs—hesitates—
O be swift—
we have always known you wanted us. (7)

While it might be tempting to see this poem as presenting a conflict between an enthralled heterosexual love and a relatively more peaceful lesbian love, for H.D. these are likely entangled. The helmsman may well be a powerful male lover, but he may also be the power of passionate love. Or the helmsman might carry the fear of the power of passionate love for a same-sex lover in a patriarchal heterosexual culture. While the lesbian lovers, or any pair of lovers, can escape temporarily into a hidden bower, a sheltered garden, they must ultimately turn outward and into a sea of unpredictable and uncontrollable forces.

Several critics have sought to locate a literary source for the intriguing figure of the helmsman, connecting him to Plato's *Phaedrus* and *Symposium*. Gregory draws attention to how the invocation of the helmsman allows for "immediate daimonic possession," and she examines its Platonic genealogy: "The urgent first assertion and desire establish a Platonic teleology, in which knowledge ('we have always known') and desire ('you have wanted us') work in inevitable, reciprocal concert . . . suggesting the intimacy of long-known erotic bondage" (*H.D. and Hellenism* 135). While "The Helmsman" also calls up the figures of Jesus and Hermes, and the romantic trope of the boat may conjure the poetics of Shelley or Rimbaud, a far more direct source for the helmsman is in Mackail. In his introduction to *Select Epigrams*, Mackail paraphrases an epigram by Meleager: "Love the Helmsman steers the soul, like a winged boat, over the perilous sea of desire" (xii). Although Mackail does not include the actual epigram in his volume, a translation in Paton's *Greek Anthology* reveals a far less decorous statement about love, in which both Cypris (another name for Aphrodite) and Love (presumably her son Eros or Cupid) steer a boat that drives the speaker into a "Pamphylian sea of boys": "Cypris is my skipper and Love keeps the tiller, holding in his hand the end of my soul's rudder, and the heavy gale of Desire drives me storm-tossed; for now I swim verily in a Pamphylian sea of boys." "Pamphylian" is glossed at the bottom of the page: "as I did when my passion made me abject" (17).

While "The Helmsman" attests to a powerful masculine presence, the poem immediately following, "The Shrine," conveys a magisterial feminine presence. Combining both iconic and pursuit modes, "The Shrine" is most likely addressed to Aphrodite and influenced by Mackail's translation of an epigram by Anyte about the Cyprian Aphrodite: "This is Cyprian's ground since it was her pleasure ever to look from land on the shining sea, that she may give fulfillment of their voyage to sailors; and around the deep trembles, gazing on her bright image" (211). As in the preceding poems, this poem's projective love and libidinized field poetics are constituted through a listing of phrases. Moreover, as with the helmsman, this "spirit between the headlands" is predator and protector. "When the tides swirl," her "boulders cut and wreck." Even so this "bright shaft" gives special passage to the "we" of this poem:

> we passed the men in ships,
> we dared deeper than the fisher-folk
> and you strike us with terror
>
> .   .   .   .
>
> Flame passes under us
> and sparks that unknot the flesh,
> sorrow, spitting bone from bone,
> splendour athwart our eyes
> and rifts in the splendour,
> sparks and scattered light. (9)

By daring to approach the rocks, the "we" find feminine remonstrance and safety with this "land blight":

> Though oak-beams split,
> though boats and sea-men flounder,
> and the strait grind sand with sand
> and cut boulder to sand and drift—
> your eyes have pardoned our faults,

your hands have touched us—
you have leaned forward a little
and the waves can never thrust us back
from the splendour of your ragged coast. (9–10)

Although "The Shrine" may be read as both an iconic and a pursuit poem, in most of the poems one or the other of these dispensations dominates. In "Sea Lily," the action of sea, wind, and sand on the iconic flower is severe:

sand cuts your petal,
furrows it with hard edge,
like flint
on a bright stone. (14)

As in "The Helmsman," defined furrows evoke female sexuality. H.D. begins "Sea Lily" by reflecting on how "great heads as yours / drift upon the temple-steps" (14). While flowers as "heads" recall "heads" of state or religion, the "drift" cuts into this institutional circuitry. As in "Sea Rose," references to "drift" and "drifting" define the poem's metonymic propensities. Mackail titled one of the translated epigrams "Drifting," and that epigram likely informed several of the poems in *Sea Garden*, including "The Shrine," given its reference to "delicate Scylla": "Bitter wave of Love, and restless gusty Jealousies and wintry sea of rev-ellings, whither am I borne? and the rudders of my spirit are quite cast loose; will we sight delicate Scylla once again?" (115).

That H.D. is deliberately taking on lesbian or homoerotic references is amply evident in "Sea Violet." Her speaker's preference for the "white violet" and the "white root" is likely a homoerotic reference, since "white" often signaled homo-eroticism in the nineteenth century.[6] The speaker compares the white violet that fronts the sea to the "blue violets" that "flutter on the hill," asking "who would change for these / one root of the white sort." The answer:

Violet
your grasp is frail
on the edge of the sand-hill,
but you catch the light—
frost, a star edges with its fire. (25–26)

The sense that something which is small and frail, which is not "overly painted, over lovely," may bear the greatest beauty echoes H.D.'s descriptions of Frances Gregg in her novels. In *Paint It Today*, Josepha (Gregg) is described as wear-ing the wrong kind of clothes, and her "face was slightly spotted. Her color was bad." Yet despite these qualities, Midget marvels, "It was her eyes, set in the un-wholesome face . . . her hand, small unbending, Stiff with archaic grandeur; it was her eyes, an unholy splendour" (9). That these poems were inspired by or intended for Gregg is validated by Gregg's response to *Sea Garden*: she wrote her own poems "on the paper wrapper, and on the flyleaf, also over the title page, fi-nally filling in the empty back pages" (Guest *Herself Defined* 81).

In H.D.'s poems of pursuit, there is a double sense of "pursuit" as both pur-suing and being pursued. The poems are often quite mysterious about the iden-tities of their speakers and who is referenced by "you" and "we" and about the precise nature of their actions—who is doing what to whom and why. In sev-eral of the poems, a path or action disappears into transparency or sublimity. "Mid-Day" and "Pursuit" each effect a moment of paralysis in which the "I" is "spent," followed by a pursuit in which the "I" tracks the "you" through his or her footsteps until "I can find no trace of you." In "Mid-Day":

> The light beats upon me.
> I am startled—
> A split leaf crackles on the paved floor— (*Collected Poems* 10)

In "Pursuit," the "I" follows the "you," who appears to have been either pursu-ing or pursued:

> But here
> a wild-hyacinth stalk is snapped:
> the purple buds—half-ripe—
> show deep purple
> where your heel pressed.
>
> . . . .
>
> This is clear—
> you fell on the downward slope,
> you dragged a bruised thigh—you limped—
> you clutched this larch. (*Collected Poems* 11–12)

The speaker asks if "you" have disappeared into the realm of the "wood-daemon," which seems to satisfy the speaker in some way, as if this pursuit has of neces-sity entered into a different realm:

> For some wood-daemon
> has lightened your steps.
> I can find no trace of you
> in the larch-cones and the underbrush. (*Collected Poems* 12)

"Huntress," a pursuit poem with the same sense of broken earth and furrow as in the pastoral scenes of "The Helmsman," concludes with a haunting address to this "you":

> We climbed the ploughed land,
> dragged the seed from the clefts,
> broke the clods with our heels,
> whirled with a parched cry
> into the woods:
>
> *Can you come,*
> *can you come,*
> *can you follow the hound trail,*
> *can you trample the hot froth?* (24)

H.D. would seem to be echoing Pound's well-known and much-touted "The Return," a poem published in 1912 before Pound's discovery of Imagism that Guest claims likely aided H.D. in her own more concerted writing of Imagist poetry (Guest *Herself Defined* 45). But "Huntress," written as a past action projected into the future, is more impassioned, more unbound.

"She Herself Is the Writing"

H.D. did not return to write the same quality of sustained love poetry evinced in *Sea Garden* until *Trilogy* and *Helen in Egypt*, written some thirty years later. In both of the later poems, as in *Sea Garden*, there is the sense of direct seeing, what H.D. referred to in her letter to Cournos as her poetry of "clairvoyance." While *Trilogy* is readily categorized as an epic or long poem, critics have debated whether to characterize *Helen in Egypt* as epic, drama, or lyric. *Helen in Egypt* includes characteristics of all three genres, but it, along with *Trilogy*, evinces a projective love and libidinized field poetics. Both works constitute a writing in which perception leads directly to further perception, language phrase to language phrase. If in Pound's cantos, the forward movement of a projective-introjective poetics is most prominent, in H.D. the introjective or backward work is intense as she reworks her field of "that" so she can accomplish a writing of "this." In both works, H.D. takes on a writing of the present to realize a changed reality, to make "real what is most real." "Making real" involves H.D. in emotional and intellectual responses in which the experience of sexual love is both a generative force and the subject matter of her poetry. Both long poems were directly inspired by people whom H.D. loved in her actual life, although these relations are more defining for *Helen in Egypt* than for *Trilogy*. In *Helen in Egypt*, by projecting her existence onto a cast of godly and heroic figures, H.D. creates a highly charged libidinal field.

In *Trilogy* H.D. searches for a reparative vision in light of the traumatic destruction of World War II. In the initial section of this three-part long poem, "The Walls Do Not Fall," H.D. uses the metaphor of "walls" to investigate the ruins that remain and the psychological barriers erected to survive this trauma. *Trilogy* does not, as it has been reductively credited, "redescribe loss as something triumphant, character-building, transformative" (Detloff 8), but rather, as a writing of the present, it connects the immediate past with the present, so that H.D. can go on. *Trilogy* is sometimes compared to Eliot's *Four Quartets*, but the poems' ultimate vision and language philosophy are very different. Eliot states as his aim "the use of memory" for "expanding . . . love beyond desire" (36). Moreover, he is frustrated by how words "will not stay in place." For H.D. desire and love are not opposed and thus do not need rectification, and the figures of the Virgin Mary and Mary Magdalene are divided more in name than in reality. For H.D. language is a rich trove of palimpsestic meanings that do not need to be controlled, but rather explored: "I feel / the meaning that words hide; // they are anagrams, cryptograms, / little boxes, conditioned // to hatch butterflies" (*Collected Poems* 540).

In the second and third sections of *Trilogy*, "Tribute to the Angels" and "The Flowering of the Rod," H.D. unites the Virgin Mary with the biblical "whore" Mary Magdalene as a love for female figures becomes a series of distilled words and shifting sounds:

Now polish the crucible
and in the bowl distill

a word most bitter, *marah*,
a word bitter still, *mar*,

sea, brine, breaker, seducer,
giver of life, giver of tears;

now polish the crucible
and set the jet of flame

under, till *marah-mar*
are melted, fuse and join

and change and alter,
mer, mere, mere, mater, Maia, Mary (*Collected Poems* 552)

H.D.'s shifting configurations explore how changed word associations lead to transforming psychologies, as "*marah*" morphs into "Mary." The passage brings together mother and beloved, and sea and matter, and is followed by a meditation on three goddesses connected with eros, "Venus, Aphrodite, Astarte." Through similar strategies of interacting semantics and sounds, puns and rhymes, H.D. repairs the misogyny to which these goddesses are subjected. For H.D. the objective of *Trilogy* is to create new conditions of belief, of affirmation, as an effect of the writing itself: "We have too much consecration / too little affirmation" (540).

Helen in Egypt takes on the exploration of actual love relations and produces them as a sustained epic, drama, and lyric. In *Sea Garden*, H.D. moves almost imperceptibly between same-sex and different-sex love; *Helen in Egypt* is decidedly more queer. Not only does Helen, as female lover and beloved, pursue her desires with minimal regard for the wishes of the heroic and desolate Achilles, but she does so in relationship to a character known for his homosocial bond to Patroclus. H.D. enacts the drama of this unlikely love relationship in Hades, long after the primary events of these mortals' and immortals' lives are over, and they conduct their love affair as a kind of life-in-death or death-in-life scenario. H.D. describes her consciousness in writing *Helen in Egypt* in ecstatic terms, as existing in an "Eternal Present": "the work has made me so very happy. . . . The work must write itself." Having read *Helen in Egypt* out loud for a radio production, H.D. relates her experience: "I was alone and felt that I had an alter-ego, this Helen, speaking with my own voice. . . . I seemed to lose myself, to be myself as hardly ever in my life before. . . . This is myself, Helen out of the body, in another world, the eidolon of the legend. But she is not alone. There she meets the legendary Achilles, a phantom but a reality" ("Compassionate Friendship" 15–17).

If *Helen in Egypt* is a cross-genre work, it also crosses a more traditional love poetry with a projective love writing. As in traditional love poetry, Helen as lover takes center stage, but in placing her there, H.D. vitiates any prescribed situatedness of this lover. On the one hand, Helen's speech is so vatic that she produces a different set of economies than those of the earth-bound lover of most lover-beloved poetries. On the other hand, Helen's speech is so multiple and self-canceling that she exists less as a single figure than as an omniscience. H.D.'s characterization of her experience of reading Helen as being "out of the body, in another world" and of Helen herself as "*eidolon*" does much to suggest what in contemporary parlance would be called the "posthuman" subjectivity of this work. Indeed, this poem's consciousness or omniscience at times resembles a Greek chorus and is reminiscent of the consciousness of Virginia Woolf's novels in its implied "we," constituted through shifting authorial and character consciousnesses. H.D.'s Helen as a composite figure is sometimes the "mouthpiece" of this "we" and sometimes of an individuated Helen. DuPlessis usefully analyzes the set of writer and reader relationships joined in the figure of Helen, who is "writer, reader, and main character, a curious status which has at least one theoretical effect—of collapsing subject-object distinctions between the thing scrutinised and the viewer. For the main character to be [a] rank projection of H.D. herself—while bearing so interestingly her mother's name—and for a female character to be a serious reader of her own desires ('I am instructed, I know the script') not an object or symbol of desire for others starkly cedes from a number of conventions of poetic depiction. . . . This Helen is a site of resistance by being plural. . . . The poem allows icon to become critic, yet remain icon; object to become subject yet remain object; interpreted to become interpreter yet remain interpreted" (*H.D.* 109).

Helen in Egypt is made up of two different types of writing: the sections written in poetic verse composed initially by H.D. over a two-year period and the later prose sequences written by her to provide an orientation to the poetry, which she calls "captions." But the prose sections are hardly glosses on the poetry, but rather something more like midrash, or actions on actions. DuPlessis, who uses the concept of midrash in her discussion of *Helen in Egypt*, emphasizes the interpretive aspects of the captions, but as actions on actions they also extend the poem's figural field, as language leads to further language. While DuPlessis emphasizes H.D.'s resistance to problematical gendered scripts, *Helen in Egypt*'s complex delivery system enables H.D. to engage gendered scripts while successfully evading their implicit hierarchies. These rather diverse strategies and agendas make *Helen in Egypt* difficult to read. With the predominant focus on Helen as enunciation and enounced, the reader cannot identify with either the poetic speaker or the character in any consistent way, resulting in a multidirectional reading experience that foreshadows the later writing experiments by Leslie Scalapino, whose avant-garde practice often entailed confounding her audience's capacities to process her work. Insofar as this multiple attention forms around a female character who is primarily known in Western civilization as the object of a love quest and who is usually seen as falling far short of Achilles's heroic stature, the poem's apotheosis is always threatening to break apart.

Particularly important for *Helen in Egypt* are the figures of Hugh Dowding as Achilles and, secondarily, Erich Heydt as Paris. In "Compassionate Friendship," H.D. lists both Dowding and Heydt among the seven male initiators who have enabled her writing. As a man of war who engaged in séances to recover pilots lost under his command at the Battle of Britain and who shared something of these searches with H.D., Dowding provided the quintessential love experience—of entering into love relations with another by engaging a shared imaginative space. Although moved by Dowding's emotional searching for his lost pilots, H.D. came up against a decidedly more guarded figure when it came to interactions with her.[7] In one sense, the plot of *Helen in Egypt* is rather simple: to realize that the man of war is also a man of love and that the love between Helen and Achilles is real. While this plot ultimately involves H.D. in difficult intellectual and emotional questions about war and love, the sword and the pen, *Helen in Egypt* has as its basis H.D.'s love for people in her actual life.

While the first and third sections of the poem are largely focused on Achilles, two psychoanalysts serve as models for the middle section: Paris is Erich Heydt and Theseus is Freud. Heydt was H.D.'s analyst during the time she was writing *Helen in Egypt*. He was employed at the sanatorium where H.D. elected to prolong her stay after her breakdown immediately after World War II, because of what she experienced as its simultaneously restful and charged atmosphere. For H.D. Heydt was not only an analyst, but also a paramour; the two went on outings together and engaged in a playful flirtation. One of the more revealing types of encounter concerned a kind of play with language in which Heydt claimed to have read words in H.D.'s works that were not there. These interactions would send H.D. into a tailspin of word associations and questions as to why Heydt was playing these word games with her. In describing Heydt as one of her seven initiators, H.D. writes: "Truly Erich Heydt is a complicated character. I myself saw the show man, the touch of a charlatan. But I was interested in the very show he put on and wondered what was back of it" ("Compassionate Friendship" 96).

One important way of understanding *Helen in Egypt* is as a palinode. The long poem takes as its source texts Stesichorus's *Palinode* and Euripides's *Helen*, both of which retell the earlier Helen stories in which she is blamed as the cause of the Trojan War and instead recount how Helen stayed in Egypt awaiting Menelaus's return while only her phantom walked on the ramparts during the Trojan War. H.D. begins her "Pallinode": "*Stesichorus was said to have been struck blind because of his invective against Helen, but later was restored to sight, when he reinstated her in his* Pallinode. *Euripides, notably in* The Trojan Women, *reviles her, but he also is 'restored to sight'*" (1). H.D.'s "Pallinode" is quite different from either of the earlier versions, which Friedman summarizes as presenting Helen either as "whore" or as "chaste wife." In her "Pallinode" H.D. creates a Helen who, as a composite figure of the two Helens, is an entirely active agent. In revising Stesichorus's and Euripides's masculine imaginations of Helen, H.D. initiates two new plot complications: Helen's agency as a character to love is made prominent, and love itself is presented as being equal to or more powerful than war, and perhaps even necessary for it.

Stesichorus is credited with creating the form of the palinode itself, which Plato's *Phaedrus* may partially imitate. There, Socrates initially defiles love by speaking against love, or at least entertaining arguments against love, but his power to speak in eloquent ways about love resurfaces once he has paid due respect to the god of love. H.D., restoring the figure of the mortal- immortal Helen as a powerful lover and author of her own destiny, gains the capacity to write this love epic. Indeed, if in Freudian psychoanalysis an analysand's "talking cure" can be considered to be a palinode of reclaiming a repressed love, the abating of hysterical symptoms of paralysis, such as blindness and speechlessness, might be seen as the grace afforded by the retraction. In her "Pallinode" H.D. places considerable attention on Aphrodite, who, according to many accounts, including Homer's, initially set in motion the events that led to the Trojan War by promising Helen to Paris. H.D. brings out how Aphrodite guides Paris's arrow that kills Achilles, and she configures these events as beneficial to Achilles because Paris's "dart" breaks through Achilles's armor, his fixed warring impulses, creating a "new Mortal" freed by "Love's arrow" from his iron encasement (10). Taking on the legend of how Helen's walking on Troy's ramparts during the war enraged the Greek forces, H.D. makes Helen an active agent of war, not its foil. And it is while Helen is walking on the ramparts that she exchanges glances with Achilles, transfixing him with an eternal love for her—a love that at the beginning of the drama he has forgotten and by the end has affirmed.

While in contrast to more open-ended projective poems discussed in this book, this poem is structured by a dramatic apparatus established at the outset and a restricted set of characters, its projective love poetics produces changes in its psychological orientations. Moreover the poetry in the individual books and sections moves through a processual writing often constituted by an amassing of appositional questions and phrases. Toward the end of *Helen in Egypt*, H.D. describes the epic drama's changing orientations: "*Helen of our first sequence was translated into a transcendental plane. . . . Helen of our second sequence contacted a guide near her in time. . . . our third Helen . . . is concerned with the human content of the drama*" (255). Elsewhere, H.D. describes the second section as based on an "*intellectual or inspired*" Helen and "*the third Helen as numb with memory*" (258). Thus, while in "Pallinode," H.D. seeks to understand an ultimate kind of contact with Achilles as "a flash at midday" or the "Sun / hidden behind the Sun of our invisible day," in the final section, "Eidolon," she affirms more simply that "the ecstasy of desire had smitten him" and that he loves Helen (34, 260). In addition to affirming its own writing as an ultimate good, "*a rhythm as yet unheard*," the poem arrives at a sense of human limitations: men go to war because men go to war and no one wants Helen. It reverses Freudian psychology by conceiving that "*my first lover was created by my last*" and that "the dart of Love / is the dart of Death"—suggesting most simply that we are born and die, but also that love and death are inextricably bound together, as the metaphor of a piercing arrow has long indicated (215, 303).

There are several outrageous assertions made or questions raised in the poem that almost under any other circumstances would run afoul of human credibility. Yet, it is precisely the rapid-fire delivery of the projective poetics that allows for not only the articulation of these thoughts but also their effectiveness in presenting the power of passionate love. At one point, H.D. presses the outsized claim that the Trojan War served to mediate Achilles and Helen's love at first sight, since without the ships of war this transfixing love would have self-destructed: "*Helen only knows that without the souls or 'the sails of the thousand ships,' her encounter with Achilles would have 'burnt out in a flash' or burnt her out, like Semele, when Zeus at her request, 'revealed himself'*" (45). While Helen is in search of love, as Helen of Sparta she claims that the war itself is hers—she caused it, as one version would have it. The sails of the warships and the petals of a rose and a lily coalesce into a single image:

> they were mine, not his,
> the unnumbered host;
>
> mine, all the ships,
> mine, all the thousand petals of the rose,
> mine, all the lily-petals,
>
> mine, the great spread of wings,
> the thousand sails,
> the thousand feathered darts
>
> that sped them home,
> mine, the one dart in the Achilles-heel,
> the thousand-and-one, mine. (24–25)

Through this series of appositional phrases, rose, lily, sails, darts all combine into a single image that makes the claim that this war does not belong to Achilles, but to Helen, a distinct possibility. While Helen, an agent of love, declares the war to be hers, Achilles's capacity to wage war, to strengthen his command, is based on his capacity to love. Midway through the first section, Achilles abruptly changes from hating to loving Helen. While he initially asks, "Are you Hecate, witch" and tries to choke her, he then suddenly remembers that he loves Helen: "all things would change but never / the glance she exchanged with me" (54). Throughout her drama, H.D. studies how the passions of war and of love are inseparable. The poem provides a vision of ultimate reality as a kind of veil, or a series of folds, of interrelated realities that cannot be penetrated: "*Is the 'veil of Cytheraea' or of Love, Death? Is the disguise of Death or the 'veil' of Death, Love? This is too difficult a question to answer*" (45).

Helen in Egypt begins and ends by calling up languages and scenarios from *Trilogy* and *Sea Garden* and takes them further. In *Trilogy* H.D. invokes Amen

(Amon) to aid her in a fresh beginning; in *Helen in Egypt* she enters the "Amen-temple." Whereas *Trilogy*'s movement forward is based on changing figures that are transmogrifications of the self, *Helen in Egypt* recasts its figures again and again. *Helen in Egypt* begins with H.D.'s preoccupation with "walls," which recur throughout her late writing, as suggestive of what is architecturally concrete as well as psychologically prohibitive, of building and of ruin. Beginning with "hosts / surging beneath the Walls," H.D. describes, as if in a séance:

> I hear their voices
> there is no veil between us
> only space and leisure (1–2)

The passage brings together a sense of transcendent reality with a modern quotidian "leisure," not as a yoking that creates bathos, but as a "clairvoyance" that arises through a shared liminal space. Immediately after creating a location for her drama in the "Amen-temple" H.D. turns to the sea, drawing on figures and languages that she first initiated in *Sea Garden* and linking them with the Trojan War:

> the glory and the beauty of the ships
> the wave that bore them onward
> and the shock of hidden shoal,
>
> the peril of the rocks,
> the weary fall of sail,
> the rope drawn taut,
>
> the breathing and breath-taking
> climb and fall, mountain and valley
> challenging the coast.
>
> drawn near, drawn far,
> the helmsman's bitter oath
> to see the goal receding (3)

Many of the references in these lines recur throughout *Sea Garden*, most notably perhaps in "The Shrine" and "The Helmsman." While a "helmsman," as Gregory points out, is associated with "immediate daimonic possession," in *Helen in Egypt* he is bereft of this possibility of presence since there is now a "goal" that is "receding." The figure of the helmsman recurs throughout H.D.'s works, often through references to the "captain." Achilles as the captain of his ship is associated with Dowding, who is linked to the Viking Hallblithe, H.D.'s séance circle's spirit guide. In "H.D. by Delia Alton," H.D. meditates on several diverse captains, including one anonymous captain from her actual life who mysteriously disappears and whom she links with the figure of the "Eternal Lover" (185).

Although in the second of the three sections of the drama, "Leuké," Helen finds companionship with Paris, described as *"agent, medium, intermediary of Love, and Troy's great Patron, Apollo the god of song,"* the poem's final section, "Eidolon," affirms the attraction of Achilles (112). One of Theseus's (Freud's) challenges to Helen as he tries to supplant memories of her lover Achilles with those of Paris is to goad her with *"Even a Spirit loves laughter, did you laugh with Achilles?"* (160). But while Theseus reminds her of the benefit of a more earthly passion, Helen ultimately chooses Achilles, referring to her contact with him as the "Absolute" and *"brighter than the sun at noon-day, yet whiter than frost"* (196, 160). Saying that Paris "renewed her youth," she elects what she perceives as Achilles's greater power, "only the memory of the molten ember / of the Dark Absolute claims me" (196). H.D. summarizes: *"Achilles is a 'sword-blade drawn from fire . . .' Menelaus, Paris had not yet been 'tempered'"* (198). *Helen in Egypt* concludes with an "Eidolon" to its third part, which is also entitled "Eidolon":

> But what could Paris know of the sea,
> its beat and long reverberation,
> its booming and delicate echo (304)

In its affirmation of Achilles, the final section connects the sea and land imagery of *Sea Garden*: *"the hill and hollow / of billows, the sea road"* (304).

Concluding that the ultimate meaning of the poem may be in a "rhythm as yet unheard," H.D. in *Helen in Egypt* realizes how the extraordinary inheres in the ordinary, transcendence in immanence. Helen's enlightenment necessarily entails the knowledge that Achilles *had* loved her. Helen pronounces this the "treasure beyond treasure," which she wishes to contemplate "forever":

> if only God
> Would let me lie here forever,
> I could assess, weigh and value
>
> the secret treasure, as I count
> the seven and the seven slats of the ladder
> or the bars of light on the wall. (283)

For H.D. the "treasure" of Achilles's love is inseparable from her actual writing of *Helen in Egypt*, as the reference to "the seven and the seven slats of the ladder" introduces a visual mnemonic of the writing of the poem. (The first two sections of *Helen in Egypt* consist of seven books, and the third section is made of six books and a concluding seventh part, "Eidolon.") *Helen in Egypt* allows H.D. to discover and to retain Achilles's love—this transfixion through the captain.

Near the end, the poem seems to state its ultimate vision. The speaker pronounces:

there is not before and no after
there is one finite moment
that no infinite joy can disperse

. . . .

the seasons revolve around
a pause in the infinite rhythm
of the heart and of heaven (303–4)

While the poem seems to affirm the possibility of simple mortal death, it also makes way for the possibility of a death caused by transformation of the self into another state through love: an absolute fixing, the sun behind the sun, an eternal kiss. Indeed, it may well be this transfixing that is the "pause" in the "infinite rhythm."

Of this epic-drama, Barbara Guest remarks, "*Helen in Egypt*, although difficult, narcissistic, cloudy, obsessive, is high theatre" (*Herself* 293). Much like Virginia Woolf in *Between the Acts*, H.D. avails herself of the artifices of a staged drama—a casting that offers her various kinds of deus ex machina and forced "quits." Through a sense of the staged nature of reality, H.D., through her surrogate, Helen, can follow her own love inclinations in a far more precise way than in a writing that must attain to realistic decorums. While the formal pattern of the work (three sections of six or seven books with each book consisting of eight parts, all written in triadic stanzas) heralds a procedural verse, the writing itself is projective, a present tense. H.D., casting her writing ever further, has achieved a poetry of "clairvoyance" where "this" is "this" through supple machinations. She affirms her early contention that "Love is writing."

"The First Beloved"

ROBERT DUNCAN'S OPEN FIELD

A man writes "I love" on a wall. He hopes to escape from his mistake by
not signing his name. But a glamour radiates from the letters and has
illuminated his being as he writes.

—Robert Duncan, *Letters*

In *The H.D. Book*, Robert Duncan relates how he "found my life in poetry" to be
made up of three defining elements: "my falling in love or conversion, my loving or company in the art, and then something quite different it would seem,
setting all into a new motion, my first intimations of an historical task with the
modernist imperative" (69, 70). Duncan creates this outline for his "life in poetry" at the outset of writing the essays that comprise *The H.D. Book*, a few years
after publishing his groundbreaking *The Opening of the Field*. Although in *The
H.D. Book* Duncan lists these three commitments to understand his preceding
life, his assured linkages between falling in love, relationships with other poets and artists, and modernist directives should be attributed to his success in
bringing these together in *The Opening of the Field*.

Although Duncan was drawn to modernist poetics early on, in his initial poetry he seemed more to mimic than to engage these poetics.[1] His early poetry
was often written through willful (and occasionally diffident) poetic speakers,
who manifested much "interference of the individual as ego," although this poetry also struck impersonal and universalizing poses. Moreover, it was a poetry
in which mourning and melancholia served as the dominant emotional modalities and in which binary oppositions constituted his poetic field. In a turn-
around in his subsequent volumes, *Writing Writing* and *Letters*, Duncan deliberately took on Gertrude Stein's experiments as a corrective to his early poetry and
found an enchantment with writing itself. By *The Opening of the Field*, Duncan
found a way of writing his poetry through complex psychological and physical
orientations that engage the writing of poetry as an event, which he often characterized as a dance. He quotes John at Ephesus: "To each and all it is given to
dance. . . . He who joins not in the dance mistakes the event" (*The H.D. Book*
537). No longer writing primarily through poetic speakers who held definitive

stances or through an enchantment with writing itself, Duncan creates a poetry of process and collage—a writing that allows for an increment of association, both temporally and spatially. As Duncan describes in the preface to *Bending the Bow*, he "works with all parts of the poem as *polysemous*, taking each thing of the composition as generative of meaning" (ix). For Duncan, the poem becomes a kind of imaginative holding "of thought and feeling in which we may participate but not dominate, where we are used by things even as we use them" (*Fictive* 91). Duncan brings issues of submission and dominance to Olson's universalizing sense of how the "objects" of a poem must be handled within a "field," such that they "are made to *hold*, and to hold exactly inside the content and the context of the poem which has forced itself through the poet and them, into being" (*Selected Writings* 20).

In creating his poetics of interactive elements, Duncan produced a poetry in which proprioceptive relations are operative, a concept developed by Olson and summarized by Don Byrd as a writing "which arises directly from the physical body and the space which it inhabits" (Byrd 42). Duncan celebrates getting his body into his poetry, punning in "The Dance" how "the numbers have enterd [his] feet" (*Opening* 8), and conveys a sense of bodily motion through an inventive syntax and page arrangement, or what Fraser described as Duncan's "connection to [the] *page* as a graphically energetic site in which to manifest one's *physical* alignment with the arrival of language in the mind" (*Translating* 186). Duncan brings all of himself into his poetry—body, emotions, intellect—and finds a way to write poetry in which the diverse aspects of himself could find dispensation through a poetics of interactive, rather than willed, relationships, or what he commends as a "total freedom in the interaction . . . by which the meaning of each term of the poem has been charged by the total composition" ("Interview" by Faas 4–5).

In creating *The Opening of the Field* and his later volumes of verse, Duncan came to understand how loving and poetry writing are parallel practices that bring about acceleration. In an interview with Steve Abbott and Aaron Shurin, he commented: "you're not capable of love til you've found out how it's practiced and you find out how you love. You don't love straight out. Or you do, but it doesn't communicate to you or anybody else. It's like writing a poem. Just the feeling of writing the poem is terrific, to find out language is suddenly speaking for you as nothing has spoken before, including yourself" (78). For Duncan, loving and poetry writing are limitless acts that are amplified in the process of performing them: "Just as Love is going deeper into the matter of love, being in love with being in love, altho, this is what makes men lovers, is viewed as a disorder of feeling by men who are not lovers, so Poetry going deeper into the nature of poetry is, not only in literature departments but in certain schools of poetry and among certain critics and leaders of the art, attackt as a disorder of art" (Fredman 28). Poetry and love bring about transformation and therefore cannot be tied to fixed definitions of manhood or of love: "We fall in love with a man, really we're reaching toward the manhood we see possible in that person. . . . manhood is not something that's there but is only there the way we then make love. So our phrase making love is the same as making poems" ("Interview" by Abbott and Shurin 94).

One of Duncan's defining early acts was the 1944 publication of "The Homosexual in Society" in the prominent journal *Politics* when he was only twenty-four. In this essay Duncan demanded that homosexuals be included in the order of things and that social orders change to make way for homosexuals and others excluded from a presumably democratic society. This essay created much difficulty for Duncan, since he published it at a time when most homosexuals elected to keep their homosexuality outside the public purview and well before the existence of gay liberation and identity movements offered at least some protection for such announcements. Duncan noted in the essay that he was the only intellectual to his knowledge to publicly avow his homosexuality. But he wrote not only to correct a society that would demand that he deny or hide his sexual orientation, but also to abjure what he regarded as a "special culture" that had been created by homosexuals, which brought about "a tone and a vocabulary that are loaded with contempt for the uninitiated" (*Selected Prose* 41). While noting that he had sought and found some solace from the hostility of the larger society in this company, he also recounts the damage: "After an evening at one of those salons where the whole atmosphere was one of suggestion and celebration, I returned recently experiencing again the after shock, the desolate feeling of wrongness, remembering in my own voice and gestures the rehearsal of unfeeling" (47). While some commentators have concluded that Duncan's distaste in this essay demonstrates a rejection of homosexuality itself, his emotional response needs to be seen in the context of his developing opus, in which he sought to create a writing that does not depend on recognizable stances or attitudes but rather conveys a set of interacting elements such that words are decontextualized from their fixed and problematical associations. Moreover, Duncan's concern with "untruthfulness," which arises elsewhere in his work, is his way of marking how at this point in time different aspects of his life were out of sync.

By the time Duncan began *The H.D. Book* in the 1960s, shortly after publishing *The Opening of the Field*, he had found an important articulation of his love through the concept of Eros as a force or a god and he claimed that Eros "lie[s] at the heart of our study here" (*The H.D. Book* 79). Important to this articulation is the Psyche and Eros myth, in which Duncan understands Psyche to be the poet and Eros to be the demonic force that she seeks to possess or to be possessed by. Duncan writes, "the would-be poet stands like Psyche *in the dark*, taken up in a marriage with a genius, possessed by a spirit outside the ken of those about him" (80). And he elaborates: "There is no way then but Psyche's search, the creative work of a union in knowledge and experience with something missing. At the end, there is a new Eros. . . . We are drawn to Him, but we must also gather Him to be. We cannot, in the early stages, locate Him; but He finds us out. Seized by His orders, we '*fall* in love,' in order that He be; and in His duration, the powers of Eros are boundless. We are struck by His presence, and, in becoming lovers we become something other than ourselves, subjects of a daemonic force" (82).

By making Eros into a force that exists through lovers falling in love, but that exceeds the reality of this dyadic formation, Duncan articulates how in love one becomes other than oneself. Moreover, Duncan claims that the arrival of the demonic is connected to how "the old orders . . . move to speak in the new" and how we find "the story of one Eros . . . entering the story of the other Eros" (94). Not content to let the Psyche and Eros myth and Christian traditions inhabit different spheres, Duncan through his own essayistic myth-making links them: "Love wounded for the sake of Love, and . . . taken up to heaven, because of a Disobedience" (94). For Duncan, "Paradise is the inexorable power of Eros" (87), and the palace of Eros to which Psyche travels is like the richness of imaginative culture, an open secret available to all: "And the Palace of Eros has [a] likeness to the world that exists in works of art—'No single chain, bar, lock, or armed guard protected it,' the story tells us. It lay an open secret for those who discovered it to live in" (81). While some may question the ineluctable romance of such an assertion, it is a romance wrought through Eros. Duncan quite unromantically links the palace of art to the sexed body and sexual love.

In "Eros," Duncan laments what he understands as the changes wrought by the New Testament pronouncement "in the beginning was the Word," finding in this statement a division between "inner" and "outer." Duncan analyzes the effect of this historical transformation: "Now a language that originated in the Word, the speech of man, was to be the true universe. The *vis imaginativa* in which the things of men's souls and the things of the actual universe dance together . . . the magic world of resonances and freely associating rhymes—is disowned. And what appears is a world of two opposing possibilities—dogma and heresy" (*The H.D. Book* 88). Duncan's criticism of the New Testament's beginning with "the Word" presages this book's concern with how the sense of language as transcending everything that it names creates an impoverishment, including of eros. Moreover in objecting to a division between "inner" and "outer," Duncan provides an implicit critique of a love that defines itself through an introspective lover and an objectified beloved. This ontology devalues or diminishes the state of falling in love or being in love because of how the self, conceived as being separate from the beloved, must negotiate a relationship rather than participate in a greater energy field.

In response to a limited Christian ontology, Duncan sought out other traditions, such as the Celtic, in which he found that "Within and Without dance in interchanging patterns." He notes that such traditions contain a multiplicity of beliefs and symbols: "The sacra of the Church and the magic treasures of ancient kings, the sexual emblems and ritual objects of chthonic cults, have been stolen to furnish the changeling mysteries of a Romance in Poetry" (*The H.D. Book* 95). While for Lacan such sacra and emblems mask desire, for Duncan they produce eros.

Duncan concludes the chapter "Eros" with a description of how the creation of poetry should occur as a kind of projective-introjective writing, in which meaning, sound, and image produce more of the same: "That one image may recall another, finding depth in the resounding, is the secret of rhyme and measure. The time of a poem is felt as a recognition of return in vowel tone and in consonant formations, of pattern in the sequence of syllables, in stress and in pitch of a melody, of images and meanings. It resembles the time of a dream, for it is highly organized along lines of association." And "the impulse of dream or poem is to provide a ground . . . beyond what we know, for feeling 'greater than Reality'" (*The H.D. Book* 99).

More than any other poet examined in *The Transmutation of Love and Avant-Garde Poetics*, Duncan provides extended commentary in interviews, essays, and prefaces to his work on the relationship between his love experiences and the form his writing takes. For the young Duncan even to say "I love you" in the context of a relationship caused considerable consternation: "The shattering experience when I was in love is why couldn't I say 'I love you' and saying was impossible for me. I was struck dumb because the depth of feeling was so fundamental that if you advanced to the level of speech, the network of things drawn into that fundamental point was so complex you couldn't speak from it. It was felt throughout the entire body and you could not find within it any actual confidence of loving" ("Interview" by Abbott and Shurin 77). Or, as he wrote with some despair in an early letter: "I can make no real connection between what I mean by sex, by lust, and what I mean by love" (Faas 205).

Along with not being able to speak his love, Duncan criticized his emotional deportment in his early relationships: "In 1938, when I was nineteen, I had fallen in love and left college in my sophomore year, following my lover East. That first experience of a sexual relationship took over my life. I was moved by violent conflicts and yearnings, a need to be reassured in love that all but obscured any expression of loving" (*Years* 1). Not only was this love relationship marked by failure, but the poetry writing that emerged in relationship to his early love relationships was also troubling: "Going back over my earliest poems, I am still dismayd. What a time I had finding speech for the feeling I wanted, and how often I seem to have found speech for feeling I did not want at all. . . . This sense of untruthfulness and lies surely reflects upon an uneasiness I felt in my own stance in writing. . . . A menacing, desolate and overwhelming world of feeling, over-charged, was only too ready to take over in the poem" (vi). Yet although Duncan felt his early poetry to be marked by "untruthfulness" and an "overwhelming world of feeling," he also understood it as leading into his later poetry of a realized eros. The early work brought his psychology and body into his writing: "The opposites playd in me: male and female, love and hate, tenderness and jealous anger, hope and fear. Here too there had been the awakening of a rhythm, the imprint of a cadence at once physical and psychological, that could contain and project the components of an emerging homosexuality in an ardor that would prepare for the development of Eros" (i).

Duncan linked his mature art to his creation of a sustained relationship with Jess Collins. This relationship, based on a "deep accord" between the two men, enabled Duncan to go beyond "contending" "opposites." Duncan explains: "I had fixed in my account of falling in love that union of opposites . . . of contending forces united in their contention by love. . . . But I broke through that fixation to admit that I was in love with him where the sense was of a deep accord, not of winning or losing, but of going on with him in a common life" ("Interview" by Abbott and Shurin 78). In his relationship with Collins, Duncan was able to create the "household" he had long sought, which he characterized as based in a "practice of love" that included room for "falling in love" and its "seizures" (78).[2]

Duncan celebrated the "household" he had managed to create with Jess, and poetry itself became a kind of "house" or "holding." Duncan, who wished to bring not only all the parts of a poem, but all parts of his life, into interactive relationships, found a calling to household or form to be a way of creating a space for objects or things previously overpowered by an obsessive desire or universalizing will. Michael Auping has suggested that the actual house shared by Duncan and the visual artist Collins was an extension of their joint commitment to collage practices: "The association between Jess and Duncan [was] itself a collage that extend[ed] beyond Duncan's poetry and Jess's art to an interactive collage encompassing the house they inhabited, itself symbolic of the products of their combined imaginations" (qtd. in Fredman 88). Jess's visual collages become an important accompaniment to Duncan's poetry, which enabled him to define his poetics as freeing up separate elements through their interactions: "The painter works not to conclude the elements of the painting but to set them into motion, not to bind the colors but to free them, to release the force of their interrelationships" (qtd.in Johnson 5).

It would be wrong to think of Duncan's distinction between early obsessive desire and his "household" love as evincing the usual dualities that separate one kind of love from another: love from lust, mature love from falling in love. For while Duncan queried the differences between sex, love, and eros, he also came to understand them as interrelated. Moreover, his sense of each was inventive and rather different from common usage. He commented that falling in love, rather than a transient or ephemeral state of being, "is bringing something out at a deeper and deeper level" ("Interview" by Abbott and Shurin 93). For Duncan "caring" and "eros" are not opposites, but linked: "Caring in itself becomes an adventure of the imagination that is wed here to the great adventure of Eros and desire." And he notes how for Plato, "Eros and even Dionysus, desire and intoxication . . . are daemons of the Good" (*The H.D. Book* 85, 86).

In the remainder of this chapter, I trace Duncan's poetry through three different stages: the early poems based on willful poetic speakers for whom a dichotomized relationship between lover and beloved and other binary definitions often prevail; the intermediary deliberately experimental poetry of *Writing Writing* and *Letters*, in which Duncan began to shift in the direction of a field poetics; and the poetry of *The Opening of the Field* and *Bending the Bow* in which he created a projective love writing and libidinized field poetics. In each of the three stages, Duncan explored how to write love, conveying in multiple ways how for him the experience of love and the writing of love are inseparable. When Duncan discovered a projective love and libidinized field poetics in *The Opening of the Field* and developed it in *Bending the Bow* he found a writing that brought together his physical, intellectual, and emotional responses.

"Moves I, I, I"

Like Pound's early poetry, Duncan's initial work was marked by his engagement with different modes of writing and his considerable ambivalence about love. But while Pound's dissatisfactions with love stemmed from a vacillation about how to value love's inspiring, but seemingly fickle, powers, Duncan focused his unhappiness with love on what he conceived as his own incapacity to experience and know love. Most of Duncan's early poetry was written through willful poetic speakers whose mournful and melancholic stances serve to entrench his poem's subject-object dichotomies and is at considerable remove from what he came to identify as the aim of his later poetry: "total freedom in interaction" ("Interview" by Faas 4).

Attempting to write through a poetic speaker as lover, Duncan found himself inhabiting an isolated subjectivity in relationship to isolated others. In "An African Elegy," Duncan created a melancholic or death-dealing subject, initially through utilizing Africa and its inhabitants as a kind of foil, and then by identifying with a murderous Othello whom he associated with a black Orpheus and with Virginia Woolf in her election of suicide. Duncan's poetic speaker quite blatantly uses the idea of Africa to create a sense of his own darkness:

> I know
> no other continent of Africa more dark than this
> dark continent of my breast. (*First Decade* 13)

While the first section begins with African wives and husbands preparing for the hunt—"let loose through the trees / the tides of Death sound"—Duncan ultimately seeks "a complete black-out," void even of "negro armies" and "women and birds." In the latter part of the poem, a fully melancholic subject emerges as "the towering Moor of self" consumes all, including a Desdemona who "wails" from within this Moor:

> Desdemona
> like a demon wails within our bodies, warns
> against the towering Moor of self, and then
> laments her passing from him. (13)

Thus "Moves I, I, I," at once Othello and black Orpheus, stalking as well as stalked, a figure of "Death singing": "Then it was I, Death singing, / who bewildered the forest" (13, 14). Yet, Duncan does not end the poem with this apotheosis, with a victory of the melancholic, death-dealing subject. He concludes that this ferociously and stereotypically imagined Othello-Orpheus figure is a barrier to a darker and deeper dream: "the rooms deserted at the roots of love." And he turns his poem of melancholy into one of mourning:

> There is no end. And how sad then
> is even the Congo. How the tired sirens
> come up from the water, not to be toucht
> but to lie on the rocks of the thunder.
> How sad then is even the marvelous! (15)

While Duncan, who published this poem in 1944, the same year he published "The Homosexual in Society," may be lamenting the difficulty of his love in a homophobic society, he expends most of his effort in the poem in creating a fully melancholic poetic speaker who spurns or finds himself alienated from more nuanced emotional and sensate experiences.

In "An Apollonian Elegy," Duncan turns from his exploration of darkness in "An African Elegy" to Apollo, whose "lyre strings" "burn white the black bodies of lovers, burn black / their white souls in the awake of night" (25). Duncan's masculine Apollo has the power to "pierce" "the Muses, dim ladies, / until they blaze" and to raise "litanies / to break, to crack, the unlighted sky" (25). Drawing opposites into unholy alliances, Duncan attempts to express a divine strength that connects to an earthly love. The poem links emotional and physical being, in part through repeated uses of the verbs "rock," "rocked," and "rockt." The sun rockets over the sky and bodies rock:

> Return you, Apollo, to ride your old sun
> Across that nemesis world, the night. In our dark,
> In our human, we rest, we rock. (25)

The sense of the sun riding across the sky, stopped rhythmically by the concluding "we rest, we rock," casts the poem into cross-currents of diurnal and sexual rhythms. In the poem's tense relations, "each lover hears / pluckt from the string, the strain, of his body, / by the lustful beak and claw of his hunger, / that music, love" (25) Conceiving of an eros composed of conflictual love and hunger, Duncan draws together light and dark, burning and searing:

> In Apollo's grove, the sunless night,
> grave and pale, his body, the burnisht steel,
> gleams, bright as a sword to reflect the blaze,
> to burn, to sear, my body's dark. (26)

In this passage, "his body" refers to a preceding "angel" or "lover," whose body like "a sword" has the power of cutting across "my body's dark." If one of Duncan's intentions in the poem is to realize eros as a form of apotheosis through its contradictory and conflictual formations, he also wishes to address a mortal love. Early on, the poem victoriously declares, "And trembling, I face my lover. / He is more beautiful than the sun," but later Duncan changes his orientation away from Apollo's light, made of darkness and his "devil-strummd" music, to something darker, namely a mortal love, for "We live in a night broken by the sun" (*First Decade* 25, 26). Indeed, by changing the sense of the "sun" from a source that relieves darkness to an entity that breaks up the night, Duncan intensifies the poem's darkness, since the sun is now presented as a force of disruption.

To further explore this darkness as elegy, as mourning, Duncan turns to the myth of Apollo's accidental killing of his beloved Hyacinthus. Repeating Apollo's mournful refrain "AI AI" several times, the poem ends, like "An African Elegy," by turning to mortal loss. In this poem, however, the lament is more extended and draws mortal together with immortal:

> See!
> the beloved mouth, to be kisst, is closed.
> The eyes are closed. The beloved body lies,
> to be seized to your body, broken.
> As in the early morning from their wet meadow
> one gathers up the iris, blue tears of heaven,
> eager to hold love's very fragrance
> close to the heart, as one cuts them down from their stems
> and they perish (27)

The vivid depiction of broken bodies and irises cut prematurely from their stems is reminiscent of H.D.'s image of the hyacinth in "Acon," in which "The light of her face falls from its flower." Duncan's poem concludes with a tribute to Apollo that further binds together mortal and immortal through its high declamation:

> Deathless Apollo, Thou too hast loved, and Thou
> immortally must bear
> mortality's bourne. (28)

While Duncan's early poems are marked by a searing intensity, they also at times evince diffidence. The sequence of poems in the Berkeley Poems brings to the surface a multiplicity of problems that Duncan had in writing love poetry. The initial, untitled poem that begins "Among my friends love is a great sorrow" was written from the perspective of a generic "we," which, especially in contrast to the "we" of the somewhat later *Medieval Scenes*, manifests as a mere place-holder for a speaking position, rather than as an active constitution of group subjectivity. Duncan characterizes this "we" as lacking intensity: "we do not burn hotly, we question the fire." For these "friends" "love is a painful question," and it is also "a payment" for "an old debt for a borrowing foolishly spent," and "we go on borrowing and borrowing from each other" (*Collected Early* 77). A strong sense of impoverishment, which is related to the lovers' sameness, threads its way through the poem: "We stare back into our faces / We have become our own realities" (77). Although the final poem of the Berkeley Poems seems to conclude positively, with an affirmation of "a most fleshly man," whose beloved's "spirit is intimate of my hand / . . . intimate of my parted lips," much of it is written through the conditional "would," and it concludes with "I would embrace you in that flame" and "we should lie brought then to rest" (82, 83).

In between the initial and final poems of the Berkeley Poems, Duncan develops figures that might mediate the impasses of the work, although they also serve to entrench them. Duncan enlists the presence of a "drunken woman" and envisions himself as "a sphinx." The "drunken woman" is able to "love" and "to drink deeply of thy soul," but only through a deranged sensibility (80). The sphinx attempts to mediate the binaries of the poem by identifying itself with unanswerable questions:

> Questioning females, answering males!
> Question that shall never fathom its answer!
> Answer that shall never fathom its question! (*First Decade* 31)

While these figures cross over the gender and sexual dichotomies that troubled Duncan's quest for love, they do not answer the deeper questions of the poem: about what love might be and how love might lead to an enrichment of being. Duncan addresses at some length his precarious love and ambivalent relationships with women, with whom he sometimes identifies and whom he occasionally seeks as love partners. He invokes commonplace hierarchical relations between a masculine lover and a feminine beloved that propagate into additional binaries:

> Did you not hear in the music as we danced
> the sigh as of a lover before whom appears
> the weeping and stricken form of his beloved?
> She is like a white deer in the foliage hidden,
> that, panting, heated, fixes upon him
> her innocent gaze. Asks me, asks me,
> are you the lover? are you the hunter? (30)

The problematics of an active lover and a passive beloved spin into a more sinisterly construed hunter and hunted, as the feminine beloved morphs into "a white deer." Elsewhere in the poem, the poet addresses two women, who are unable to hold beauty and passion:

> *If only my sense of your beauty*
> *could flow back and fill you.*
>
> . . . .

If only my sense of your passion
could flow back and fill you. (33)

While here Duncan is projecting the inability to "hold" "beauty" and "passion" as defining for each of the two women, respectively, these failures are the larger problematic of the poem itself since Duncan both in life and in this writing was unable to bring together "making love" with the excitement of sex.

If there is one early poem sequence that indicates the direction that Duncan's poetry will take in *The Opening of the Field*, it is *Medieval Scenes*. In *Medieval Scenes* he engages language as a medium and avoids the dichotomies and binaries of his earlier poetry. Duncan wrote this poem in a séance-like atmosphere, amid a coterie of Berkeley acquaintances who regularly visited his house at 2029 Hearst Street, including several of Duncan's homosexual attractions and admirers. After dinner, Duncan "received" this poetry at a *table parlante*, flanked often by Jack Spicer and Hugh O'Neill, sometimes by Robin Blaser and Robert Curran. Duncan began the poem each night with a "literary *objet trouve* or found text" (Faas 227–31). In the author's notes to *Medieval Scenes*, Duncan wrote how he "had the sense for the first time in poetry not just of 'having' a poem . . . but having a work to do and knowing that work as I did it" (qtd. in Anderson 48). In *The H.D. Book*, Duncan described his experience of writing *Medieval Scenes*: "I . . . thought of myself as artisan and medium of the poem in one, receiving certain scenes and reworking them in language" (440).

Duncan wrote *Medieval Scenes* shortly after composing the Berkeley Poems. While in the Berkeley Poems Duncan is most decorous in the telling of love's dissatisfactions and would-be love, in *Medieval Scenes* he creates a hypercathexis between the imagined participants and language in which "Love's questions" disappear into the immediacy of the exchange itself. While he initially refers to "Half-loves / kept short of love's redeeming fire," he does not emphasize the dissatisfaction of these half-loves but rather creates a more resonant space in which to explore disconnection and connection as inseparable from each other (*First Decade* 51). Initially, Duncan included the line "My lover swims and glitters in each face," but he later changed "My lover" to "The daemon," suggesting that in writing this sequence Duncan began to locate a powerful rather than a diffident or desperate love (Faas 227). Indeed, while the Berkeley Poems recount a not fully expressed or felt love, *Medieval Scenes* creates the conditions through which diverse people and things can interact. The Berkeley Poems advocate and practice an Adamic speech and naming; *Medieval Scenes* at the outset speaks of "sleep" and "lethargy":

Sleep lingers all our lifetime in our eyes
as night at midday hovers

. . . .
It is the magic of not-touching,
not-looking sharpenings of the eyes,
dim thunders of imaginings. (*Selected* 11)

Rather than displaying a resolute will that serves to expedite his poetic explorations, this poetic speaker seems to hold a multiplicity of sayings near to
him, so that they may gestate in relationship to each other. The poem deposes
the patrician or patriarchal value of clear-sightedness and the plain speech of
the goodly, "fleshly man," insisting on its own simultaneously myopic and far-
sighted vision. As opposed to the love that "strikes" "steel" in "An Apollonian
Elegy," this poem makes way for "bearish" presences holding onto and bump-
ing into each other (*First Decade* 26; *Selected* 11). "The magic in convolutions of
our company" underwrites "lightnings in half-sleep of furry storm" and creates
an environment in which all things "swim and glitter" (*Selected* 11).

While the first section of the poem, "The Dreamers," might be seen as a kind
of calling together of "the company of love," in the next section, "The Helmet
of Goliath," the speaker alternately identifies with David, Goliath, and Goliath's
helmet, which itself sings, "There is a secret wooing in the night, / a fine adultery of voices talking" (*Selected* 13). "A fine adultery of voices talking" wrenches
the transgressiveness of adultery from its usual associations, suggesting how
voices and sayings mixing with each other create a collocation apart from conventional social rules, while keeping at bay the usual jealousies and betrayals
that accompany adultery. Duncan's personification of the helmet is indicative of
his changed relationship to "things" and "persons," as the helmet and the speech
of the poets take on presences of their own:

The poets at their table speak of love
The waves of an uncomprehending sea
washing between each lover and his love.
The words are drowned of meaning in that roar.
. . . .
The speech of the poets seems to deny
all love. They listen to forbidden music.
And in that darkend helmet
each poet's face is curious. (13, 14)

In imagining the poets as curious, Duncan would seem to be describing a kind
of speech animated by sexual desire that partakes of a Lacanian economy in
which signification carries desire apart from love relationships. This moment

is reminiscent of Pound's translation of Cavalcanti's sonnet in which the poetic speaker declares, "New is the face that's set in seigniory," although for both Pound and Duncan this Lacanian desire is just an initial stage of discovery on their way to a fuller speech.

In *Medieval Scenes*, years before Duncan created his open field poetics in which he voids the "interference of the individual as ego," he discovered a poetics of interacting elements. The change this poem realized was due to his willingness to stay his writing through a set of enchanted relations with his collaborators and the romance of the evolving poem. Rather than the poet being the prime mover of the poem, song itself and an array of associations create the poetic speaker: "Created by the poets to sing my song / or created by my song to sing" (*Selected* 19). *Medieval Scenes* envisions enchantment as a living "brocade" that includes its makers, unconscious of their "signature":

> The poets weave themselves as the erotic hunters.
> They wear bright jerkins of a rich brocade
> and silk of forest green upon their thighs.
> .   .   .   .
> They seem unconscious of the signature. (*Selected* 14–15)

Plumbing feelings and truths toward which he had strived, but which he had failed to realize, in his earlier poems, Duncan in *Medieval Scenes* created an enchantment that dared to speak its name.

"Writing as Writing"

The change between Duncan's emotionally and rhetorically fraught early poems and the work in his 1950s volumes *Writing Writing* and *Letters* could not be more marked. In these two volumes, Duncan entered into experiments in which he concentrated on "writing as writing." He opened up a space for poetic exploration apart from what he characterized as the "menacing," "over-charged" "feeling" of his early writing (*Years* vi). In *Writing Writing* and *Letters*, Duncan continued his investigations into love, only now as a writing of love as a writing of love. In this work, he gained considerably more sense of the possibility of his agency as a writer, and he engaged language primarily as a material. Two months after publishing *Letters*, Duncan began *The Opening of the Field*, in which he joined his newly discovered alacrity in "writing as writing" to his earlier entrenched intellectual and emotional issues.

One of the biographical events that may have catapulted Duncan into these experimental volumes was his prolonged, torturous relationship with Gerald

Ackerman, a considerably younger man who was prone to infidelities, as was Duncan. And while Duncan's preceding relationships were tumultuous, as his biographer Ekbert Faas points out, the jealousies, misunderstandings, and remonstrances of his relationship with Ackerman surpassed the others' and became just too much for Duncan. Faas draws on the observations of psychoanalyst Hilda Burton, who witnessed the breakup of this relationship, which was "truly painful and crazy-making" for Duncan: "I think it produced an identity crisis in him, and he came out a different person at the other end. A different part of him became constellated" (Faas 267). Within a year of this breakup, Duncan entered into his lifelong relationship with Jess Collins. Faas comments about this transition: Duncan's "difficulties with Jerry [Ackerman] . . . helped him understand the vicious circle of quarrels and reconciliations which seemed to plague his rapport with those he had chosen as partners for his ideal of a sacrosanct household. Whatever the case, the pattern was not repeated in the union with Jess" (267). Duncan characterized the changes in his relationship with Jess as having direct parallels for his writing life: he gave up his "fixation" on a love based on "contraries" for a love of "deep accord," "going on [with Jess] in a common life" ("Interview" by Abbott and Shurin 78).

Duncan's primary exemplar for *Writing Writing* was Gertrude Stein. He explained in an interview with Faas, "I had the instinctive feeling that what I really needed was Stein," noting that what he sought was a "discipline" not a "guru." He qualified this distinction: "Discipline is perhaps a poor word. It was to open the range. I was really in a way designing a non-sequitur field of influences which would balance off the intensity of the Pound, Williams, Eliot, Stevens directive I had taken." He commented that his election of Stein was for "a force that's foreign enough while you can still recognize it as a power," although he did not ascribe to "Steinian common sense." Moreover, he sought out Stein because of her experiments with syntax: "I wanted to go to Stein to see if I could single out syntax as the local plan for anything," noting that in following the lead of Stein's syntactical emphasis it was impossible to write fiction ("Interview" by Faas 10, 11).

In *Writing Writing*, Duncan explores different sets of relations regarding writing, no longer insisting on an alignment between his person and the words he writes, his emotions, and his speech. The titles of the various pieces reveal how individual works are an experiment in bringing forward some aspects of writing while stilling or ignoring others: "The Beginning of Writing," "Imagining in Writing," "Writing as Writing," "An Imaginary Letter," "Descriptions of Imaginary Poetries," and "The Feeling of Language in Poetry." In the first piece of the volume, "The Beginning of Writing," Duncan makes the need for beginning and sustaining the energy of a poem the subject of the poem itself. With Stein's confident sense of a "continuous present" informing his experiments, Duncan is able to let the writing itself do the expressing. While in his earlier poems, Duncan often felt a need to begin writing a poem over again to develop and sustain its initiating energies, now, by getting his subject out into the "open," his dependence on a compulsive writing has lessened (Faas 228):

> Beginning to write. Continuing finally to write. Writing
> finally to continue beginning.
>
> To overcome the beginning. To overcome the urgency. To
> overcome writing in writing. (*Collected Early* 449)

By engaging writing as writing, Duncan constitutes his writing as part of a continuous present that bypasses his previous need to write out of an emotional crisis. He finds through the activity of writing the sensations of advancing, including, overcoming, and continuing, which he equates with loving:

> Love is sometimes advancing and including. Love is some
> times overcoming and not beginning. Love as a continual
> part of some writing is imagining expansion of loving to
> include beginning as continuing.
>
> . . . .
>
> When I imagine not overcoming but including, loving takes place in the
> place of desiring. (449)

Here, Duncan through the activity of writing reformulates questions about love that plagued his early writing—replacing desiring love with staying love, or replacing what some might call "narcissistic *parry*" with "narcissistic *economy*" (Kristeva 267–68). "Writing as writing" replaces Duncan's earlier ruses of the "sphinx," the "drunken woman," "deranged sensibilities," and "magic-making" with the forward, looping nature of writing itself. Thus, while in *Medieval Scenes*, for example, he questions the ethos and aesthetics among his peers of "the magic of not touching" with the querulous contention that "beasts at least would touch each other," in "Imagining in Writing," the question of "not touching" is answered by language itself: "touch touches" (450).

While *Writing Writing* opens up important spaces for Duncan, these spaces also threaten to make writing an exercise in writing—or a lopsided investment, with the poet using language and only rather tepidly being used by it. Although in "The Beginning of Writing" Duncan eases writing, frees it from its compulsions, he also makes the difficult subject of love tauntingly easy:

When I imagine myself a lover
—love is again here, here I say:
coming forth by Day once more
from all mere longing, belonging
to saying. (450)

Duncan immediately passes judgment on these lines: "A soliloquy! A soliloquy! / Such idle talking in different colord lights" (450). Yet, he cannot resist the ease and freedom of this writing, and in the next piece, "Imagining in Writing," he advocates "pretending":

Not in believing, but in pretending. Not in knowing, but in pretending. Not in undergoing but in pretending.

At last, at last, all of reality: We find we are only what we pretended to be. We realize. (450)

In "Descriptions of Imaginary Poetries," the poet warns that monstrous birthings of words may arise with considerable agility but limited meaning:

Where giant wordlings interrupt the stuttering machine-gun-wit; the pale insensible bland body phrases loom, as islands in the line-of-fire. Not targets, but meaningless casualities. Luminous blobs in a splattered night scene. Too accidental for inspiration, too clumsy for lyric. (*Collected Early* 469)

In *Letters*, Duncan continues the deliberate distancing from his early work, although he engages not only the constructive aspects of writing and language, but also an inspiring "company of peers," who are addressed, albeit indirectly and obliquely, through a corresponding set of letters or, as Duncan writes in a preface, "Your signature in mine" (*Collected Early* 638). Duncan's use of the title *Letters* is undoubtedly meant to cast attention on letters as literature and letters as correspondence; in other words, to create literature is to correspond with prior literature and other writers. In the preface, the named exemplar not to be followed is Artaud. While in the later *Truth and Life of Myth*, Duncan entertains the possibility that psychosis and poetic meaning may be interrelated, in *Letters*, as in *Writing Writing*, he upholds certain limits. Duncan sees Artaud as being "torn apart by actual excitations which are intolerable to his imagination and his material. Neither his desire nor the object of his desire can endure his excitement" (*Collected Early* 636). As opposed to Artaud's out-of-control "excitations," Duncan elects to work at a "threshold . . . with a constant excitement at play." And he presents the excitements of "making love" and "writing poetry" as interacting playfulness: "A lover makes love, and may use poetry to do so. A poet makes speech and may use love to do so" (635). At some remove from his later dynamic admonition—not only to use things but to be used by them—he asserts, "These poems are evidences of the desire for speech" and are based on "a process which sets self-creation and self-consciousness in constant interplay" (635–36). While Duncan in his later writing makes "self-consciousness" just one of many elements, here "self-consciousness" serves as a kind of bedrock, keeping the poems on track through a writing in which rationality and whimsicality are interrelated.

The Opening of the Field

Two months after completing *Letters*, Duncan began writing *The Opening of the Field*. In that work, he returned to his "world of feeling" and linked it to "writing as writing," creating a projective love and libidinized field poetics. By Duncan's own account, *The Opening of the Field* was the first time that he conceived of writing poems specifically for a book. As such, it was a place where he could "put / therein first things"—a set of injunctions or "permissions"—and this new way of holding things became a way of making love. By conceiving his poetry writing through the larger project of a book, Duncan was able to hold in relationship discrepant things that are brought "into being" through his writing.

No longer simply the feeling drudge or the writing impresario, Duncan positions his poetic speaker as both master and servant of writing, used by things as he uses them. Indeed, the things in this volume direct the poetic speaker through their particular insights, or incites. The "Sentence" in "The Structure of Rime I" commands:

Speak! For I name myself your master, who come to serve.
Writing is first a search in obedience. (*Opening* 12)

The "Wood" counsels:

Lie down, Man, under Love. The streams of the
Earth seek passage thru you,

. . . .

Look behind you, courageous traveler! you will see that past where you have
never been. See! These are not your footprints that fall from your feet. (20)

He who is "under Love" is born newly unto himself, since as he looks into his "past" it has been transformed, and his "footprints" are no longer his own. While in the early poetry, Duncan's poetic speaker sought love as a "pained," "proud," and "animal self," who sings in a "lonely monotone," now he depicts love as a force that moves through, connects, and changes things:

> the beloved turning to his beloved in the dark
> create love as the leaves,
> create from light life (17)

In this set of changed relationships, "there is no touch that is not each / to each reciprocal" (10). Or in more general terms: "all beings into / all beings pass" (24).

The Opening of the Field is distinguished from his earlier work by two important changes. Love and strife are brought together, not as abstractions to be unified, but as dispositions to be held simultaneously. There also are increased proprioceptive relations.[3] Mackey has written about how in *Bending the Bow* there is a "confounding of love's fire with the flames of strife." And he comments that both of these dispositions are defining for Duncan's writing: "Duncan, who acknowledges war to be a 'great theme' of poetry, proposes love as an alternative mode of intensification, falling in love as a way of coming into an order of intensities, a richness of intent otherwise unavailable" (*Paracritical* 152). Yet, while in *Bending the Bow*, Duncan, writing during the Vietnam War, brings these to a new pitch, this duality is explored as mutually defining in *The Opening of the Field*.

In the first poem of the volume, "Often I Am Permitted to Return to a Meadow," Duncan names "the First Beloved" as his instigating figure and engages several new defining elements for his verse. The poem begins with an exploration of its "made place" as "an eternal pasture folded in all thought." And it draws together "light and shadow" with a sense of falling:

> a made place, created by light
> wherefrom the shadows that are all forms fall. (*Opening* 7)

This falling then precipitates the line discussed in chapter 1, "Wherefrom fall all architectures I am," a kind of falling into and through love. Although the immediate reference for Duncan's "First Beloved" is likely the beloved in Diotima's speech in Plato's *Symposium*, its proprioceptive relations recall the *Phaedrus*. While in Diotima's famous staircase metaphor the movement in time and space is one of ascent and transformation, in the *Phaedrus*, eros, depicted as sublime and aloft, also moves into the realm of memory and the past, "down under." In this opening poem and in *The Opening of the Field* more generally, Duncan engages proprioceptive relations occasionally of ascent but most often of descent as well as a movement against, widdershins. Mark Johnson defines "widdershins" as "moving in a direction opposite to the usual especially in a direction contrary [to] the apparent course of the sun. Considered unlucky, such motion is irresistible nonetheless" (76). Duncan's invocation of a "field" and its folding down "Under" is reminiscent of the Kore, Persephone, and Hades myth with its "rent" field and connection to the Eleusinian mysteries. Duncan commented in a 1959 lecture in which he discussed his plans for *The Opening of the Field* that "the meadow is the place where one enters the gate of otherness—the other world" (qtd. in Jarnot "from The Ambassador from Venus" 1).

After the initial summons of his "made place" and its animating figures, Duncan further explores this space through an invocation of one of his recurring dreams, which partakes of widdershins:

It is only a dream of the grass blowing
east against the source of the sun
in an hour before the sun's going down

whose secret we see in a children's game
of ring around of roses told. (7)

These much remarked on lines convey a sense of physiological shifting into a mythic or dream space created by a child's game, an event in which the sense of the body's relation in space, or proprioception, is vivid because of the dizziness that comes from circling around. Most of the preternatural aspects of this moment come from how, in this passage, just before sunset, the sun is going down quite wrongly in the east, conveying a sense of life-in-death or death-in-life—further brought out by the omitted concluding line of the ring-around-the-roses game, "ashes, ashes, we all fall down." The omission of this line is made all the more prominent because this stanza is made up of only two lines, whereas the rest of the poem consists predominantly of three-line stanzas. Indeed, this sense of a poetic or dream event creates an untoward disturbing coincidence of self with that which is outside the self, as the self becomes other than what it was. The poem concludes by announcing the significance of this morphing sequence as providing Duncan with a "place of first permission, / everlasting omen of what is" (7).

In the poems immediately following "Often I Am Permitted to Return to a Meadow," other kinds of movement and proprioception prevail. "The Dance" tells and enacts a rhythm of dancing. Borrowing some of the pounding, rounding syntax and rhythms of Williams's "The Dance," based on Breughel's *The Kermess,*

Duncan's "The Dance" creates correspondences among dance movements, poetry writing, earthly fecundity, and orgasmic joy: "Lovely their feet pound the green solid meadow" (*Opening* 8). But the poem also explores Duncan's particular set of issues in finding this new fulsome rhythm. It includes a figure called "old Freidl," which refers to a woman out of Duncan's past. Faas describes Duncan's relationship with Freidl, who when Duncan knew her was working on a new translation of Wilhelm Reich's *Die Funktion des Orgasmus*: "Occasionally Robert had found himself impotent when sleeping with women. . . . Sex with Freidl was not simply sex but the culmination of an orgiastic experience" (Faas 171). "The Dance" includes a dialogue between Freidl and Duncan, which manifests both an earlier Duncan and Duncan as the poetic speaker of this poem:

> I remember only the truth.
> I swear by my yearning.
>
> *You have conquered the yearning*, she said
> *The numbers have enterd your feet.*
>
> turn   turn   turn
>
> *When you're real gone, boy, sweet boy . . .*
>
> Where have I gone, Beloved?
>
> *Into the Waltz, Dancer.* (8)

Duncan learns that he has entered the dance through the voice of Freidl, as if knowledge of one's participation for those truly involved in the dance must be announced from the outside. Freidl pronounces him "*Dancer*" through the heavy "somnambulistic language" of "*Waltz, Dancer*," and Duncan conveys through this sounding what he writes in "A Poem Beginning with a Line from Pindar": "the information flows / that is yearning" (*Opening* 69).

In the next two poems, "The Law I Love Is Major Mover" and "The Structure of Rime I," Duncan explores proprioceptive relationships between standing one's ground and moving. In "The Law I Love Is Major Mover," Duncan begins with a sense of the necessity of judgment and of a stable, consistent witness, conveyed by the poem's semantics and syntax, "*I, John, testify: / I saw*," and then he insists that "he who judges must / know mercy," a syntactical arrangement in which the subject, "he," flows into his actions. Duncan concludes with "the Angel that made a man of Jacob" "was the Law" and "was Syntax," and "Him I love is a major mover." Rather than the construction "I love him," the object, this beloved, has first place in the sentence, subject as well as object, and both entities are marked by a capital letter. Duncan embeds "Him" and "I love" in such a way that the movement between "Him" and "I" is not unidirectional and fixed but circular and continuous, not straightforward but looping (10–11).

In "The Structure of Rime I," which may well be a precursor to the "New Sentence," Duncan engages the containment and predictability of the structure of a sentence as it is crossed with movement.[4] "The Structure of Rime," a serial poem that appears throughout *The Opening of the Field* as well as in later volumes of Duncan's work, is both about "rhyme," as that which repeats or corresponds, and "rime," as a frost or a crystalline, self-propagating formation— or the generative, ongoing production of this serial poem. In "The Structure of Rime II," which immediately follows, Duncan further defines "The Structure of Rime" not as a "melody" "to charm the beasts" but as "a melody within this surfeit of speech that is most man." Thus "rime," or poetry more generally, is *"an absolute scale of resemblance and disresemblance* [that] *establishes measures that are music in the actual world"* (13). Duncan defines poetry as a relational art in search of a music based on the differences between things, on perception leading directly to perception, language phrase to language phrase, in which through careful attention *"an absolute"* can be attained. Indeed, the only absolute may be the bringing together of resemblances and disresemblances into a new music.

While the initial poems of *The Opening of the Field* present their love and strife through proprioceptive relations registered through an altered syntax, "A Poem Beginning with a Line by Pindar" is created through a forward movement pushed from behind and takes on considerable thematic complexity. Widdershins becomes a way of discovering the light and dark of passion through a movement toward the ashes of an earlier day:

There is the hero who struggles east
widdershins to free the dawn   and must
                woo Night's daughter,
sorcery, black passionate rage, covetous queens,
so that the fleecy sung go   back from Troy,
    Colchis, India . . . all the blazing armies
spent, he must struggle alone toward the pyres of Day

            The light that is Love
rushes on toward passion. It verges upon dark. (66)

In discussing this poem in *The Truth of Life and Myth*, Duncan recounted his writing in a manner reminiscent of Olson's "INSTANTER" writing, although *The Opening of the Field* presents a slowed-down projective-introjective writing as the figures in one poem become reworked as figures in later poems. He described how in writing this poem, he utilized the "revelations flowing out of" the Eros and Psyche myth, which depend on a recognition of an "I" apart from "the interference of the individual as ego": "I cannot make it happen or want it to happen; it wells up in me as if I were a point of break-thru for an 'I' that may be any person in the cast of a play. . . . When that 'I' is lost, when the voice of the poem is lost, the matter of the poem, the intense information of the content, no longer comes to me, then I know I have to wait until that voice returns. The return is felt as a readiness, a body tone. . . . The creative nexus or the true poem that moves the poem—is the source, not the product." In describing this "source," he noted that it is made up of three elements: "the words . . . alive in their resonances of sound, pulse and meaning," "the life experience and imagination of the poet," and "the actual body of the poet—the reservoir of his lifestyle" (*Fictive* 17–18).

Throughout "A Poem Beginning with a Line by Pindar" love and strife contend and "confound," creating an eros defined through its mixed "holdings." For instance, Duncan writes, "In Goya's canvas Cupid and Psyche / have a hurt voluptuous grace / bruised by redemption" (*Opening* 62). Interpreting Goya's canvas as a conflictual presentation between the classical myth of Cupid and Psyche and a Christian redemption story, Duncan notes that the latter enters into the painting as the bruising of the two lovers. Duncan's sense of this bruising likely manifests his critique of Christianity as creating a division between "inner" and "outer," a pervasive cultural force that is inescapable by all who live amid it, whatever one thinks of it. The colors and shadings of this bruising tinge other depictions, stimulating emotional and physical responses, as perception leads directly to further perception:

> A bronze of yearning, a rose that burns
> > the tips of their bodies, lips,
> ends of fingers, nipples.
> .   .   .   .
> hot luminescence at the loins of the visible.

All aspects of the lovers' situation, including their responses to it, create their mythos, their passion, and "serve them":

> That she is ignorant, ignorant of what Love will be,
> > serves them.
> The dark serves them.
> The oil scalding his shoulder serves them,
> serves their story. Fate, spinning,
> > knots the threads for Love.
> Jealousy, ignorance, the hurt . . . serve them. (62–63)

Through his emphasis on how these different aspects "serve" them, Duncan reads the myth backward, widdershins, and the past is valued in the present for how it creates the present.

Near the end of the poem, Duncan returns to his "first things," reworking the opening dream sequence in "Often I Am Permitted to Return to a Meadow" as well as reconsidering the derivation of his poem in Pindar. Through the projective-introjective process that has resulted in the "upwelling" of this poem, Duncan now envisages his dream as more pulled apart and more directly meaningful, more singular and more cosmogonic, as its grass separates into singular blades and as its movement becomes part of a larger dance:

> On the hill before the wind came
> the grass moved toward the one sea,
>   blade after blade dancing in waves.
>
> There the children turn the ring to the left.
> There the children turn the ring to the right.
>   Dancing . . . Dancing . . . (68)

Now rather than the unidentified "it" of the "She it is Queen Under The Hill" and other "its" meant to suggest the ineffable, "the lonely psyche goes up thru the boy to the king." Duncan also revisits the immediate source for the poem in Pindar's work: "a line from a hymn came in a novel I was reading to help me." Ultimately his return to these "first things" leads Duncan to a reseeing of the children, now as a past event, apart from him: "I have seen the willful children // clockwise and counter-clockwise turning" (68–69). The poem concludes not with a final event, but with the pastness of Duncan's own seeing, his envisioning through a past tense.

In many ways the preface to *Bending the Bow* may be seen as announcing and consolidating the discoveries of *The Opening of the Field*. While Duncan's immediate concern with the writing of poetry during the Vietnam War gives urgency to his preoccupation with strife in relationship to love, he also insists on an interactive poetics, naming them a "*grand collage*": "The artist, after Dante's poetics, works with all parts of the poem as *polysemous*, taking each thing of the composition as generative of meaning, a response to and a contribution to the building form" (ix). Duncan insists on an "abundance" of purposes and cross-purposes working in tandem. He quotes Heraklites: "*They do not apprehend how being at variance it agrees with itself. . . . there is a connexion working in both directions*" (iv). In a separate section of the preface titled "It," he links his poetics of grand collage with eros: "the trouble of an Eros shakes the household in which we work to contain our feeling in our extending our feeling into time and space" (vi). In this section, he vacillates between naming a love of two "he's" or trans-gendered identities as defining for this eros: "Man His-Her-Self" (viii). In either case, both the preface and the poetry in *Bending the Bow* exhibit a new confidence in man-to-man love, arising out of Duncan's projective love writing, in which feminine and masculine dispositions rather than being delineated as separate identities morph into each other.

Duncan comments further on "the trouble of an Eros": "The nearness of this shaking—[of] our own actual city built as it is high on the ground of a history written in earthquakes—makes for an almost womanish tenderness in orders we are fierce to keep. A girlish possibility embarrasses the masculinity of the reader. . . . In the poem this very lighted room is dark, and the dark alight with love's intentions" (vi-vii). Duncan elaborates that his writing is best expressed as an "It," which he links with "*grand collage*" but which exceeds any naming of "It": "*It* is striving to come into existence in these things, or, all striving to come into existence is It—in this realm of men's languages a poetry of all poetries, *grand collage*, I name It, having only the immediate event of words to speak for It. In the room, we, aware or unaware, are the event of ourselves in It" (vii). Duncan bypasses entrenched identities and references. He emphasizes that the "words" of his "*grand collage*" do not so much name as indicate the "event of ourselves" and "our" connection to eros (vi-viii).

In *Bending the Bow*, tender love statements between lover and beloved are part of a larger structure that enables the poet to get beyond his individual ego. Eros in "The Collage, *Passages 6*" moves between "I" and "we," personal and im-personal, one body and many bodies:

How long have I been waiting,
                    the language, the sea, the body
     rising above
          sleep
       above
                         and leaves us
     fallen back
                     above sleep
   .   .   .   .
until the reefs upon which we live are exposed,
     the green water going out over
                    the rock ledges,
   body upon body
       turning keys as the tide turns
   and reaching up into . . . (19–21)

The proprioceptive movements of this writing, back and forth, rising and descending, falling into and out of, are pronounced, manifesting Duncan's commitment to the creation of meaning as inseparable from a moving language in all its senses. In "The Collage, *Passages 6*," Duncan calls on a poetics of "paste-up," which includes graphically distinct presentations of signs and letters. Duncan asks about the intermixing of sign system and bodily fluids: "Can consonants / so crawl or blur to give . . . / contrive to imitate juices, excretions, the body's / spit?" (20).

Throughout the volume, Duncan's writing draws power and confidence from the relationship between first beloveds and other lovers. He calls on "music," "where other / lovers in intermingling figures / come and go" and recalls "the First Partner," "in Whom / you are most you" (5). In "Sonnet 4" and "5th Sonnet," Duncan would seem to be creating a more personal love lyric, yet even in these poems, Duncan's writing moves between personal and impersonal address. "Sonnet 4" begins with an indirect address to the lover:

He's given me his *thee* to keep,
secret, alone, in Love's name. (3)

The poem proceeds to find its measure at some remove from the beloved, while recalling the enclosure of this liaison. Conjuring a rose that scatters its petals as well as "the perfection of the rose," Duncan creates an analogy:

I would know the red *thee* of the enclosure
where thought, too, curls about

. . . .

until it falls away, all the profuse allusions let go (3)

One of the most famous poems of this volume, "The Torso, *Passages 18*," addresses a man through his body parts—"*the clavicle*," "*the nipples*," "*the navel*," "*the pubic hair*"—creating at once a "universal man" and a "lover," whose "locks" are his "keys" and whose self "gathers" selves. The poem both states and conveys the proprioception of rising and falling, as the lovers rise and fall into each other:

<blockquote>
In your falling

I have fallen from a high place.   I have raised myself

From darkness in your   rising (64)
</blockquote>

The poem concludes by honoring the poetic speaker's love for a man, naming this love in no uncertain terms, seemingly apart from any agitations arising from gender or sexual codes:

For my Other is not a woman but a man
the King upon whose bosom let me lie. (65)

At a great distance from Duncan's earlier "Buggery stirs enmity, unguarded ha-
tred / Cocksucking breeds self-humiliation," "The Torso" names its love with confidence (*First Decade* 90). Throughout *Bending the Bow* the sense of a "gathering,"
rather than a controlling or being controlled by, is defining—repudiating through
its different economy Duncan's earlier melancholic "I, I, I" and the mournful
strains of "An African Elegy." Sadness is now just one emotion among others in
his poetry, and the poetic speaker professes, "I let sadness gather" (*Bending* 58).

Thom Gunn has written a succinct overview of the relationship between
Robert Duncan's love life and his writing that corresponds in very broad out-
lines with the account here, except for Gunn's tendency to see this "life in poetry" through entirely normative terms. Gunn describes the young Duncan as
initially writing love as an "act of will," and his mature poetry in *The Opening of
the Field* as based on a love that is the "real thing," which is like "moving from
a series of rooms into open country" (146, 147, 151). As Gunn sees it, an important accomplishment of Duncan's mature verse was the production of a homosexual love not marked by homosexuality but by the experience of "love [as]
merely the occasion for a poem which would be just about the same if it were
about the relation between a man and a woman. . . . love of one's own sex, just
as much as love of the opposite sex, is the start of that training that reaches to
the god's presence" (147).

While by *Bending the Bow*, Duncan did seem to have achieved an at once
equanimous and passionate love, the volume had behind it decades of written
explorations that brought to such terms as "lover" and "beloved," "men" and
"women," "falling in love" and "desire," "sex" and "eros" a changed sense not
only of these terms but of the very act of what it means to write. While Gunn
produces his own poetry through a deliberate naming, for Duncan Adamistic
naming is simply not adequate to writing love.

Kathleen Fraser and "Falling into the Page"

There was, as it turned out, a place in language—even in its zero
beginnings—to put one's trust.
                          —Kathleen Fraser, "The Blank Page: H.D.'s Invitation
                            to Trust and Mistrust Language"

In many ways, Fraser's and H.D.'s writing trajectories parallel each other. Fraser early on found a way to write a nascent projective love and libidinized field
poetics. Then she turned away from this coalescing of subject and object, which
H.D. referred to as her needed "clairvoyance" for writing poetry, to address the
problematics of the "sex-gender system." Relatively late in life, Fraser, like H.D.,
returned to write a projective love and libidinized field poetics through an expanded field of references and through the compositional space of a complete
book. Both poets from the outset of writing love poetry did not create poetic lovers
in the throes of singular emotional states—say, enchantment or melancholia—as
did Duncan and Pound, but rather they displaced emotional stances onto erotic
topos. H.D. created *Sea Garden* through a poetry of pursuit and of stasis. From
the outset, Fraser was concerned with absence and presence. But while in Fraser's early poetry these exist in opposition to each other, in her later poetry they
interrelate.

   While the similarities between H.D. and Fraser might on the surface seem to
stem from shared temperamental and personal attributes, they are rather the result of each poet's desire to write her love within a patriarchal and heterosexual
society and set of love practices. Indeed, H.D. and Fraser are quite different
women and poets. H.D. was bisexual and reclusive; Fraser is heterosexual and
far more public, initiating and participating in collaborative enterprises.[1] However, H.D. and Fraser share an early intention to engage how being in love leads
to poetic transport as well as a sustained commitment to write love. Moreover,
they both have expended considerable effort in exploring the cultural and social
problematics of gender and sexuality. Historically, they have engaged different
moments: for H.D., an emerging feminist critique and new sexual discourses;
for Fraser, increasingly vocal and articulate feminist and sexuality movements.
Although Fraser has found considerable definition and impetus through femi-

nism and through related gay and lesbian movements, she also has found herself at odds with the often identity-based poetry that accompanies them.

At the outset of her poetic career, Fraser claimed that "Lust" is the "first virtue," without which poetic transport does not happen (*Change* 15).[2] Yet while her initial poetry evinced this transport, it was stopped short in poems in which lover and beloved exist in opposition and in which a disappointed female lover bespeaks dissatisfaction with the love she has not been able to create with her male lover. Fraser's first book, *Change of Address* (1966), begins with two love poems that manifest her frustration at her emotionally unavailable beloved. In "Glass," discussed in the introduction to *The Transmutation of Love and Avant-Garde Poetics*, the poetic speaker asks for transparency and clarity, describing her "need for you": "shining / the way sun does." The poem then turns to a meditation about living in "a house with dirty windows" and concludes, "Knowing you in the dim-light, / loving the half-light, / how safe it felt / to see only partly" (3). In the second poem, "Song for a Man in Doubt," dedicated to "Jack," the poet addresses a man's "impassable space[s]," in contrast to her own responsiveness: "Look / you touch my arm and you've touched // all of me, waves inside my skin." But in this relationship, "talk of dark places // becomes a conjecture" (4). Fraser concludes this poem about a hypostasized relationship by offering her own grounded existence: "I am here to fill and be filled / My feet grab the soil like radishes" (4). At this point in her work, she defines "conjecture" in opposition to presence, an opposition she will unsettle in her subsequent projective verse.

In her third volume of verse, *Little Notes to You, from Lucas Street* (1972), divisions between lover and beloved are much diminished, and Fraser initiates a nascent projective love and libidinized field poetics. The frustration expressed in the earlier verse is gone, and there is a coalescing between lover and beloved, subject and object. While this volume bespeaks a different love relationship and lover, a requited and returned love, it also evinces a different poetics in which the individual poetic speaker as ego is largely voided for a cathexis with the objects and others of her attention as well as language itself. Finding herself in what she experiences as a deeply reciprocated love relationship, Fraser is propelled into a present-tense writing of enhanced presences. Yet, while Fraser found and practiced these poetics early on, she abandoned them in her subsequent volumes of verse and did not return to engage these poetics until the 1990s, when she published *when new time folds up* and *WING* along with several essays exploring an ecstatic relation to language.

Between writing her *Little Notes* and *when new time folds up* (1993) Fraser engaged in a protracted exploration in which she attempted to address the critique of romantic love ushered in by 1970s and 1980s feminism through exploratory forms of writing. This feminist critique of romantic love, whether in

consciousness-raising groups or in theoretical treatises, created epochal transformations as women came to distrust the love relations in which they were involved. Adrienne Rich's 1980 essay "Compulsory Heterosexuality and Lesbian
Existence" created a highwater mark both within and without the academy as
Rich persuasively argued that heterosexuality kept women imprisoned and that
all feminists should seek a "lesbian continuum," whether or not they sought
same-sex love. While Rich did not demand that all women become lesbians but
rather enter into a sisterhood, the strength of her argument meant that many
women left male partners and sought out lesbian relations. At the same time, many
lesbians were outraged by the idea of a "lesbian continuum" that elided sexual difference. Fraser, recognizing the importance of both the feminist critique of heterosexual love and the need to create common cause with other women, kept her
distance from the divisive identity politics. Indeed, throughout this time, she not
only engaged the critique of romantic love, but also sought a way to write love
without forgoing her heterosexual orientation. Eileen Gregory has commended
Fraser for her "continuous" "examination" of "life practice" and "poetic practice"
and her commitment to correlate these ("Poetics" 16). For Fraser, this commitment has meant that her writing of love and her practice of love must correspond.

In the mid-1990s Fraser wrote two essays that define her version of a projective love and libidinized field poetics: "Barbara Guest: The location of her
(A memoir)" (1994) and "Translating the Unspeakable: Visual Poetics, as Projected through Olson's 'Field' into Current Female Writing Practice." (1996).
The Guest essay is in many ways the more significant description of Fraser's
version of a projective poetics, although she does not engage the concept of the
projective itself. Fraser draws out the "processive" and "conjectural" aspects of
Guest's poetics in ways that are consonant with a projective and open field poetics and that are descriptive for Fraser's own poetry. Fraser recalls at some length
her first transformative personal encounter with Guest in 1964 at a public event
at which Guest read her poem "Parachutes, My Love, Could Carry Us Higher":

Having exercised our arms in swimming,
Now the suspension, you say,
Is exquisite. I do not know.
There is coral below the surface,
There is sand, and berries
Like pomegranates grow.
This wide net, I am treading water
Near it, bubbles are rising and salt
Drying on my lashes, yet I am no nearer
Air than water. (Guest, *Selected Poems* 16–17)

While in a traditional love lyric, a lover seeks to possess or unite himself with his beloved, this poem projects an uncertain eros moving through the poem, transforming, for instance, "coral" and "sand" into "berries" and "pomegranates." Fraser observes: "The speaker's hold on language is at stake: Guest's location of self is structural" (*Translating* 128, 129). She describes how Guest's "horizon of the page" creates a space "where almost anything might conjecture itself into language . . . and leave, as suddenly" (125). Fraser comments on the draw of "Parachutes": "What was it about that poem that captured people with its labdanum resins? It was, I think, the precariousness of emotional suspension . . . the condition of the tenuous, spoken out of a peculiarly interior experience, yet as far afield as one could imagine from the battering 'confessional' model much favored in certain East Coast poetry circles at that time" (127).

Although Guest is rarely linked with Olson's projective verse, "Parachutes" appears in Donald Allen's anthology *The New American Poetry*, in which the lead essay is Olson's "Projective Verse." In extending Olson's apt definition of the projective to poets and poetics not typically grouped with him, my book draws attention to how a projective writing formed throughout the twentieth century, quite independently of Olson, however useful his articulations. Indeed, Guest's protracted attention to H.D. as well as to Pound provides a rather different genealogy for her writing than the New York School and L=A=N=G=U=A=G=E poetries with which she is commonly associated. Guest's writing is probably best analyzed as existing between movements and schools, rather than being confined to any one school, especially since movements and "isms" are almost always initially defined through their male practitioners and then applied backward to others, who inevitably are at least partially outside those definitions.

Fraser utilizes an analogy with painting that well conveys the projective *and* introjective aspects of Guest's projective and processive poetics: "There is a word in Italian, *distacco*. . . . Its meaning is recorded in the step backwards a painter makes when, having placed a mark on the canvas, she stops to observe how planes of light or color have massed and shifted as a result of that last placement of pigment. Whatever mark or brushwork may or may not follow takes its counsel from this moment of cool observation. This action and accretion, where mortal touch replaces stern inevitability, might describe the processive experience of Barbara Guest's compositions" (*Translating* 125, 127). These poetics are much tempered from Olson's "INSTANTER" and "push" poetics, but importantly the inspiration for the poet's ongoing composition is in the preceding "mark or brushwork" she makes. This processive composition, created by a series of responses, is generated through a composed subjectivity that projects itself in "action and accretion."

In her essay on Olson, Fraser acknowledges "the immense, permission-giving moment of Charles Olson's "PROJECTIVE VERSE" as leading to experiments with the page so important for women's writing practice because of the ways the space of the page enables the writing of otherwise "unspeakable" experiences, including those of female "longing" and eros. She credits Olson's injunction to get "rid of the lyrical interference of the individual as ego" as allowing for "a writing practice that foregrounds the investigation and pursuit of the unnamed" (175). However, she also distances herself from Olson because he devalues women by not addressing them and turns to Robert Duncan and Susan Howe for the ways that they mediate Olson. Indeed, Fraser, like Mackey, concentrates her enthusiasm on Olson's engagement with the visual page rather than on his mythical hero Maximus. Fraser commends Olson: "The excitement Olson generated, the event of the *making*—the hands-on construction of a poem being searched out, breathed into and lifted through the page, fragment by fragment, from the archeological layers of each individual's peculiar life—revealed the complex grid of the maker's physical and mental activity. Its *it*" (*Translating* 176). Fraser comments that the example of Olson's "play with typographical relations of words and alphabets, as well as with their denotative meanings, has delivered visual-minded poets from the closed, airless containers of the well-behaved poem into a writing practice that foregrounds the investigation and pursuit of the unnamed. The dimensionality of the page invites multiplicity, synchronicity, elasticity . . ." (175). Finding Laura Moriarty's poem "Birth of Venus" to be an example of an Olsonian engagement with the page, Fraser describes Moriarty's poem in ways suggestive of her own 1990s poetry, as a "determination to inhabit the present, while marking absence" (188).

Although in *Little Notes* Fraser first approached a projective love and libidinized field poetics, immediately following this volume her work was increasingly informed by systemic critiques of romantic love and no longer sustained the present-tense erotic writing of *Little Notes*. This alteration is evident in her ambitious inquiries into love writing in the 1970s and 1980s, bearing such temporally troubled titles as "Now That the Subjunctive Is Dying" (*New Shoes* 9) and "Energy Unavailable for Useful Work in a System Undergoing Change" (*Something (even human voices)* 24). Later, Fraser rediscovered the "presencing" of *Little Notes*, extending this writing into much longer poems.[3] Defining for this writing is a movement among eroticized persons and a changed relationship to the sensorium of poetry itself, in which language as medium and material has agency. In this later work, gendered and sexual relations are unsettled, and Fraser's prior concerns with absence and presence become mutually defining. Fraser's poetry assumes the mobility described by Mallarmé and quoted by Agamben in *The End of the Poem*: "Words rise up unaided and in ecstasy. . . . Our mind . . . sees the words not in their usual order, but in projection (like the walls of a cave), so long as that mobility which is their principle lives on, that part of speech which is not spoken" (46).

Little Notes to You, from Lucas Street

In *Little Notes to You*, Fraser first wrote a love poetry in which the bifurcations between lover and beloved, subject and object, were greatly diminished. The "impassable" spaces of *Change of Address* gave way to poems in which presence and absence interrelate. The titles of the volume's three sections, "Little Notes," "Loving," and "Presences," suggest a trajectory of ever-increasing elision between lover and beloved, subject and object. In the first two sections, Fraser presents her lover through ephemeral traces, lessening, if not undoing, the separations between lover and beloved that are articulated through the poem's "I" addressing a "you." In "Territories," the poetic speaker is haunted by the absence of the beloved, who remains present in his traces:

> My finger touches your absence in this room—
> a difference of space. A chair not used today
>
> still announces you as a face,
> as a face behind leaves,
> as leaves. (2)

While the poetic speaker may be looking at actual leaves in a vase that might obscure the beloved's face were he sitting in his chair, the remembered face tells of different kinds of "leaves," an absenting of the beloved from "this room." Rather than existing in separate "territories" from her lover, as in "Glass" and "Song for a Man in Doubt," "leaves" echoes as linguistic residue.

In "Now," Fraser, writes about the difficulty of representing the beloved in her poems: "your body refuses my poem / will not fit / but springs from the dark with an overpowering scent" (3). The poem invokes "joy" and reports an intensified perception—in the "flexing," "articulate," and "sharp bites" of "flowers." Fraser concludes with a poetic speaker who locates her lover in the space she has cleared for him:

> I inhale you through your loose clothing
> where there is space to feel myself
>
> . . . .
> I inherit you as a resonance
> who fully inhabits
> the field I have taken years to clear (3)

Fraser seems to be announcing the possibility of a "field" poetics in this clearing, but she sustains an "I" apart from this field.

In "Love Poem Written in the Swimming Pool," Fraser engages Guest's swimming metaphor for sexual and liminal relations. But while the poem goes a great distance to achieve liminality, the address of the poem to a "you" introduces a bifurcated rhetorical dynamic, however much Fraser aims to undo it. The physical environment of the swimming pool provides Fraser with "Reflecting, curving surfaces," an aquamarine environment of "shimmering gallons," a perfect place to stage her interpenetration of "I" and "you." The poem concludes:

> Then you are there. On the ceiling, I mean.
> Your face
> is pacing mine. Your arms are streaking
> with neon and your tender mouth
> gives off the contained silence of noise-proof ceilings
> where thought is roared.
> I see you.
> Am entered.
> And swim effortlessly. My body changed. Flowing. (6)

The "I" imagines, as she swims on her back, his face and arms above her, pacing with her, which leads to an intensified aurality in the "silence of noise-proof ceilings / where thought is roared." But while the poem conceives of interpenetration, it asserts the individual existence of the poetic speaker: "My body changed," although it is "Flowing."

In the final section, "Presences," Fraser further undoes the bifurcated "lover" and "beloved" through erotic acts of attention that tip her poetics into a projective love and libidinized field poetics. In "Sun, Three Rays," Fraser forgoes the poetic speaker as "I" and approaches the "clairvoyant" exactness of H.D.'s finest Imagist poems, recording a moment of slowed erotic witness: "his attention / going out of / focus" (12). And in "Sensing the Presence of Butterfly," Fraser utilizes the page as a visual composition. But in by far the most remarkable poem of this section, "Day and Night," Fraser neither forgoes an "I" (albeit the "I" is more cipher, or "structure," than speaking subject) nor utilizes the page for visual composition.

"Day and Night" locates emotional and physical responses in the movement of the poem itself—not only through semantic meanings but through intruding visual and aural materialities. The poem creates a meditation in part through its focus on ducks and feathers—feathers being an erotic site for Fraser in other work. "Day and Night," in its frivolous as well as "deep"—bodily—transformation, recalls Guest's "Parachutes" as the poetic speaker, while staging herself in the poem as "I," is eclipsed into a "duck." This poem foreshadows Fraser's later work in which projections create projections, not only as a series of changing perceptions, but through their introjected sounds and appearances on the page. "Day and Night" is a study in alternation, day and night, black and white, in which the coded nature of animal and human life reveals itself in abstract patterning. It begins with the speaker identifying herself with the "duck," and its many short rhyming and partially rhyming words virtually "Quack" on the page:

> My eye rises in the white duck's
> eye. I ferment. Extend
> myself, itself
> into a flat kiss of feathers.
> I am duck,
> and look! (15)

As the poem proceeds, the speaker's identification with the duck intensifies; the duck becomes two, then three ducks, defined by "codes" and "digits" and "details of fields . . . furrows, pockets of seed." In a panoply of echoing aural and visual relations, of hard, breaking sounds and many four-letter words, the ducks increase:

> Now four. Now four.
> The sound of Quack moves out
> of black ink. Four. More. (15)

Throughout the poem Fraser creates an enlarged sensorium in which thing, word, and page interrelate. She concludes with the poetic speaker playfully protesting that she is being lost to the poem she writes:

> Wanting not to disappear.
> Now in hot pursuit of what is left of me.
> The river below shines white. Tiny ships row and wave smoke.
> Their flags unfurl the red yellow blue in my wing beat. (15)

This "unfurl[ing]" at the end of a poem of day and night, code and digits, provides unexpected color. Speaker and world, speaker and poem, are interpenetrated, linked through the erotic transport of a "wing beat."

"His Romance"

From the early 1970s on, Fraser's work was increasingly informed by systemic critiques of romantic love. The immediate effects of these critiques can be seen in the title and structure of a volume of Fraser's selected poems, *What I Want*. She eliminated the mid-1960s poem "Lust" and other early love poems, and placed "Glass" and "Song for a Man in Doubt," not at the beginning of the volume, as in the evocatively titled *Change of Address*, but in a section declaratively named "Access." Fraser's new focus on "I" in the title *What I Want* manifested the feminist commitment that the "I" of each woman is the most potent place of political oppression—and potential liberation.

In Fraser's poem "4 A.M." in *New Shoes* (1978), which bears echoes of Adrienne Rich, Fraser associates her own frustrated or disappointed love with the terror of an unidentified woman running in the streets, "begging for help."[4] The poem concludes with the poetic speaker going to the door with her lover, at first seeking his assistance and then identifying more fully with "a scream," perhaps that of the running woman, or perhaps an internalized scream of her own:

> I ran to the door, straining to locate her terror.
> I called your name.
>
> You were standing next to me naked
> in the cold air, both of us helpless.
>
> A car door slammed. At that very moment
> I felt the scream enter my body, changing me finally. (30)

What differentiates Fraser's work from Rich's at this inceptive moment of feminism's critique of romantic and heterosexual love is a far greater inclination to include men, "both of us helpless," within the systemic terror of love relations, rather than as its perpetrators. In the opening poem of *Each Next* (1980), the poetic speaker's earlier "clear" sense of erotic response is now troubled by damning critique: "That rush. How I've wanted it. His romance" (13).

Yet if Fraser was compelled by and registered the critique of what Adrienne Rich called "compulsory heterosexuality" (203), or what Rachel Blau DuPlessis described as "romantic thralldom" ("Romantic Thralldom" 406–7), she also continued her investigation into love and love writing in different registers. As in her early poetry, the poetry of Fraser's middle period divides between work in which there is a pronounced bifurcation between lover and beloved, which often centers around absence and loss, and poetry in which the gap between lover and beloved is lessened—a poetry of presence and hope. Yet in almost none of her poetry through the 1970s and '80s were the ecstatic moments of subject-object coalescing, as in the "Presences" of *Little Notes*, repeated.

In *Each Next*, Fraser enlists a kind of projective writing, but perception leading to perception resulted in juxtaposed, fragmentary narratives (Quartermain 114). Throughout this work, Fraser's critique of romantic love and her inclination toward narrative structures, if often fragmentary, do not incline her to a sense of joyful presencing but rather entangle her in questions of temporal duration. In her later work she will rediscover how to create this present-tense ecstatic writing and how to sustain this writing over multiple linguistic registers and multiple temporalities, but her middle period was more often marked by a "subjunctive" that was alive and living than by a present love.

One of Fraser's inventions in the 1970s, through which she explored the bifurcations between female lovers and male beloveds, was the creation of small and large female personae who take on far less and far more agency than Fraser typically assumed for her poetic speakers. Assuming this differentiated agency enabled Fraser to query the romantic or ecstatic responses between unequally advantaged lovers, but also set this work in a fictitious or mythic direction and therefore apart from Fraser's writing of presence, of the present, in *Little Notes*. In prefatory comments to "The Story of Emma Slide," Fraser remarks: "a name fell into my mind. The name was Emma Slide. . . . [This] long poem . . . would be an investigation of romantic love, as it was breaking down in the life of a baffled confused woman" (*New Shoes* 41). By locating this dilemma in a figure smaller than herself, Fraser was better able to explore her own vulnerability: "I took on the persona of Emma Slide like a costume or mask that expressed some very real part of me—some voice that had been too small and baffled to risk its nakedness as *my* voice in my 'regular' poems" (*Translating* 41). Fraser created a fantastic, playful caricature of a woman so diminutive she is dissolving within herself: "Emma . . . // was so small / so small / she was / all in a pool / in an overflowing of help me. // Emma's confused. The water's too much. It comes down in / tiny perfect seeds all the day long" (*New Shoes* 42–43). The poem registers a "disappointment" that "He's not a phenomenon to be in awe of," as Emma, at the end of the poem, veers away from the possibilities of romance to a renewed commitment to the vicissitudes of her daily existence (51).

If one of the strategies in *New Shoes* is to invent a "small" persona, another is to create shadowy, large personae, as Fraser engages surrealistic fantasies in *Magritte Series*. These fantasies create a female protagonist capable of changing her male others through violent action. In this volume, the color red seeps and signals the presence of a kind of life-in-death or death-in-life eros. Male figures are rendered as vulnerable through actual blows to their bodies: "his flesh / had received blows / distinct enough / in precisely those spots / he understood now / as tender" (56). In "*La Baigneuse du Clair au Sombre* / Bather between Light and Darkness," a female figure "slowly / puts a dagger through the bones // in his chest. She puts lights / in his chest. Her arm / is a big cloak. Pieces of him glow // all over the room" (*New Shoes* 60). While at times the change pressed on the male beloved is presented as positive, at other times it is simply disturbing. It is uncertain, for instance, in *"La Baigneuse,"* whether the glow of light from the parts of the man's body (he is possibly an Osiris figure) is life-giving or is the banked coals of an underworld. *"La Baigneuse"* concludes, "Now she's giving me // the big present" (60). Is this death or orgasm?

If in "Emma Slide" and *Magritte Series* Fraser increases the space between lover and beloved, querying romantic thralldom and compulsory heterosexuality, in other poems she attempts to write an ecstatic love through a poetic speaker who is much closer to herself. But although these poems seem to wish to attain the kind of "Presences" of *Little Notes*, or what Fraser refers to as "a seizure of voice" in "Energy Unavailable for Useful Work," they remain apart from these potentialities. "Now That the Subjunctive Is Dying" begins with a sensuous description of her lover's body after love making and then all but disappears him:

> We are lavish
> rooms with many doorways that open out.
> Your face, if that is your body standing
> there, suggests the hand on a knob that could be
> possibly
> turning. (*New Shoes* 99)

While Fraser engages a sense that after love making, "this is," the poem concludes with the poetic speaker in a state of reverie, imagining her lover:

> you, on your back, in air, above the couch in the other room,
> discover your body below and a girl dreaming of a door. (100)

These lines resemble the conclusion to "Love Poem Written in the Swimming Pool," only now the earlier interpenetration of lovers' bodies through imagined reflections is reduced to parallel bodies floating in a kind of miasma that sustains them. In contrast to her earlier love writing, not only is Fraser bent on getting descriptions of her lover's actual body into her poem, but the poem is made up of multiple narratives that engage several temporalities. And while the interpenetration of lovers in the earlier poem yields such lines as "your tender mouth / gives off the contained silence of noise-proof ceilings / where thought is roared," this poem's present is not as linguistically complex or aroused.

One of Fraser's most ambitious poems of the 1980s, "Energy Unavailable for Useful Work" in *Something (even human voices) in the foreground, a lake* (1984), flirts with presence, juxtaposing fragmented narratives in which past, present, and dream world are interwoven. The poem is haunted by the desire for an increased dimensionality in "this world" through a repeated refrain from a Creeley poem: *"There is a world / underneath, or / on top of / this one—and / it's here now"* (25). As do other Fraser poems, it engages the Leda and Swan myth, bringing into the poem a phallic neck and inhabitation by the phallus. Moreover, "Energy Unavailable for Useful Work" reintroduces Fraser's repeated engagement with winged creatures and feathers as erotic substrate. While the poem seeks flight and ascent, it often moves downward, paying homage to the "earth's insistence":

> Taking off. A *swan*, she thinks. She has harbored in her mind a duckling
> who honks awkwardly and swims in circles, who forgets the long stretch
> of the imagined neck, the rising into air, leaving the earth's insistence. (30)

Pulled between ascent and descent, the poem includes two women, "I" and a "dark-haired, smart-mouthed woman" (27). In one of the dream sequences, a male protagonist, Karl, abandons the "I" for the "dark-haired" woman, and the poetic speaker later surmises that both women may be herself. But although Fraser attempts to bring her diverse visions together, the present-tense, ecstatic experiences are at best moments in larger narrative fragments, a sought-after but finally momentary "seizure of voice":

> She felt new strength in each bit of flesh grown wily with feathers.
> Her power was in eiderdown. Her power was in a sudden rush from
> the mud, into bright air hovering. A shaking-out of golden light. A
> phoenix in her with a different sort of song. A reclassification of duck
> into swan. . . . Her desire was on a grand scale and she empowered it
> as vision. Slowly belief. Then a seizure of voice. Asking for, saying *this*.
> This is what I want. And it's here now. (33)

Although the poem asserts this moment of ascension as one of presence, later augmenting it with "It is so," Fraser concludes with a dream in which the swans are grounded:

> They did not glide on water but traveled in packs on flat dirt beneath the
> trees which were green, large of leaf and effulgent. (34)

The swans relocated "in packs on flat dirt" require food, and Fraser is reminded of another dream, in which "There is nothing to eat but a dish of white buttons" (35). It is with this food, at once magical and mundane, glistening and dull, that Fraser concludes her poem, a hoped-for present realization contained by the subjunctive, or what is just about to be:

Now the swan food arrives on its wooden trays. The words unloose in me. . . . I want to be in the company of swans, catching my own currents. My dream has provided the peculiar glistening food. My mouth waters. Something outside is pulling. (35)

"Falling into the Page"

In the 1990s Fraser entered into a new stage of her writing of "ecstatic response." "Etruscan Pages" (in *when new time folds up*) and *WING* extend the erotic intensity of Fraser's early verse, only now the eros is located more definitively in the writing itself.[5] In *Little Notes to You, from Lucas Street*, Fraser inscribes a writing of presence, of a present love; in the later poetry, she sustains direction over multiple temporalities and entire volumes of verse.[6] At this time, Fraser names several new directions and influential sources. She remarks on "Duncan's profound connection to Olson's *page* as a graphically energetic site in which to manifest one's *physical* alignment with the arrival of language in the mind" and H.D.'s "invitation to trust and mistrust language" (*Translating* 53). Throughout the 1980s and 1990s, Fraser found stimulus in L=A=N=G=U=A=G=E writing and poststructuralist perspectives, including French feminism. As she writes in the 1991 introductory essay in *Translating the Unspeakable* (which was published in 2000), "Things that do not exist without words", the poet is "a field charged with sound. The page begins revising its surface" (10).

Written in relation to multiple others, the late poems contain passages that speak to singular erotics and grief that are often hidden or obscured.[7] In the penultimate page of "Etruscan Pages," Fraser writes of absence as disappearance, lamenting the loss of "your face":

Grief is simple and dark

as this bridge or hidden field
where something did exist once

and may again, or
your face receding behind the window

a possible emptying (*when new time folds up* 33)

In *WING*, "there are two men, they are tall men, and they are talking softly / among the disintegrating cubes" (1). In the penultimate page of this poem, a single line about these two men occupies an entire page: "There are two men without feet, they are tall men swimming through matter" (9). Fraser engages "swimming," her prior metaphor for sexual liminality, in describing these angelic men who pass through matter.

If some untold or hidden set of emotions partially motivates this writing, it is also a writing that responds to itself, builds on itself, through multiple others. "Etruscan Pages" and *WING* address Fraser's earlier concerns with absence and presence, but gone is the rhetorical dynamic of lover-beloved bifurcations—now replaced by an extended erotic field. Both works draw together absence and presence as they interpenetrate. "Etruscan Pages" explores a celebratory sexual culture that has largely disappeared, leaving only archaeological remnants, and *WING* engages tensions between ethereal angelic figures and the concrete compositional space of the page, between what is hidden and what is made manifest.

By Fraser's own account, "Etruscan Pages" was created out of complex circumstances that included a visit to three Etruscan necropolises with her husband and women friends; subsequent writing about this experience in letters; and additional contact with Etruscan culture through museum visits and archaeological research. Initially, Fraser queried whether she could create poetry out of her profoundly nonverbal experience of the Etruscan necropolises: "I *did* feel as if I had dropped through time" ("Interview" 5). Then, through a visit to the Villa Giulia, the primary Etruscan museum in Rome, and a letter to someone named Susan, the poem began to take shape.[8] Fraser comments, "The poem slowly began to rise to the surface of my listening mind . . . something much more layered and much less personal than any account of my own private experience" (*Translating* 56). In the letter to Susan, she writes of transport between "this world" and "the other world" and of the Zagreb mummy: "When they found her in Etruria, her body had been wrapped in this shroud made of pieces of linen, written on through centuries . . . used as 'pages' for new writing whenever the old text had faded" (*when new time* 27). Fraser recounts how her ability to write this poem was furthered through the example of H.D.'s attempt to decipher Egyptian hieroglyphs ("Interview" 5). She comments on her attraction and resistance to D. H. Lawrence's famous "Etruscan Places," noting how her "new word PAGE over the old word PLACE . . . tip[s] the reader's attention in the direction of an optional reading introduced through a formal shift of perception" (*Translating* 58).

"Etruscan Pages" begins in a way that is reminiscent of Duncan's initial poem in *The Opening of the Field*, in which through the instigatory presence of a "First Beloved" he creates a sense of widdershins, a backward or reversed motion. Fraser's "Etruscan Pages" also begins with an opposing movement:

Norchia, day of error

. . . .

Same wrong direction, again, olive groves
running backwards through rented window

"bearded" as in grain's awn, gold oats. (9)

"Grain's awn" creates widdershins in its sound, which is reminiscent of "yawn,"
a kind of gaping, in counterdistinction to its actual meaning: "a slender, bristle-
like appendage found on the spikelets of many grasses."

But if the eros of "Etruscan Pages" inheres partially in its sense of the untoward, its "wrong direction," there are passages that are directly sexual descriptions of Etruscan "urn pictures":

sex erect under rough shirt (15)

· · · · · · ·

man who's down on
all fours
like a table top

he gives it to her
unreservedly (15, 16)

In contrast, in the section titled "Vulci," Fraser calls up the qualities of a highly
wrought erotic art in passages that forge fabrication and signification:

Fibula: pin; clasp. *The bone in man is a clasp.*
Sanguisuga: leech. *The leech in man is a clasp of blood* (28)

In many ways, this is a poem of glimpses and phrases that, unmoored from
larger structures, create a sense of bodily, erotic response: "your clumsy lavish-
ness and heavy mascara," "such breathing," "Randy sea," and "audacious poppy /
late, and everywhere red" (14, 23, 31, 34).

Fraser sought the Etruscans through their writing, a strange, often backward-
slanting script, handwritten with berry juice onto tufa stone: "My page wanted
to be inscribed as if it were a canvas, my own linguistic motion and visual no-
tation appropriating the Etruscan alphabet as subject and object" (*Translating*
57). Extending the love writing of *Little Notes*, she speaks of "wanting messages,
'little sentences / freely written in red paint or black'" (11). Relatively early in
"Etruscan Pages," when Fraser first introduces the subject of Etruscan script, she
describes and then replicates it—a physical remnant of what was once freshly
minted that unsettles the visual sensorium of the page and that needs to be attended to as a visual thing and puzzled over for its meaning:

wind sifts iron filings'
carelessly drawn script

downhill writing
carved with metal object

or red and black brushed with finger
into soft stone recess

.   .   .   .

we know what each mark is equal to
but not, in retrospect, what was intended (11)

The page concludes with handwritten Etruscan script.

This poem creates its eros, in part, through a playful crossing between multiple registers—semantic meaning, aural evocation, and visual display. Fraser comments that "unorthodox compositional strategies" allow a culturally resisted "otherness to intrude" into poetry—including an othered feminine eros and sexuality (Boland and Fraser 393). In the section of the poem titled "Norchia," Fraser inscribes an Etruscan letter *A* (approximated here) and writes:

The letter A is a plow
(mare pulling into *ma*re)
   horse plowing sea
   Maremma (20)

Fraser explains: the "Etruscan 'A' . . . reminded me of a drawing of an ancient wooden plow. That visualization came directly from the drawing or shape of the letter. The word 'plow' then gave me 'horse,' then 'mare,' pulling, plowing into the 'sea,' which is *ma*re in Italian" ("Interview" 8). Fraser refrains from addressing the eros of a mare, of horse plowing sea, such that mare becomes *ma*re, a mobile and penetrated sea. The sound of the Italian place name "Maremma" further develops this erotic sense, as I discuss in the introduction. Throughout this poem, gender and sexuality are unsettled through the sensorium of the poem, as the presented language asks to be read through multiple registers and as the poet introjects her projections to reproject them. In these ways, Fraser "discovers a perpetual motion on the page" (*Translating* 12).

In *WING*, Fraser further addresses her concerns with absence and presence, abandonment and hope. While *WING* investigates the possibilities of erotic presence through two angelic figures, it also registers a sense of their complete withdrawal, or absence. *WING* enacts interpenetration by creating a work in which semantic meanings are inseparable from page composition. The poem presents angelic inhabitation, described in Fraser's "La La at the Cirque Fernando, Paris," written a few years earlier:

> he dropped
> one night in the dark
> inside her, unfolded
> his golden wings . . .
> and that was enough
> gold for me (*il cuore* 158–59)

While the earlier poem describes this erotic indwelling, *WING* enacts it.[9] Indeed, the very title *WING* suggests the poem's commitment to a projective eros—a winged desire. And in *WING* this inhabitation involves both figurative angels and visual composition, which manifest, alternately, erotic presence and absence.

In *WING*, eros and the creation of art are conveyed as inseparable. The poem begins with a discussion of the creation of "the New" that to be itself must not only be "violent" but "attached." One of the defining tensions here is the intersection between the "made," or fabricated, and living human beings:

> its feathers cut as if from tissue or stiffened cheesecloth
> condensed in preparation for years of stagework
>
> attached to it historic tendons; more elaborate
> the expansive ribcage, grieving, stressed, yet
>
> marked midway along the breastbone with grains of light (1)

Reminiscent of the light "stabbed" into the man's chest in *Magritte Series*, this poem does not need to stab an unresponsive man to create light but finds "grains of light" in the stresses of human fabrication. A few pages later, the poem defines "the New" as "tender," characterized by "attachment" and connected to "the shimmer of wing":

> Even the New is attached or marked by attachment
>
> the shimmer of wing, which claim may tell us everything
> in a white blink
>
> just as in troubled moments it disappears

[A young girl in Arkansas, the quill of an angel in
warm light, from orange and yellow regions, falls] (5)

The evidence of this envisioning, the falling "quill of an angel," serves as a re-
minder of the multiple registers this poem crosses. Yet if there is a connection
between the "New" and a broadly construed eros, it is inseparable from actual,
singular experiences of love. In the section titled "Fall Out," Fraser encapsulates
a history of a disappearing, nominal "I" overtaken by erotic experience:

now and melt with rush all   in one place nothing changed   I
did not grow up I   went away in one phase   brooded I over
skier   in black the flyer, forces   that dive far yet he
persists (7)

While "skier" may refer to the memory of a particular lover, this skier morphs
into his effects as "melt" and "rush" "persist" in a poem that makes presence
and absence, love and death, its abiding subject.

In creating this work, Fraser comments on the importance of Mel Bochner's
art and of responding to the death of the poet and artist Joe Brainard and the
grief of his lover, Kenward Elmslie. Fraser is responding to two of Bochner's art
projects, one of which includes drawings of cube forms "hurtling through space"
on canvases constructed into cubes, a work that is both flat and sculptural ("Interview" 25). In the other project, Bochner installed an artwork in an apartment
where, Fraser recounts, "Italian Fascists and Nazis had imprisoned Jews, Gyp-
sies, and resistance fighters during World War II before sending them off to
the camps. . . . Against an army blanket placed as 'a canvas' on the floor of each
room, Bochner had constructed three six pointed stars formed with 365 burnt
matchsticks—one for each day of the year" (25). Fraser notes that "the forms
were extremely precise geometrically," and Bochner's artworks "began to cata-
lyze memories . . . of all the loss I had been feeling particularly for Joe [Brain-
ard] and the lover who was losing him. . . . Later I realized that the cubes had
depicted for me the breaking up of matter and its reformation" (25). While Fraser's public comments on this poem place it in the realm of grief over willfully
destroyed peoples and over the death of her poet and artist friend, it is also about
the grief of unnamed lost lovers or, more simply, lost love.

In WING's black quartet sections, delimited forms create an eros that is
deathly. In "First Black Quartet: Via Tasso," four blocks of type forming a cube
can be read either across or down. Specific line lengths create a reading experience of abrupt endings, while circuitous passages that emerge through reading
variously across the poem's spacings enable rather different readings. For example, in the upper left-hand corner, Fraser squares off her language this way:

A cube's clean volume
its daily burnt mark
backwards into match
day's oxygen, common
the remaining light
nothing changed yet
have a way of crash (2)

This block then connects to other language blocks, forming the possibilities of multiple readings, such as "he persists as does pain // have a way of crash // ing in on you, swimming // through heart matter // are two men." Or "ghost or angel // sent to tell us what // we didn't want to know" (185). The block-shaped forms contrast with the "swimming" variations, as love and continuity, death and curtailment, are made manifest.

WING concludes with "Vanishing Point: Third Black Quartet," a concrete poem that manifests the shape of a wing through its negative space, that is, the space not taken up by the words. Fraser has remarked that this shape was created accidentally, or serendipitously, through a set of procedures she had created for adding and subtracting words on the page ("Interview" 26). The interpenetration between page composition and semantics is taut as the writing constructs and communicates different meanings simultaneously:

little tasks of pain had tried to lift
and little tasks of pain had tried to lift
decision and little tasks of pain had tried to lift
lucent decision and little tasks of pain had tried to lift (10)

To consider Fraser's work in any simple way as a changing poetics or as an expression of love is to fail to attend to her evolving "erotic-emotional innovation" (H.D. "Notes on Euripides, Pausanius, and Greek Lyric Poets" 1) Developing a projective field poetics that takes on the material aspects of language and the page itself, Fraser transmutes love. Initially discovering the possibilities of love writing as "presence" in *Little Notes to You, from Lucas Street*, Fraser extends these relations in her later work. For Fraser, as Agamben remarks in *The End of the Poem*, "Poetry matters because the individual who experiences [a] unity in the medium of language undergoes an anthropological change that is, in the context of the individual's natural history . . . decisive" (94).

Nathaniel Mackey and "Black Sounds"

Song so black it
                burnt
my lip . . .

—Nathaniel Mackey, *School of Udhra*

Pound, Duncan, and Mackey found early instruction in melancholic love poems. Yet for all three writers melancholic stances proved to be inadequate for their larger poetic ambitions. Mackey, initially meditating on the advantages of a Petrarchan melancholic love, soon turned his concerns with loss and desire, failure and aspiration, in other directions.[1] In melancholic love poems, a poetic speaker as lover subordinates himself to a beloved who is unavailable. Or as Freudian analysis would have it, the subject jettisons his egoistic self for a superego that finds all meaning in an "object ideal." Petrarch's poetic speaker, Schiesari analyzes, is a melancholic lover par excellence, since the dead Laura is an entirely unavailable other. Melancholic love poetry in creating oppositional stances in relationship to unattainable objects at once depends on and tends to fix symbolic orders. In many ways, Lacan's overall theories are melancholic, given his postulation of a desiring subject who will never attain his love but rather must locate his "real" desire in a symbolic realm, secured by an unavailable beloved, the *objet petit a*. While at times Mackey's poetry conveys melancholia and seems propelled by Lacanian lack, it ultimately refuses these fixations.

In "Call Me Tantra: Open Field Poetics as Muse," which was Mackey's PhD dissertation at Stanford, he meditated on the advantages of Petrarchan melancholic love. Mackey notes: "What the Petrarchan lover fears most is a favorable response from his Lady. Her unattainability is the basis for his . . . *canzone*" (14). Mackey finds a Petrarchan economy in the work of both William Carlos Williams and Charles Olson. He quotes Williams: "It is to assert love . . . not to win it that love exists. If the poet is defeated it is then that he most triumphs, love is most proclaimed" (14). Turning to the poetry of Olson, Mackey notes how "defeat" in love allows poetry to "triumph": "The dividedness of desire—in part for the woman yet as well for the poem that extols her—proposes the poetic as in fact impeding the sexual act, and vice-versa" (27). Mackey claims that failure is good for poetry: "Loss, deprivation, and even defeat come to be embraced as among the terms of a pact or accord whose aim is longevity of aspiration" (90). Although Mackey is troubled by this relation, because of how it denies "touch," "comfort," and "sex," he notes its efficacy. But while early in his career Mackey considered the advantages of a Petrarchan love economy, he soon turned to a redistribution of privileged stances and idealized objects. His early insight into this love economy and his set of abstract considerations bespeak both his strong engagement with melancholic love as well as how he, at least in part, is outside of its economies.

In previous chapters I addressed the ways that gender and sexual dispensations determine different poets' possibilities for writing love, but I paid minimal attention to race. While love poetry, given its subject matter, is clearly inflected by gender and sexuality, race is much at play in what Mackey refers to as "unevenly allotted orders of agency," perhaps all the more so in love poetry (*Discrepant* 284). This is evident in the ways that US society at large responds to African American men, in contrast to white Anglo Saxon men, as lovers and sexual beings—exoticizing, delimiting, and punishing them. And while African American men have had considerable leeway to engage and explore a love idiom in diverse forms of music, including assuming the stance of lover in some song lyrics, there is not the same latitude or empowerment for African American men who write love poetry. Indeed, the whole scenario is complex, with African Americans figuring as towering jazz and blues musicians, but finding less acceptance as rock stars. (While there are clearly exceptions to this claim—say, as in the cases of Jimi Hendrix and Michael Jackson—the disproportionate number of white male rock stars who take on the role of lover and top the charts reveals the ways that love is racialized.) Poetry as a written art is intermeshed with literacy and educational hierarchies, and it thus may be more restricted than many popular forms, all the more so because poets often figure in the creation of national identities and because of the presumed permanence of print. To put it bluntly, African American male poets have not had the same possibilities of saying their love publicly with either the aristocratic privilege of Lord Byron or the demotic assuredness of Robert Creeley.

In *Abandoned Women and Poetic Tradition*, Lawrence Lipking strongly differentiates the lyric of abandonment from the lyric of pursuit (xv–xxvii). While Lipking speculates socially and politically about why abandonment lyrics, in counter distinction to lyrics of pursuit, might be very important for women writers, he does not address whether writers marginalized by other determinations, say, by race or sexuality, might find recourse for their erotic expression through this orientation. Nor does he address the rhetorical problem of a marginalized poet in the role of lover, given the hierarchical relationship between empowered poetic speakers as lovers and comparatively disempowered beloveds in lover-beloved poetry. For nondominant poets to write a poetry of pursuit, to take on the assured stance of being a lover seeking an indifferent or rejecting beloved, is problematic. Pursuit poetry underscores not only the poet's perceived, socially scripted powerlessness but also, conversely, a feared powerfulness. Socially, nondominant lovers are out of bounds—subjects who are either pathetic or threatening, self-destructive or destructive of others. For African American men the legacy of lynching, especially given its message of sexual punishment, hardly makes questing after an unavailable beloved an attractive literary genre.[2] Although from this vantage, abandonment might be seen to be a default legacy, Mackey names abandonment as the defining condition of an Orphic poetry that he links with an orphaning resulting from "social death."[3]

In turning his interests from melancholic love to abandoned and unrealized love, Mackey queries the potentially false allure of loss. In "Song of the Andoumboulou: 5" in *Eroding Witness*, a muse figure addresses the poetic speaker:

> "Sad bringer of love,
> born singer of sorrow,"
>   she warns
>   me, "beware the false beauty
> of loss.
>
> . . . .
>
> The least eye's observance of
>   dawn will endanger what
>   of love
>
>   you take as one with 'love's bite.'" (44)

The muse figure informs the poetic speaker that love is far greater than "love's bite" and that one only needs to observe the dawn, even through the "least eye," to know this. Rather than finding solace in either seeking or grieving for a lost beloved, the poetic speaker is directed to register the splendor of dawn, or of love itself. Later in this poem, the poetic speaker suggests that the "aye" of the beloved or muse figure and the "aye" of dawn may be inseparable. The poetic speaker declares, "Dawn so belated . . . / having been denied / Erzulie's inmost / *aye*," and then goes into a crisis: he weeps and conjures "cut" "tongues" (46). Erzulie is a figure that recurs throughout Mackey's poetry, and he has identified her as "the *loa* of love and beauty in Haitian *vodoun*, sometimes referred to as the Haitian Aphrodite" ("Interview" 217). As a love figure, she is source, not object.

If there is an aesthetic, ethical, and political dilemma that threads its way through Mackey's work, it is how to engage loss and desire, failure and aspiration, without giving short shrift to either. He responds to this dilemma through engaging art forms that synergistically combine these oppositions, most importantly jazz—a reconstitution of earlier "sorrow songs" in a dissonant, syncopated rearrangement that depends on recalling previous musical passages as these are caught up in a forward movement of mournful, aspiring sounds. Immediately following "Song of the Andoumboulou: 5," in which Erzulie, the muse figure, atypically speaks, Mackey writes poetry in the form of letters to the "Angel of Dust" in "Song of the Andoumboulou: 6" and "Song of the Andoumboulou 7," the first of his epistles that leads to his multivolume, cross-genre fiction *From a Broken Bottle Traces of Perfume Still Emanate*. In these poems, the poetic speaker defends his poetry of loss by insisting that "*absence* [is] unavoidably an inherence in the texture of things (dreamseed, habitual cloth)" (*Eroding* 50). He thus refuses a dichotomous absence and presence that articulate a binary dynamic conducive to "social othering" and initiates a poetics of "aesthetic othering" (*Discrepant* 265–68). Mackey concludes these initial letters with the poetic speaker recommending a specific piece of music for its "certain arch and / or ache and / or ark of duress, the frazzled edge of what remains 'unsung'" (*Eroding* 54). The poetic speaker signs these letters "N," a nomination that uses the initial of Mackey's first name and that results in the fictional persona N, a composer-musician who serves not only as the letter writer but as one of the characters in Mackey's cross-genre endeavor.

Somewhat perversely, N's initial letters to the Angel of Dust consciously defend his poetry of absence or of lack, his "seed" "cloth," but they also give rise to the profuse fictional and thought exposition *From a Broken Bottle Traces of Perfume Still Emanate* and bring to the fore the possibility of an apposite plenitude in the comedy and antic humor of his fictional endeavors. As H.D. through creating prose fiction sought to remedy how her personal self was interfering with the impersonal and clairvoyant vision she needed to write poetry, Mackey seems to need to write to the Angel of Dust about his collaborating and aspiring jazz band as a necessary accompaniment to the often vatic singularity of his poetic voice. Mackey's prose provides him a way of exploring experience, thoughts, and aesthetics within the socially more explicit realm of fiction writing, a writing of "this" is "that" in contrast to his poetry of "this" is "this."[4]

Throughout Mackey's poetry, a sense of ecstasy, or a standing outside of himself as author and poetic speaker, prevails. He writes in *Whatsaid Serif*: "Some / ecstatic elsewhere's / advocacy strummed, / unsung, lost inside / the oud's complaint"(3).[5] A dispossession derived from large-scale social injustice as well as from failed love reverberates throughout his work. Mackey describes one jazz rendition in the first book of his epistolary fiction, *Bedouin Hornbook*: "he went from grief, as it were, to grievance, from lover's lament, one might say, to slave narrative—to some extent erasing the line between the two" (*Broken Bottle* 120). He writes in "Song of the Andoumboulou: 7": "leg irons gave our voices their weight" (*Eroding* 54). But if loss and its correlates are defining, Mackey also insists on the possibility of fulfillment. The Guyanese novelist Wilson Harris is an important figure for Mackey because of how Harris envisions an attainable fulfillment amid signifying systems that perpetuate the conditions of social injustice as they attempt to ameliorate them. Harris claims that although one must write through existing categories, it is precisely how those existing definitions structure existence that constitutes, in part, the "anguished ground" of poesis, or making. Mackey writes, "such terms as *deprivation* and *dispossession* are subject to quotation marks," since Harris "sees any 'fixed assumption of things' (and correspondingly the 'monumental architecture' by which it is symbolized) as an impediment" (*Discrepant* 165, 167).

Having begun "Call Me Tantra" with an inquiry into Petrarchan models, Mackey takes on a protracted examination of eros through Federico García Lorca's related concepts of "*duende*" and "*cante moro*," which Lorca also refers to as "*cante jondo*," or "deep song." By focusing on artistic practices deemed to possess duende, Mackey produces a rather different sense of the interrelationship between poetic possession and erotic dispossession (or, more broadly, artistic possession and erotic dispossession) that does not depend on a dynamic of lovers who are divided from their beloveds but inheres in the fabric or texture of the work of art. Mackey first considered Lorca's "*duende*" in his 1980 essay "Limbo, Dislocation, Phantom Limb: Wilson Harris and the Caribbean Occasion," and then elaborated on this concept at some length in his 1994 essay "Cante Moro." The concept of duende has a rich set of coordinates for Mackey; he likely first encountered it in Lorca's essay "Theory and Function of the *Duende*," anthologized by Donald M. Allen and Warren Tallman in *The Poetics of the New American Poetry*. Lorca relates the concept to an "Old World–New World connection" between "black song in Spain, cante moro, and black song in Cuba, the music of the Yoruba-Catholic mix known as *lucumí*," and then links these traditions with the African American music he heard in Harlem. Of the music in Harlem, Lorca claims, "Only the *cante jondo* is comparable," and in North America "blacks . . . are the most delicate, most spiritual element" (*Paracritical* 183, 189). Mackey notes that early in his essay Lorca quotes the Gypsy singer Manuel Torre, "All that has dark sounds has *duende*," and then draws attention to a more recent translation of this line, "All that has black sounds has *duende*" (*Paracritical* 182).

While duende is not the same as eros, it is enmeshed with it. Mackey comments on how for Lorca it is foremost a musical concept, which Mackey then links with poetry. Lorca provides an example of a singer who achieved technical virtuosity but failed to move her audience because her singing lacked duende. To affect her audience, La Niña de los Peines had to abject herself to her song, become "crazy, torn like a medieval weeper. . . ." Lorca connects duende with the singing of *Saeta*, which "means 'arrow.' The song is piercing, heartrending. We hear the singer singing from a position of being pierced" (*Paracritical* 192). Mackey elaborates on this concept through an example from his own work, "Ohnedaruth's Day Begun," in which John Coltrane speaks of playing "Out of This World": "the riff hits / me like rain and like a leak in my / throat it won't quit" (*Eroding* 73). He comments on these verses and their inspiration in Coltrane's music: "This has to do, among other things, with a surge, a runaway dilation, a quantum rush one often hears in Trane's music" (*Paracritical* 191). Mackey connects duende with "an exegetic refusal to be done with desire" and analyzes: "It is the breakage in the song beyond which the voice cannot go and it is something more than technical virtuosity that may require a rejection of technical perfection if one is to attain it. . . . *Duende* often has to do with a kind of longing that has no remedy, not simply loss, unrequited love and so forth, but what Lorca calls 'a longing without object'" (185).

The concept of a "longing without object" may be seen to cross between Lacanian and Freudian theories of love and sex. While "without object" inclines toward the Lacanian concept of how lack promulgates desire, especially in light of Mackey's emphasis throughout his work on "unquenchable thirst," the very word "longing" places the production of art back into a field of objects and object cathexis, if through an experience of their absence. In Mackey's work, it is possible to understand how distinctions between mourning and enchantment, and between melancholia and mania (see chapter 2), may implode when the possibility of a socially sanctioned or sustained possession is out of the question. He writes: "meaning manic, / want without remedy" (*Whatsaid Serif* 5). Indeed, in both melancholia and mania, as distinct from mourning and enchantment, the subject, no longer governed by his managerial, egoistic self, is consequently more taken over by the others and objects to which he is attracted. But rather than maintaining his attention on a specific object or beloved, as does Petrarch, Mackey extends aspiring desire and debilitating loss into artistic forms that hold both.

In relating the concept of duende to Duncan's poetry, Mackey notes how Duncan associated Spicer and his work with Lorca because of how all three men shared "the trouble" "with being gay" (*Paracritical* 186). He evaluates, "It is not that Lorca advanced a gay poetics, but that they saw in him and his work some of the trouble, for him, of being gay—a certain depression and self-censure, a censuring of his own homosexuality" (186). Duncan associated duende with the demonic possession by eros conveyed by Plato as necessary for the highest reaches of art. Mackey draws out Duncan's inference: "That is what Duncan means by 'the trouble of an unbound reference'—an inordinancy, a lack of ad-equation that is to language what *sin remedio* is to a longing without object. . . . One has worked beyond oneself. It is as if the language itself takes over. . . . [It] is a sound of trouble in the voice. The voice becomes troubled" (182, 186–87). Through "the divine madness of daemonic inspiration," Duncan moves beyond "bound reference," which Mackey connects to sexuality itself. As Mackey notes in "Call Me Tantra," "the boundedness of society is most emphatically clear in its containment of sexuality" (57).

Although Mackey initially drew his projective and open field poetics from concepts articulated by Olson, Duncan's poetry has been a far more important example for Mackey than Olson, as evidenced by the many essays Mackey has written on Duncan in comparison to his one essay on Olson. He analyzes Dun-can's *Bending the Bow* as a combined production of strife and love, commenting how for Duncan "falling in love [is] a way of coming into an order of intensities, a richness of intent otherwise unavailable" (*Paracritical* 152). Moreover, he links Duncan's work with that of Wilson Harris and Harris's comment that the "in-stant of arousal . . . abolishes the 'given' world," holding at bay problematic fig-ural or representational orders in which any writer at odds with the hegemonic signifying system finds him- or herself. Mackey notes that for both Duncan and Harris negative capability is most important, and he quotes Harris on "the irony of self-sufficiency," which he glosses as ironic in its admission of "an otherness residing in the self" (*Discrepant Engagement* 98–99).

That Mackey ascribes to an ars poetica that finds sexual love to be productive of art is most clearly brought out in *From a Broken Bottle Traces of Perfume Still Emanate*. Of the music recounted in this five-volume series, the most "ontic" is almost always performed through the auspices of sexual love. In order for the composer-musician N to engage fully the demands of the jazz standard "Body and Soul," he seeks a "door" through a remembered love affair (98). In *Atet A.D.*, the third installment of Mackey's epistolary fiction, an unrealized love affair at the moment of its eclipse leads not only the two band members most immedi-ately involved in this "post-expectancy," but also the entire band, to make great music: "we made some of the most ontic, unheard-of music we've ever made" (430). Mackey describes this music as composed of a "blistering heat" and "ar-ticulacy," possessed of a "finesse" and "the nuanced ability to speak." At the peak of its expression, this musical rendition of unrealized love, of "outrageous articu-lacy," speaks "so exquisitely" that balloons begin to emerge from the bell of the horn, bearing printed messages: "*Having heard flamenco singers early on, I wanted in on duende. . . . All I wanted was to bury my head between her legs. . . . Something I saw, thought I saw, some intangible something led me on*" (426–27). Mackey not only published this narrative as an episode in his fiction, but used it as an exemplary piece in the title essay for his critical collection *Paracritical Hinge*.

Jazz offers Mackey a love genealogy that competes with poetry in its insistence on sexual love as indelibly linked with artistic production, a genealogy that is amply conveyed by the multiple musical titles in the "Discography" included at the end of *From a Broken Bottle Traces of Perfume Still Emanate*: Charles Mingus's "What Love"; Sonny Rollins and Coleman Hawkins's "Lover Man"; Jackie McLean's "I'll Keep Loving You"; Earl Zero with the Soul Syndicate's "Get Happy"; Yusef Lateef's "Love Theme from Spartacus"; Arthur Prysock's "Someone to Watch Over Me"; the Ornette Coleman Quartet's "Embraceable You"; Miles Davis's "I Fall in Love Too Easily"; Charlie Parker's "What Is This Thing Called Love?"; Ben Webster and Coleman Hawkins's "Prisoner of Love"; Clifton Chenier's "I Can't Stop Loving You"; John Coltrane's "Dearly Beloved"; and many more (*Broken Bottle* 543–54).

In discussing the origins of his epistolary fiction, Mackey recounts a biographical incident. Intrigued by an advertisement for an "outside" music group called "A Love Supreme," Mackey went to their concert to find that he was the only audience member: "It was a strange experience, as though I was there on a special assignment or by special appointment, an appointment I didn't know I had, an odd appointment of an almost mystic sort . . . . I felt as though I had been summoned. It felt almost as though I was part of the band, had been inducted into the band. It started me wondering, at least, what being in such a band might be like" (*Paracritical* 213). While Mackey does not comment on how "A Love Supreme" is the title of one of Coltrane's revered and best-selling albums, it would seem that Mackey's jazz-inspired writing is indebted not only to the expectancy, resolution, and irresolution of jazz tempo but to the ways sexual love inheres in these processes and musics.

Four for Trane

Barbara Guest remarked about H.D. that she had an unerring capacity to find what she needed for her art and to engage it (Guest, *Herself* 44). The same could be said of Mackey. In "Call Me Tantra: Open Field Poetics as Muse," he engaged open field poetics through what he referred to as "an open field critical practice," but in a few years he had bent these poetics to his own ends (*Paracritical* 346). In his 1978 essay "Robert Creeley's *The Gold Diggers*: Projective Prose," he identifies the Creeley he wishes to engage and critiques Creeley's use of female figures as foils. In "The Changing Same: Black Music in the Poetry of Amiri Baraka," which appeared in the same year, he relates these poetics most assiduously to jazz and the "new thingers" by engaging Baraka's descriptions of them in *Blues*

People. At the same time, Mackey published his first chapbook, *Four for Trane*, beginning this collection with a jazz-inspired projective love poem, "Dearly Beloved." Soon thereafter Mackey extended these poetics in full-length volumes of poetry; his ecstatic poetic speakers or, more accurately, speaking positions are located in what Jack Spicer practiced and Robin Blaser defined as an "outside." For Mackey, this "outside" has expanded over time: within his poetic speakers as a space of affection and disaffection and without as his libidinized field takes on an enlarged set of historical and geographical references.

Mackey has remarked that while he was an undergraduate in the late 1960s he was influenced by Robert Creeley's *For Love* and wrote poems in the manner of Creeley, although no publication of this work exists (*Paracritical* 286–87; "Interview" 214). In his Creeley essay, Mackey turns from Creeley's poetry to his stories because they provide a better model of projective writing. Although Creeley's stories are written through the perspective of individual protagonists, Mackey notes that Creeley does not create individuated characters (*Discrepant* 107). In his stories, Creeley "insist[s] upon the *diffuseness* of feelings, and of possible sources of feeling. He makes use of a field, rather than a focal, approach" (113). Since feelings issue not "*from*" but "*through*" "events," "their ultimate sources [are] as much a mystery as those of life itself" (114). However, despite the many advantages of Creeley's projective prose, Mackey found it wanting because of its use of binary female and male figures: "In a binarism that is not innocent of sexist equations (man = mind, woman = matter) the female characters function as foils for the ruminations of men" (109).

The ostensible reason for Mackey's essay on Amiri Baraka was to query Baraka's rejection of his earlier experimental poetry in *The Dead Lecturer*, published when he was LeRoi Jones, by showing how Baraka's statements about jazz and the "new thingers" in his later *Blues People* replicated many of Olson's statements on projective verse. In doing so, Mackey forged a relation between open field poetics and jazz for his own evolving poetics. Baraka, then Jones, was the only African American poet to be published in Donald Allen's *New American Poetics*, although he came to reject this affiliation. *The Dead Lecturer* was among Mackey's earliest influences and he attempted to show in his essay on Baraka that there was a continuity of endeavor from Baraka's experimental writing to his later overtly polemical engagements. Mackey comments that Baraka's "description of the music of Ornette Coleman and Cecil Taylor, with its emphasis on 'total area' as the determinant of form, is highly suggestive of the Projectivist notion of 'composition by field." (*Discrepant* 31). He further links Baraka to Olson's poetics by drawing out how the new jazz is "an assault upon the ego" (36). He quotes Baraka, "Find the self, then kill it" (36).

An important quality in Baraka's early poems, as Mackey sees it and as Baraka commends in liner notes for "Rufus" in Archie Shepp's *Four for Trane* album, is their quick change from one musical phrase to the next: "'Rufus' makes its 'changes' faster. *Changes* here meaning, as younger musicians use that word to mean, 'modulations.' . . . They change very quickly. The mind, moving" (*Discrepant* 40). Mackey analyzes Baraka's early poetry: "The closeness of improvised music to the primacy of process is the quality Baraka strives for in his poems" (32). He theorizes that what Baraka achieved in his early experimental way of writing was actually a way of addressing the "enraged sociologies" that motivated his subsequent polemical work, since this early poetry was "*un*learning modes of speech that impede the speech he is reaching toward" (45). As Mackey sees it: "Obliquity or angularity . . . challenges the epistemic order whose constraints it implicitly brings to light" (43). And while Mackey himself does not always write nor advocate composing "INSTANTER" or "faster," he practices a poetics in which one perception leads directly to another perception, one language phrase to another.

Mackey began his first chapbook, *Four for Trane* (1978), with a projective love and libidinized field poem. "Dearly Beloved" consists of three stanzas replicated verbatim, seemingly spoken by an unidentified poetic speaker, although from the title of the chapbook one might presume this horn player to be John Coltrane or his amanuensis:

> Took
> between my lips
>   Her cusp of
>   tongue's
>   foretaste of
> Heaven   (Heaven) (*Four for Trane*)

Mackey has noted that the poem takes its title from a Coltrane composition on the *Sun Ship* album and that it is "vested in the facts that a horn player takes the horn into his or her mouth, and that the mouth itself is an instrument, the instrument of speech, as well as that mouths initiate or announce the initiation of romance with a kiss or with an 'I love you,' often both . . ." ("Interview" 216). The perspective of the poem is oblique since it ostensibly asks for an identification with the poetic speaker, but provides little orientation by which to accomplish this; moreover, its exact replication calls into question its verisimilitude. "Dearly Beloved" occurs between a past and a present tense, as the horn player "Took" and then commences presumably to play. The poem takes on medieval love tropes while intimating sexual contact and calls up "Heaven" before reiterating it in the negative space of parentheses. The "(Heaven)" might be heard as a softer, second intoning of the initial "Heaven" or as critiquing it, thereby simultaneously extending its allure and voiding it. Mackey remarks on how he created "Dearly Beloved" specifically for the *Four for Trane* chapbook, the title of which was taken from Shepp's album of the same name. "Dearly Beloved" is "preceded by a snippet of Trane speaking to the other musicians, ending with the question, 'Ready?' So it was resonant, for me, with ideas of readiness and anticipation, not to mention speech, language, the primacy of the word" ("Interview" 216).

"Dearly Beloved" may well be a predecessor poem to Mackey's "Mu" series, as Mackey himself has commented, given "the conjunction of terms, images and ideas . . . of mouth, myth, muse, music," which this poem initiated ("Interview" 216). Most of Mackey's poetry belongs to his two series: "Mu" and *Song of the Andoumboulou*. As he has developed these series over several decades, they cross and "braid" and conceptually keep his concerns with aspiration and failure at the forefront of his writing (*Splay* 1). The "Mu" series with its attention to "lingual and erotic allure" aligns with aspiration, and *Song of the Andoumboulou*, based on a "flawed earlier form of human being from Dogon myth," makes failure a constant. Mackey's initial poems dubbed as "Mu" were written in relation to Erzulie, and his *Song of the Andoumboulou* reference an "underness" (*Splay* xi). Mackey first encountered "Song of the Andoumboulou" on the album *Les Dogon* while hosting a "musical mix program" for a noncommercial radio station in Los Gatos, California, KTAO ("Interview" 212). He discovered the album in the station library and played it, also reading on the air from Marcel Griaule's book on the Dogon, *Conversations with Ogotemmêli*. The Andoumboulou, who are born of and smaller than the Yeben, both the progeny of incestuous relations, inhabit the interior of the earth. Mackey quotes from his source text, Marcel Griaule and Germaine Dieterlen's *The Pale Fox*: "The Yeben [are] small creatures with big heads, discolored bodies, and frail limbs who, for shame of their condition, hide in the holes of the earth" (*Udhra* 1).

Eroding Witness

Initiating his projective love writing with "Dearly Beloved," Mackey extends this writing and its outside in his first three full-length volumes of poetry. In *Eroding Witness*, Mackey composes additional poems that channel jazz players, which as "witnesses" are "eroding," perhaps Mackey's equivocal response to Baraka's declamatory title *The Dead Lecturer*. In *School of Udhra* and *Whatsaid Serif*, Mackey's takes on a set of new geographies and historical concerns and increased kinetic and proprioceptive relations. The title of *School of Udhra* is from the seventh-century Bedouin school of poetry, in which poets "loving die," a tradition that Mackey associates with Provençal love poetry.[6] While in this volume he calls on a love poetry constituted through lovers' address to or about their beloveds, he engages this love poetry through a set of deracinated poetic speakers. This poetry in focusing on a "School" or a tradition addresses love writing through a composite tradition or aesthetic practice that exceeds its basis in individual poems. *Whatsaid Serif* takes on a love marked by social, cultural, and economic relations of indentured work and the so-called free labor markets of capitalism, beginning, as identified by Paul Naylor, in Andalusia, Spain. Naylor explicates the relations of *Whatsaid Serif*: "There is no remedy for lost love, when humans are the objects and subjects of sale" (599). While Naylor remarks on this work's increased, finely textured thickness, it in many ways possesses a greater openness, a more pulled-apart weave, than Mackey's preceding works. Mackey's poems' proprioceptive and kinetic energies culminate in *Whatsaid Serif* with its emphasis on travel and locomotion. Yet, although the volumes in some ways can be differentiated from each other, there are significant overlaps as concepts and phrases that appear in one volume are recontextualized and inflected differently in a later volume, in a slowed-down projective-introjective writing in which perception leads directly to further perception, language to further language.

As do each of Mackey's first three volumes, *Eroding Witness* begins with what might be loosely categorized as a muse or beloved poem. The figure in "Waters . . . ," however, disappears into the concrete instance of the poem with its segmented phrases and dynamic relations between symbolic and sensate registers:

Waters
wet the
mouth. Salt
currents come
to where the
lips, thru
which the tongue
slips, part.

At the tongue's
tip the sting
of saltish
metal rocks
the wound. A
darkness there
  like tar,

like bits of
drift at ocean's
edge. A slow

retreat of
waters beaten
back upon
themselves.

  An undertow
of whir im-
mersed in
    words. (*Eroding* 3)

    While this poem may be intimating actual sexual contact, it also brings a sense
of cosmological "drift," with "salty waters" referring to the most basic and pervasive element of life, whether as oceanic plenitude or bodily constitution. The
poem's concern with "the wound" links with bodily vulnerabilities. "Waters . . ."
portrays the literal and concrete, while simultaneously conjuring "An undertow /
of whir im- / mersed in / words." Mackey has commented on "Waters . . ." in relationship to "Dearly Beloved": "'Waters . . .' gets at some of the same inferences
and implications—mouth, word, whetting, readiness—while bearing on *Eroding
Witness*'s wider scope. It shares an imagery of tongue between parted lips that's
both erotic and elocutionary and an imagery of vertical transport with 'Dearly
Beloved,' oceanic rather than celestial and more announcedly linguistic" ("Interview" 217). Both "Dearly Beloved" and "Waters . . ." are reminiscent of William
Carlos Williams's earlier poetry in their tensions between symbolic and sensate
registers and in their lineation, which places emphasis on fragmentary phrases
and individual words. In Williams's and Mackey's early poems these tensions
incline the poetry toward an allegorical reading that the work itself ultimately refuses. In the early essay "That Words Can Be on the Page," Mackey comments
on Williams's "Rain" in ways that are useful for reading "Waters . . .": "Love is
that quality of cleansed, purified perception that renews the world, bestowing
upon it the grace of an attention to concrete particulars, an almost worshipful
regard for 'the thing itself.' . . . The spacing employed in the poem is meant to
further an arousal of the love that attends to each word or each worldly object
as a thing in and of itself" (*Discrepant* 124).

    Mackey's channeling of specific musicians and musics extends the poetry in
Eroding Witness into an enriched and amplified field. Very different from Pound's
early poems, in which he creates personae by combining troubadour lifestyles
and their utterances, Mackey is engaged by musicians and their musics as me-

diums. "Ghost of a Chance" takes on a jazz standard and explores "love at / first sight." Its intense alliteration is a precursor to what Mackey calls his "anagrammatic scat," namely the breaking up of words through the rearrangement of their letters such that the aural aspects of language predominate over semantic relations, and alter these relations. In the poem, lover *and* beloved speak, commenting on their liaison. The opening lines of the poem, while telling of an ascent toward "Heaven," fall back into an erotic memory:

> I wake up snapped at by a star
>   at the foot of a ladder,   think
>   I'm on my way to Heaven, fall
> back tasting your tongue . . .
>   Robed in water, taken back where
>   one evening we met, whose hearts had no
>   mercy, you whisper, "Already it's
>   all so far
>   out of reach . . ."

"Dearly Beloved" has already drawn together "taste," "tongue," and "Heaven" in an erotic riff, but now these references are part of a dream narrative that moves from "Heaven" to a watery memory. In *Bedouin Hornbook*, an earring in the shape of a star is an important memento or signet through which N recalls a love episode in order to play "Body and Soul": "I went on to elaborate as best I could, filling in the portrait as the tiny star of an earring she wore [. . .]" (*Broken Bottle* 99). In "Ghost of a Chance" a "star" first "snapp[ing]" at the speaker is reproduced in other lines in different guises and is referred to as a "broken / shape-shifting star." The poem's initial projections are reprojected into new sequences:

>   A crowded
>   upstairs flat, a quiet would-be Miles at work on
>   "Stella By Starlight," risky stair to the
>   sky . . .
>
>   Seven reeds of a pipe the seven rungs
> on a ladder,   risky stares across the room, broken
>   shape-shifting star.   Broken music-footed
>   ghost whose low tolling of chords would make
>   the still
>   waters run, would stir the wines in their
>   cellars,   pipe a thread of complaint so complete

the stars begin to scatter,   panicky

music

I'd cut

If I could (*Eroding* 89–90)

Linking the star of the initial passage to romantic motifs and jazz music, this section's profusely alliterated *s*'s and *t*'s culminate in a "risky stair" of erotic ascent turned into "risky stares across the room." With the "risky stair to the / sky" likely alluding both to Diotima's speech in Plato's *Symposium* and to the biblical story and song "Jacob's Ladder," the "star" connects to the jazz standard "Stella by Starlight." The alliterative *st*'s, approaching what in Mackey's later works becomes the more abstracted anagrammatic scat, function in this passage to scatter the starlight as the aural relations predominate over the semantic. The final two lines draw together multiple references to "cut," a word that appears frequently in Mackey's work, alluding here, most immediately, to "cut" meaning to flee, but also to a "cut" of music and a "cut" in musical or filmic editing. Indeed, these senses of "cut" carry the proof of the passage, for if something is cut, etched into the record, it might be difficult, if not impossible, to get away from.

In "Capricorn Rising," Mackey extends his poetry's references while continuing to explore a link between his poetry and avant-garde jazz. "Capricorn Rising," along with "Aum" and "Venus," is part of Pharoah Sanders's triptych in which an otherworldly orientation is conveyed through the discordances of avant-garde jazz. Mackey links this music with the duress of indentured work and diasporic populations as well as with a need to move beyond this anguish. The expanded eros in this poem is made evident by Mackey's changed rendition of the idiom he engaged in "Dearly Beloved":

Lacking teeth but licking
the air for some
taste of Heaven,

hungered by

its name, what of
it I refuse
its name, what of
it I refuse
forks an angel's tongue
what of it I refuse awakes
the wide-eyed

stone (*Eroding* 83–84)

While the "Lacking teeth" may refer to the Haitians or "the dead," also referred to in the poem, Mackey's previous engagement with the differentially intoned "Heaven (Heaven)" is further polarized in this rendition because of an increased need for heaven's allure as well as a rejection of its sham. That is, while the name "Heaven" creates a hunger for heaven, it is insufficient to respond to the hunger it elicits: "what of / it I refuse / forks an angel's tongue." This refusal of "Heaven," of what is desired, forks an angel's tongue, turning it devilish or demonic. However, the refusal of the way heaven creates a false promise of something heavenly either now or in the future also has the power to "awake[n]" a "stone." Indeed, the negation of heaven takes all the power of heaven into itself as a site of loss and desire, failure and aspiration, voiding, at least momentarily, the false promises that cling to it.

School of Udhra

In titling his second full-length book of poetry *School of Udhra*, Mackey calls up a love poetry constituted through lovers' address to or about their beloveds, but attends to this writing as a composite "School" or tradition. Drawing on this Bedouin tradition, Mackey notes similarities between it and the Arab tradition in Spain, thought by many scholars to have been a determining influence on Provençal troubadour poetry. Mackey recounts discovering the School of Udhra in the *Encyclopedia of Islam* (when he was researching names for *Bedouin Hornbook*) through an entry on Djamil, who is credited with being "the first [poet] to speak of love as an ever-present cosmic force" (*Encyclopedia* 427). Mackey links this tradition to others in which "the idea of the ecstatic love-death . . . is both secular and sacred," including Islamic mysticism, which plays with "the confusion" between the secular and the sacred (*Paracritical* 291). The *Encyclopedia of Islam* describes Djamil as "enflamed with love for his fellow tribeswoman," whom he was not able to marry because of her father's refusal of their union (427). Djamil wrote poetry throughout his life about this lost or failed love, recounting on his deathbed the place of their meeting. But while for Mackey ecstatic love traditions have much in common, there is at least one difference between Djamil's love writing and troubadour love poetry. Troubadour poetry's lover is often of a lesser social rank than his beloved, and he engages his love quest with often minimal hope of attaining his beloved; for Djamil, the emotional tenor stays with the power of his abandoned or unrealized love for a tribeswoman of presumably equal status, which is also the dominant scenario of Mackey's projective love writing. While both modes in their emotional intensity may well spell a death to the lover, or at least to his everyday managerial or egoistic self, troubadour poetry makes unrequited desire prominent whereas the

School of Udhra, as described in the *Encyclopedia of Islam* through the example of Djamil, foregrounds lost love.

If in *Eroding Witness* the poetry tells at times of unspeakable loss, in *School of Udhra* a high-pitched sense of loss, more sublime and more troubled than in the preceding work, is sustained throughout much of the volume. Moreover, the relationship of this loss with a larger set of historical conditions is made more explicit—a set of relations that will be developed to an even greater extent in *Whatsaid Serif. School of Udhra* begins with "Song of the Andoumboulou: 8," an invocation to a muse or a beloved, presumably the *"maitresse erzulie"* of its sub-title. This invocation is written from the perspectives of "I" and of "they," identi-fied in the poem as "the oldtime people," who speak of Erzulie in the first-person singular: *"From whatever glimpse / of her I take heart"* and *"By whatever bit of her I touch / I take / hold"* (*Udhra* 3). "Andoumboulou: 8" paints a portrait of this muse and the states of being she engenders, providing a kind of pictorial over-view that is unusual for Mackey. This initial portrait is immediately followed by poems that are oblique or, to use Mackey's descriptor, "strung out" ("Interview" 214). The entire first section of *School of Udhra*, "Song of the Andoumboulou: 8–15," can be read as one projective poem, each work in the series stimulating, or leading to, the next, with the poems themselves reading forward and back-ward in their interwoven projections and introjections. Mackey initially presents Erzulie as a dance-hall figure:

> One hand on her hip, one hand
> arranging her hair,
> blue heaven's
> bride. Her beaded hat she hangs
> from a nail on the danceroom
> wall . . . (3)

The state she engenders is extreme; however, it is denoted in such a way that it can be readily grasped:

> Who sits at her feet fills his
> head with wings, oils his
> mouth
> with rum (3)

In "Song of the Andoumboulou: 9," as if responding to how this "bound" picture of Erzulie may have falsified her presence, Mackey implodes his figures as the writing gains intensity through obliqueness:

Took the dust of an eroded footprint,
    rolled as if thru dirt I'd
  see the coming forth of suns.
      Sowed ruins of what by then would
whose walls collapse and
                   crumble,
     dervished air so thin one's
               heartbeats
                    hum . . . (4)

Mackey, intimating a scene of power and destruction in which the poetic speaker's air is "dervished," depicts a state seemingly at the very edge of consciousness in which the experience is one of being knocked about by powers that exceed rational orders. The "oldtime people" in this poem express themselves far more ambiguously, saying, "hurt is light angels eat" (*Udhra* 4). In the following poem, the speaker tells of reading a "dead friend's poem," in which the line "*Rugs burnt Persian red* repeated." Later, these "rugs" are "burnt":

                   Deep
    inside one stumbles. Rugs burnt. Burning.
  No light.

       Baited lip. Love's lawless
    jaw. Said, "I love you,"   loaded
                    like
  a pointed gun. (5)

Leaving behind his initial portrait of Erzulie, Mackey concatenates his poetry's semantic, visual, and aural elements. The phrase "loaded / like / a pointed gun" may refer to the personal and social dangers of sexual love, including perhaps the proverbial shotgun marriage or other dangers accompanying passionate relationships.

Throughout the initial section of *School of Udhra*, "Song of the Andoumboulou: 8–15," a threatening "cut" slices its way: "Our Mistress's / whispers, / thrust / of a cross cut saw . . ."; "Saw myself bled, belatedly cut /. . . thunder whet the edge / of a knife"; and "Riven lip" (4, 10, 11). If this sequence of poems has a philosophy, it is "no way out / if not thru," and the poems compound imagery and sound, as in the concluding "Song of the Andoumboulou: 15":

                Cast off
  only to be called back,

cut,

sewn up again. Tenuous
throatsong, hoof to the head waking
up, plucking music from a meatless

rib . . .

Rickety tauntsong. Plum's pit.
Staining the hands with henna. (20)

A concluding introjection of this projective sequence, "song" itself is imaged
through violent and "rickety" qualities. The "cut, / sewn up again" points to both
the singer, "To be found after waiting / so long but found wanting," and to his
song, which in retrospect seems a series of cuts and sewing, "returning" "rhap-
sody to its root sense stitching together" (*Udhra*, 7, back cover). The "*Persian red*,"
first "read" in a friend's poem and later put on as a "robe," is now "henna," calling up a transmogrifying feminine figure. The semantic and aural relations of
this sequence are rich and difficult to account for entirely. For example, the consonance of "plucking" combines with "plum" to contrast with the prolonged assonance of "tauntsong," of its ribless *au* and *o* sounds that connect conceptually
with "meatless" and eventuate in a "pit," both hole and seed, the concreteness
of the latter enabling a transition to the very physical act of "staining."

If the domain of the *School of Udhra* is lost love, *Whatsaid Serif* engages the
afterburn of failed love and investigates recrimination and regret. *School of Udhra*
circles around "loss, / relatedness, lack / . . . to be free of its / memory, / This
they'd pick their / hearts out aiming / for" (23). *Whatsaid Serif* brings a more defined set of social issues to the forefront, in contrast to *School of Udhra*'s poetry
of lovers who "when loving die." In *Whatsaid Serif* Mackey addresses erotic possession and dispossession as these are marked by large-scale social, cultural, and
economic relations of indentured work and slavery in capitalism and its so-called
free labor markets. The volume can be seen to be a pulled-apart *cante moro* as
the poetry draws together the traumatic legacies of capitalism and racism with
a wounding and wounded love. While a sense of the ecstatic runs throughout
much of Mackey's poetry, it is intensified in *Whatsaid Serif* because of the work's
increased proprioceptive relations.

If in the *School of Udhra*, strife inheres for the most part in love relations
themselves, in *Whatsaid Serif*, strife is both within love and without. An im-
passe between two lovers, which is the subject of much of the book, is caught
up in the fact that she saw him struck or wounded. At times what or who is doing the striking is syntactically unclear, suggesting that this wounding is the
condition of the relationship itself, apart from any particular wounding act. In

a detailed analysis of the first poem in the volume, "Song of the Andoumbou-lou: 16," Naylor comments that its opening scene conveys the conditions of indentured work and slavery and links these to the volume's concerns with failed and lost love. Throughout *Whatsaid Serif* there is a marked sense of movement, proprioception, as the "she" and "he" travel on train, bus, and boat. Mackey has commented that in *Whatsaid Serif* "the sense of itinerary . . . is increasingly accented," and "tropes of vehicular movement—bus, boat, train—recur and senses of arrival and/or frustrated arrival are articulated over and over again" (*Paracritical* 325). Naylor links the experience of crossing over thresholds to the experience of ecstasy: "These transpositions, then can be seen as ecstatic experiences, as ways of standing outside of what or where one is" (595). Indeed, the sense of perpetual motion makes the experience of traveling with the "he" and "she" one of dislocation, in which the only mooring for the reader is the movement of the poetry itself: "what was / now most real was the 'away / from'" (*Whatsaid Serif* 23). The reader is neither inside nor outside these lovers' experiences but in the phenomenal space of the poem itself.

There are multiple entities in the poem: "he," "she," "I," "we," "they," and a "whatsayer." At times the different entities are presented as existing in some opposition to each other; at other times they slide into each other, as gender differentiation and coupledom itself are questioned: "Wanted to say of he-and-she-ness / it creaks . . . / each the / other's / legendary lack . . . / We, / who'd have been done / with both, / looked out across the wall, / saw / no new day / come" (*Whatsaid Serif* 83). The role of the whatsayer is described through an opening epigraph from Ellen B. Basso's *A Musical View of the Universe* as the necessary recipient of the story, who may ask for clarification. In *Whatsaid Serif*, the whatsayer often operates through his or her own inimicable despair: "I was the whatsayer. / Whatever he said I would / say so what" (22). Experiences in *Whatsaid Serif* often manifest in their most elemental or particle-like aspects. The remembered love between the two lovers is often reduced to its repeating traumatic and discordant elements, as phrases restricted to a seemingly plain speech repeat and morph: "The he she remembers not / the he she saw stepping into the train"; "She no longer the she who'd / arrived announced, he no longer / the he I'd been taken aside / by"; "the he-and-she / she wanted, the he-and-she / they were"; "each the / other's pronominal / elsewhere" (10, 59, 61, 81). These lovers are haunted by lovers' usual problems, which Mackey turns into states of being: "School-of-What-Hurts / her"; "Power the problem, lack of / power the problem"; "Push come to shove she'd / be with him" (11, 41, 42).

In the *School of Udhra* Mackey engages both present and past tenses; whereas, in *Whatsaid Serif* he develops a particular version of a past tense, which actually creates the illusion of a present tense, because of how the poetry proceeds through a paratactic listing of words and phrases. He thus creates a sense of events as happening neither in the present nor in the past, but rather in a kind of rarefied space, an atmosphere of claustrophobia and trance: "Voice taken up into / airlessness . . . / Conscript air, she / replied" (*Whatsaid Serif* 5). This present-past writing, which Mackey carries into his later volumes, is particularly useful in creating an "alternative space," an "elsewhere." Indeed, the uncertain temporality of this poetry combines with its undecided spatial location to intensify its conveyance of the ecstatic, since one is outside of that which one cannot locate.

In *Whatsaid Serif* Mackey constitutes his "black song" as much by sound as by semantics: deprivation and yearning are drawn together through his anagrammatic scat:

> Boat of years,
> black-orphic lament, boat of
> yearning . . .
>
> . . . .
> So that hoarseness
> bore the
> Ahtt we were after, Ttha, the most abstract
> "at"
> we'd every inhabit
>
> . . . .
> weathered fret, window
> ever out of
> Ahtt's reach (105)

For Mackey, trauma combined with desire is rendered as a sound, a "hoarseness," an excess of *ah*'s and *th*'s, "the most abstract / 'at,'" and not as a referential description. In reaching toward the emotion he wishes to convey, Mackey intimates that sound may be the best indicator. In a more salutary set of sounds, "we" becomes "wuh," unleashing an "ur-sound":

> A wuh
> sound sounding like dove-warble
> worked his throat, the we
> he, she and I were haunted by.
> An ur-sound blew thru our
> bones (19)

By tracing Mackey's "versioning" of the riffs that first occurred in "Dearly Beloved" in *Whatsaid Serif*, Mackey's projective love writing, as a very slowed-down perception leading to further perception, language to further language, can be appreciated (*Discrepant* 266). "Andoumboulou: 16" investigates multiple scenes of ravishment, countering them at one point through a feminine, if not a female, perspective, as "she" puts a child to bed, blessed by "flat sanity's / enablement." This singular incident is preceded and followed by more disturbing events, including such terrors as "charred bodies blown / about, unembalmable, / bombed" (6). Moreover, the "sane" perspective of putting a child to bed rather than staying "sanity's" course crosses over into the yearning for something more, some ravishment. This further reaching produces a "heaven" rather different from the one in "Dearly Beloved," although composed of some of the same "licks" as in Mackey's earlier poem:

> Took between her lips their
> gruff tongues' foretaste of
>   "heaven," raspy word given
> back by the newly
>   dead (*Whatsaid Serif* 6–7)

Whereas in "Dearly Beloved," heaven is associated with "the initiation of romance," in this volume it is indentured. In "Song of Andoumboulou: 24," the trope of heaven is engaged again but this time as a product of "burred / speech" and a "Not-All-There" (43):

> Took between his lips her
> cusp of tongue's foretaste
>   of "heaven,"   ravenous
>   word they
>   heard urging them on, loquat
>   spin. Teeth broke biting
>   her lip,   intoxicant meat he'd
>   been
>   warned against, took between
>   his teeth . . . Took between
> his own her bleeding lip's
>   lost
>   lustre,   ravenous
>   word

taken back, bitten into,

burst . . . (40)

Echoing the earlier rendition of "heaven's foretaste," this "foretaste" of "heaven" partakes of love's "meat"—of "lustre" lost to a "bleeding" from the "word" heaven itself. Biting into the word "heaven," it "bursts." This aporia shows the "what-sayer" in a brief noncommittal appearance as he pronounces dryly on the per-ceived staticness of the poem's pronounced proprioceptive relations: "what plot there was" was "one of / stepping on, stepping / off" (*Whatsaid Serif* 40, 41).

Occasionally in *Whatsaid Serif* Mackey approaches a realized love, although even these realizations partake of hungers. In "Song of the Andoumboulou: 22," the vision of love approaches the ecstatic: "Woven of / sun, sun woven of cloth inflaming their / bodies." But this causes the "I," or the whatsayer, to remark: "'Some / ride it sounds like' was all I could / say. . . ." (33). Song 22 concludes with a vision of "Loquat exuberance," "loquat allure," but Mackey can only find it amid "rotting / fruit" (35):

As if to say soul
seeks out low places . . . As if
to say loquat height let go,

                  rotting
   fruit lay at the foot of the
  tree, having gone to their heads.
   Loquat elixir. Ambient wine.
             Ubiq-
uitous whiff (35)

The immediate reference for "loquat" is a loquat tree, which has fragrant white flowers, pear-shaped fruit, and large seeds. "Loquat" reminds of "love" and "*loa*" as well as, in this particular poem, the "low squat" of women peeing in a field. For Mackey "low places" are not only negative spaces but a necessary "under-ness" through which life may retreat or repair, since "soul / seeks out low places" (*Whatsaid Serif* 33–35).

In *Whatsaid Serif*, Mackey engages eros through extreme dislocation. The im-plied author, who like the whatsayer assumes stances of standing outside of and apart from, approaches the ecstatic. Near the end of the volume, this projective love writing culminates in a skeletal vision of its own design:

>   we
> were beyond it, bleak skeleton crew on
>   the boat we rode, subtly in front,
>   phantom
> projection (*Whatsaid Serif* 103)

At this juncture, *Whatsaid Serif* lays bare the device of its construction. In Mackey's subsequent volume *Splay Anthem*, the poetic speaker declares, "To abide by hearing was / what love was" (*Splay* 93). Not motivated to stay his poetry's "thirst," Mackey catches up with his poetry, and his object of love coincides with the very way in which he hears his words.

Afterword

that little yes material—script pierced (& pierces)
—Kathleen Fraser, *20th Century*

In *The Transmutation of Love and Avant-Garde Poetics*, I create a new history of avant-garde poetry as based in the transforming event of being in love as it leads to a changed love writing and I claim the centrality of this altered love poetry for avant-garde poetics more generally. Creeley once formulated, and Olson often repeated, the postulate that "form is never more than an extension of content" (Olson and Creeley 79).[1] By this remark, Creeley did not mean to suggest that form is unimportant but rather that all content comes to us through a form, and is unavailable to us apart from formation, whether it is constituted as poetry or as fact. Each of the poets considered in this book has been involved in changing the form of love poetry to write their love. While I have attempted to provide a generalized description of a shared alteration in linguistic form through the concept of projective love and libidinized field poetics, for none of these poets is the form detachable from its content. These poets change love by writing love. This changed love is recondite within the formation of their poetry itself.

In insisting on a dynamic interrelation between content and form—the emotional source of this poetry and its inscription—I cross registers that are usually addressed separately, or not at all. While biographical criticism attempts to connect a writer's life to their work, it rarely links the writer's visceral or emotional responses to their formal innovation. Critical or textual studies that concentrate on formal invention focus their exposition largely on language theories and practices. They usually concentrate on what is new about the work and ignore how it draws on concepts and techniques derived from the past. Moreover, they attend to the product and not the process by which something comes about, and so tend to emphasize a stable signification and ignore the mobile and shifting nature of signification itself. By concentrating on the complex processes by which each of these poets comes to write love differently and by closely attending to their evolving writing, I disclose important relations between emotion and artistic production and between physical and linguistic response.

No discourse is more sensitive to instrumentalist interventions than love writing, since love is known to the one in love in very specific ways and often through gendered, sexed, and racialized lover's discourse. All of these poets have found a way to write love as intensely as the revered love poetry of preceding centuries, by evading restrictive social positionalities and the attendant behavioral and decorum mandates that accompany these, no more so than in a public declaration of love. These poets change love poetry by creating a poetics that opens up love writing to all poetic speakers who would engage the modalities of projective love and libidinized field poetics, thus allowing an array of persons not only to write love but to create a poetic agency outside of restrictive social roles. Refusing lover and beloved dichotomies and hierarchies, they produce a love writing that engages the power of love apart from existing social scripts. They create a poetry that works against the many binaries that create the semantic field of traditional love poetry, whether subject and object, masculine and feminine, heterosexual and homosexual, absence and presence, or stasis and motion. They thereby go a distance to achieve what some may prefer to call a queer, transpersonal, or transhuman love as not only gender, sexual, and racial distinctions but entire fields of signification become destabilized. This queering of love is most evident in the cases of H.D. and Duncan, whose writing was created in reference to their bisexuality and homosexuality. In *Helen in Egypt*, H.D. queered the warring Achilles by making him the object of her love quest and by describing his eyes as mesmerizing because they contain the sea rhythms of his mother, Thetis. Duncan refused the gendered subtexts of language, claiming: "manhood is not something that's there but is only there the way we then make love."

While all these poets write in relationship to intense feeling and desires for actual beloveds, they refuse to present this love through the form of a lover seeking unification or fusion with his beloved and as such exemplify what Jean-Pierre Vernant refers to as a "primordial eros" and George Bataille as "erotism." In Vernant's "One . . . Two . . . Three: Eros" he comments on two kinds of Eros in the ancient world, a newcomer Eros, namely Aphrodite's son, and a primordial Eros. Aphrodite's son unites lovers and beloveds, while the primordial Eros subtends existence. This Eros causes entities "to bring to light that which they have hidden within themselves" and make manifest the multiplicity included in the unity (466). It draws out the otherness which resides in the self, which includes the experience of others or "of becoming other" (476). Vernant links this eros to what the Neoplatonists call "'the fall into Dionysus,' the mirror, to which the One . . . is attracted by the image which duplicates it, which makes it two, to find itself there infinitely multiplied in a myriad of reflections" (468).

While this description reminds most immediately of the fecundity unleashed in Pound's Dionysian *Canto II*, it also conveys the multiplicity enacted by projective love and libidinized field poetics more generally.

Bataille refuses the unification of lovers as defining for erotism, but finds the power of eros to exist in the ways it aids "discontinuous beings, individuals who perish in isolation, in the midst of an incomprehensible adventure" to find their "lost continuity": "the whole business of eroticism is to destroy the self-contained character of the participants as they are in their normal lives" (17). Bataille notes that the sought-after possession of the beloved is a "fraud." Rather what lovers seek is "to substitute for the individual isolated discontinuity a feeling of profound continuity," or, as described here, the extended energies of projective love and libidinized field writing (15).

In his groundbreaking work *A Lover's Discourse*, Roland Barthes, while offering an important defense of sexual love, also replicates problematic lover and beloved formations. Barthes states that it is through the role of the lover that he writes this work, and he speaks of the beloved through a synthesized Lacanian Imaginary and Symbolic paradigm of an "image-repertoire." In doing so, he replicates many binaries of traditional love poetry, no more so than the dichotomies of subject and object, as well as absence and presence. He asks: "Isn't desire always the same whether the object is present or absent? Isn't the object always absent?" Barthes claims to be wedged between "two tenses, that of reference, and that of the allocution: you have gone (which I lament); you are here (since I am addressing you.)" While Barthes addresses the divide initiated by economies of bifurcated lovers and beloveds as well as absence and presence by enlisting the concept of an "insupportable present," Pound, H.D., and Duncan engage what Stein describes as a "continuous presence" (15). Fraser and Mackey construct new times. It is no accident that Fraser's most profound love writing occurs in a book called *when new time folds up*, and Mackey creates the sense of a present tense through amassing phrases written in a past tense.

In suggesting that this poetry is important not only as a changed love writing but for avant-garde or innovative poets more generally, I am urging the centrality of this new disposition of love to poetry writing and cultural production more generally. One of the questions this book raises regards the relationship between projective love and libidinized field poetics, and projective and field poetics, more generally. This question is made all the more prominent in this book by my engagement of Olson's terms for the projective, while not including Olson amid my discussion of lovers. Olson's vibrant terminology and exposition in fact partake of this changed love poetry, while for the most part concerning itself with other subjects. Indeed, the question of Pound's importance to Olson has given rise to a series of debates regarding Olson's originality. Yet, Olson himself readily connects his poetics with Pound—and, I maintain, derives his differently construed libidinal energies quite directly from the changed verse formation pioneered by Pound and H.D as well as others.

Projective and field poetics have increased exponentially in the twenty-first century, and are arguably the technique by which much experimental and language poetry created itself in the 1980s and 1990s—often as a libidinized field, but less frequently as projective love.[2] In Charles Bernstein's early collection of essays *Content's Dream*, Bernstein links his poetics quite directly to Olson: "Poem becoming a perceptual field / experience 'independent' of 'author' (Cf: Olson's "Projective Verse" essay: each perception instanter on the next . . . so eliminating of traditional 'inherited' forms which strip poetry of this active power)" (70–71). While despite his mocking of the introjective in his later "Introjective Verse," much of his poetry proceeds through a kind of projective-introjective libidinized field poetics as aural and visual aspects of poetry create and interrupt conceptual relations, as, for instance, his "The Klupzy Girl": "A manic / state of careless grace. Mylar juggernauts / zig-zag penuriously" (Hoover, *Postmodern* 521). While particularly West Coast Language Poetry thought to distance itself from Olson's speech-based poetics, it also partakes of his formulations. Lyn Hejinian states that "In the 'open text' . . . all the elements of the work are maximally excited" (*Language* 43). And she frequently engages a projective-introjective method of composition, as in *My Life*: "Summers were spent in a fog that rains. They were mirages not different from those that camel back riders approach . . ." (Hoover 328). Hejinian quickly takes us from a West Coast foggy summer through the concept of "mirage" as it cleaves to the desert.

In *American Hybrid*, Cole Swensen and David St. John insist that much significant poetry in recent times can be characterized by a coming together of a previously designated "raw" and "cooked," experimental and mainstream poetry. They characterize this hybridization as resulting from combined concepts of meaning, previously held apart: the poem as an articulation of a somewhat stable set of references that convey meanings already present in the society and the poem as an event in which "language, which inevitably retaining a referential capacity, is emphasized as a site of meaning in its own right . . ." (xviii). While Swensen and St. John's observation of hybridization might be interpreted rather differently, less as a coming together of the raw and the cooked and more as the success of minoratized poetics of the twentieth century now infiltrating a wide array of verse, including mainstream poetry, the problem with their primarily technique-driven analysis is that it does not account for differences in intent, politics, or history—all the more troubling since our new century promises as much, if not more, social and cultural change than the previous century. The interrelationship between form and content, between the how and the what of poetry, so defining for avant-garde interventions, is thereby rendered mute. As *American Hybrid* portrays, treating "the poem as an event" is now one formal option among others. Consequently, the emotional and innovative reach of the projective is potentially colonized within the genre of poetry itself, and the historical inventions and struggles of the poets covered by this book are harder to discern.

Olson derived his poetics from lovers and love poets. He created his "Projective Verse" in close relationship with his paramour, Frances Boldereff, and developed this essay further in the company of Robert Creeley—through what Michael Davidson has identified, borrowing from Eve Kosofsky Sedgwick, as a relationship of "homosocial" bonding and Rachel Blau DuPlessis has drawn attention to as a an eros of poesis with a strong basis in male privilege (*Guys* 16; *Purple Passages* 6). Moreover, Olson created this essay after visiting Duncan's San Francisco and, as Jarnot describes, "matching wits" with Duncan. Given his own professed influence by Pound, Shelley, and Williams, it is fair to say that Olson was surrounded by lovers and love poets in creating this essay and that the concept of the projective has much footing in sexual love, if its projected emotional field is not declared as such. DuPlessis in *Purple Passages* stresses the triangulation between Olson, Boldereff, and Creeley in the creation of this essay, and notes how Boldereff's substantial contributions have been largely erased from its historic record. She establishes how Boldereff was complicit throughout her relationship with Olson in animating and enabling his masculine powers, with Boldereff divided between asserting her own substantial intellectual gifts and electing a feminine muse role to enable Olson's dominating presence (*Purple Passages* 138–41). How different, then, the Olson love triangle in its articulation of the projective, than the love triangle of H.D., Pound, and Aldington that initiated Imagism. In Imagism, H.D. and her writing of same-sex and different-sex love poems are at the center of a diversifying poetics; in the latter exposition Olson predominates as he comes to issue a single manifesto in his name.

Other important projective and libidinized field poets of the latter part of the twentieth century, while often bypassing or even rejecting sexual love as an instigating force, partake of its energies. One would be hard put, say, to conceive of Rachel Blau DuPlessis's creation of *Drafts* without the example of Pound, H.D., and Duncan. Although DuPlessis distances herself from H.D.'s actual love affairs through the concept of "romantic thralldom," her scholarship on H.D. is extensive. (Indeed, I would suggest that feminist critics' engagement with H.D. has much to do with the allure of her love writing, the way it embeds eros, however much they parse her actual loves.) In commenting on her own transition from a more traditional poetry to her piece "Writing," DuPlessis notes the importance of reading Duncan's "A Poem Beginning with a Line by Pindar." She describes herself as "stunned": "The sound, and the scope of that particular work, the voracity and splay of it, the way he took in so much, the hypersaturation of the means were very inspiring to me" ("Interview" 104). DuPlessis's own scholarship has admirably noted the ways that actual women, often muse figures and beloveds, are erased from men's love poems as well as the historical record, yet she does not note the ways that a similar erasing of sexual love itself as productive of poetry may be part of this same patriarchal economy.[3] Lissa Wolsak, who comes to poetry amid the Vancouver poetry scene (with its multiple relations to Olson, Blaser, and Duncan), creates an occulted eros, brought out powerfully in her first published work, *An Heuristic Prolusion*: "Co-mercy, the art of harmlessness, equivocating sexual / theological, fiat, fiat lux" . . . (143). Bruce Andrews's dashed writing occurs in the gutters of love, as in "Somehow That's Just the Way It is and I Just Don't Really Care": "My brains are in my heart—Why is my heart so frail?— . . . The bad in a man—Keener reception" (Hoover 493).

There are other poets and books that would add to the exposition on the transmutation of love initiated here. Most importantly, among the poets who came of age in the 1960s and 1970s, Aaron Shurin and Susan Howe make important contributions. Aaron Shurin's early "Out of Me: Whitman and the Projective" traces projective poetics through Whitman and Duncan and his *Involuntary Lyrics* is a brilliant rendition of projective love and libidinized field poetics, as these intersect with Shakespeare's love sonnets. Susan Howe, much motivated by questions of history and civil society and instructed by Olson's poetics, finds the phenomenon of sexual love and eros defining for this inquiry in her works *The Europe of Trusts* and *My Emily Dickinson*.

In beginning my account with the Imagist writing and subsequent experimentation by Pound and H.D., I aimed to identify an important site of emergence, but not an exclusive one. Both Gertrude Stein and William Carlos Williams early on in their careers might be said to engage a projective love writing, while moving away from these poetics later on. Gertrude Stein's 1914 *Tender Buttons*, written around the same time that Imagism emerged, is now widely interpreted as love poetry, and arguably evinces a projective love and libidinized field poetics, if one somewhat chastened by her attention to the thingness of things. But while Stein begins here, her writing moves in rather different directions. Stein's "Patriarchal Poetry," declarative of an erotics of "lifting belly," has much queer and manifesto appeal, but it does not produce a writing in which, as Agamben writes, "The object sought by love would coincide with the very language in which [the work] is written" (*End* 60). And while Williams's *Spring and All*, published a few years after Pound's transformative *Canto IV*, manifests a projective and libidinized field poetics, with moments given over to projective love, in his later poetry in *Asphodel That Greeny Flower* he turns back to address his beloved, Flossie, through rather traditional lover and beloved economies. His late work *Paterson* largely eschews the libidinized field poetics of his early work.

In the 1990s there are important early books by poets discovering and working this terrain. I suggested in the introduction that an important defining moment for the direction of this book project was my discovery of commonalities between Pound and Fraser's poetics. I would be remiss not to mention three specific books by poets publishing their initial defining work in the 1990s: Lee Ann Brown's *Polyverse*, Lisa Jarnot's *Some Other Kind of Mission*, and Harryette Mullen's *Muse and Drudge*.[4] Indeed, struggling with the issues of writing sexual love as a poet just about to write her own version of these poetics in *Transducer*, I found the work of these poets uncanny. They were doing what I was trying to do.

By the twenty-first century, I think it is safe to say that projective love and libidinized poetics is one option of many for writing love. Its generative discovery as a means of writing not only love but a libidinized field poetics is now with us in many modes, as it becomes a means for conveying and even ironizing love. Brian Teare in *Sight Map* creates a rolling, roiling verse. In "To Be Two," he writes of the love poem in a series of paratactic phrases: it "shifts and clicks . . . / is split like everything / is mica-fine in silence / . . . falls for as long as." In *Down*, Sarah Dowling writes, "This yes again being all over the time you do mornings in my heart with a very secret place (place) further from me I beg you" (27). Sawako Nakayasu in "Balconic" from *Hurry Home Honey* engages the concept and reality of a balcony, as an architecture that allows for the staging of love, "the thick line between there and herein," where "it's getting to be yes, it's getting" (23, 20).

A half-century ago, Barthes proclaimed that love was an intellectual backwater, a condition that persists into the present. For many in the academy, whether as theorists, critics, or poets, the very heightened emotionalism of being in love is suspect because it is intensely experienced by the individual and hence judged to be at odds with the current emphasis on sociality and rectitude. Love itself is hardly benign. While social critiques have shown in myriad ways that sexual relations constituted through unequal power relations are *not* love (noting that rape occurs within marriages), what is largely missing from the same critiques is the ways that sexual love persists in relations of much power inequality and that it is not entirely reducible to the power dynamics through which it issues. Sexual love is a destructive as well as a conservative force in society, sustaining sometimes physically injurious relationships and often a status quo of unfair power relations. However, sexual love may also initiate radical, life-changing events that catapult persons into relating to persons entirely outside their ken, their immediate comfort zones, and may, in fact, change their hard-wiring. By rejecting or ignoring sexual love, or divisively compartmentalizing it into sex and love, this most mitigating or mediating phenomenon is as the proverbial baby being thrown out with the bathwater. Moreover, these same energies when unleashed or extended from an originating dyadic love relationship can have untold power for cultural and social creativity.

Despite themselves, many modern, postmodern, posthuman, and transhuman subjects find themselves falling in love—and amid a state of limerence that only slowly recedes. This transmutation of love is defining for poetry and poetics. Poetry is a vastly collaborative venture, and sexual love is an animating force. The example of these poets open up a writing of love to nonwhite, nonmale, and nonheterosexual lovers as never before. In a time consumed by instrumentalism that makes language into a set of predigested "counters," that uses language rather than engaging it as a medium, the poets examined in this book stay with the troubling emotions of sexual love and create a love writing for the twentieth and now twenty-first centuries.[5] Their example is "contagious," "an infectious ecstasy," as their wide-ranging influence manifests.[6] They close down the gaps between lovers and beloveds and open up the signification of sexual love.

Notes

Preface and Acknowledgments

1. For a study that investigates these relationships with a vengeance, see Kipnis.

2. Perloff urges the importance of Rimbaud and his antisymbolic poetics for a group of American poets, including Gertrude Stein, William Carlos Williams, Ezra Pound, Beckett, John Ashbery, John Cage, and David Antin (*Poetics of Indeterminacy* 3–44).

3. I am playing off Kathleen Fraser's phrase "his romance," by which she draws attention to the ways that romance and love have been largely inscribed through patriarchal cultures and privileges (*Each Next* 13).

4. Oderman emphasizes that metaphors of illumination appear throughout Pound's poetry as a trope for erotic experience.

5. I took the epigraph from a much-worked-on piece of writing in *Incapacity* titled "Offering" that I worked on for a couple of decades. The portion that became the epigraph was written in the early 1980s: "In beginning the piece she first thought about writing one morning while living the uneventful events of that morning she had decided in advance to write about, she could not decide between herself as the main protagonist or someone like her. In thinking about herself as the protagonist, her sense of character disappeared as she did not experience herself in any coherent way, and in thinking of someone like her, her sense of events disappeared, as nothing so eventful had occurred as her desire to write just this piece. Certainly she reasoned, someone like her could also desire to write *Incapacity*, but once she formulated her desire in this way, it would disappear into the confines of her piece and she would have no desire to write it."

Introduction

1. By bringing to the forefront the synergistic relationship between erotic response and poetic writing, I draw on centuries of poetry testimonies and examples, including works by Sappho, Catullus, Propertius, Ovid, Dante, Petrarch, Shelley, Yeats, Rilke, and Creeley, as well as on critical texts that explore these relations: Giorgio

Agamben, *The End of the Poem*; Roland Barthes, *A Lover's Discourse*; Philip Hardie, *Ovid's Poetics of Illusion*; Katherine Hayles, *Writing Machines*; Duncan Kennedy, *The Arts of Love: Five Studies in the Discourse of Roman Love Elegy*; Kevin Kopelson, *Love's Litany: The Writing of Modern Homoerotics*; Maeera Shreiber, *The Discourse of Love in the Lyric and the Letter*.

2. The presumption of an "introspective" subject is behind most accounts that define modern love as "companionate" or that engage object-relation theories, since these models hold that love relations are realized through negotiations between two separate lovers. In addition to the theorists and critics mentioned here, rather different accounts of love have subscribed to some version of this model for contemporary relations. See, for example, the work of Jessica Benjamin, Niklas Luhmann, and Thomas Simmons.

3. Miller argues that Sappho's orally delivered poetry has no material support for an introspective speaker, since the development of an introspective subject only became possible through a sustained poetic production, itself dependent on a material writing (53–77). In contrast to Miller, Page duBois in *Sowing the Body* claims that the individuated poetic lover of Western love writing has a beginning in Sappho.

4. Critical accounts of the hierarchical relationship between a masculine lover and a feminine beloved in love poetry are multiple and incisive: DuPlessis, *The Pink Guitar: Writing as Feminist Practice*; DuPlessis, "'Corpses of Poesy': Modern Poets and Some Gender Ideologies of the Lyric"; Easthope, *Poetry and Phantasy*; Heuving, "Gender in Marianne Moore's Art: Can'ts and Refusals"; Heuving, *Omissions Are Not Accidents: Gender in the Art of Marianne Moore*; Homans, "Syllables of Velvet: Dickinson, Rossetti, and the Rhetorics of Sexuality"; Montefiore, *Feminism and Poetry*; and Vickers, "Diana Described: Scattered Woman and Scattered Rhyme."
These accounts take on the underlying paradigm of how dominant subjects constitute themselves by othering others also engaged by critiques of race and sexuality—a rhetorical and social practice that Toni Morrison succinctly summarizes as "techniques of 'othering'" (59). For groundbreaking work that draws on this paradigm with respect to race, sexuality, imperialism, and postcolonialism, see DuPlessis (*Genders*), Edward Said, Eve Kosofsky Sedgwick, and Gayatri Spivak. Greene argues that the traditional love lyric of a poetic speaker who longs for a beloved who is absent or far away is part of an imperialistic economy. Several critics have argued that lyric poetry itself in its basic constitution unfairly situates and compromises female, queer, and nonwhite poets. See, for example, Nielsen's *Reading Race*, DuPlessis's *Pink Guitar*, and Kinnahan's *Lyric Interventions*. While Sedgwick's ground-breaking queer theory forms itself through a critique of the technique of othering, more recent queer theory, especially as a basis for social activism, attempts to override paradigms based on subject and other, self and object. In this book, my emphasis on an "open field" and "libidinized field poetics" is potentially productive of a queer ethos; "queer" itself in operating at times as an identity category can obscure painful social realities of historically situated gays and lesbians. For useful queer criticism that does not do this, see the work of Snediker and Butler (*Bodies*).

5. William Shakespeare in his sonnets utilized lover-beloved forms, sustaining their traditional positionalities of male and female while engaging them for different ends. Lynn Keller in "Measured Feet" considers how Marilyn Hacker employed lover-beloved forms to write about a lesbian relationship. In Hacker's poetry, the duo

of relatively empowered lover and disempowered beloved became an older female lover and a younger female beloved.

6. "Erotism" is Bataille's concept.

7. The bifurcation of sex and love is divisive for scholarship. Kevin Oderman's *Ezra Pound and the Erotic Medium* operates primarily under the sign of sex and sexuality and as such is worlds apart from Akiko Miyake's *Ezra Pound and the Mysteries of Love*, although they are addressing something of the same phenomenon. For a recent example of a divided sex and love discussed with much sophistication, see Lauren Berlant's *Desire / Love*. For a scientific study that finds that "being in love" stimulates different parts of the brain than mere sexual desire, see Carey.

8. In her 2002 book, *21st-Century Modernism*, Perloff insists that important twentieth-century poets from T. S. Eliot to Lyn Hejinian have in common an "ambitious" "attitude to the materiality of the text" (6). And while *Poetics of Indeterminacy* found a decisive fissure between Eliot and Pound on the basis of their symbolic and antisymbolic language, in *21st-Century Modernism* she ignores this distinction.

9. Henry Staten, presuming sublimation to be suppressive, interprets Diotima's speech in Plato's *Symposium* through this lens.

10. Both Pondrom and Jacob Korg (25–46) claim that the example of H.D.'s Imagist verse was decisive for Pound's recognition and "creation" of Imagism.

11. Both Babcock and Gregory (*H.D. and Hellenism*) discuss H.D.'s use of Mackail's *Select Epigrams*.

12. Altieri emphasizes that Pound's *Cantos*, along with other Modernist poetry, is distinguished from preceding poetry because it presents or re-presents, rather than represents (283–320).

13. For an overview of Mackey's relationship to jazz as "vatic scat," see Lazer.

Chapter 1

1. A typed manuscript copy of Pound's *Hilda's Book* is in Yale's Beinecke Rare Book and Manuscript Library; the original is in Harvard's Houghton Library. Pound's typescript presentation of these poems is much more nuanced and lively than their only extant publication as an appendix to H.D.'s *End to Torment*, in which Pound's spacing and lineation are largely ignored.

2. Oderman's *Ezra Pound and the Erotic Medium* tracks some of the same terrain as this book, especially in its validation of what H.D. calls the "fiery moment" of sexual love as being influential for Pound's entire poetic career. Oderman places attention on the figures or "ideograms" that Pound used to mark this moment and notes that for Pound two figures of erotic vision are important: "one in which the forms are seen (the gods) and one in which no forms are seen (bright void)" (88). Oderman uses a vocabulary primarily of sex and sexuality rather than sexual love, although he seems to be referring to the latter when he notes, for instance, that for Pound "sexuality stood at the threshold of the *mysterium*" (7).

3. In "Projective Verse," Olson credits Pound, but not H.D., as an important precursor for his poetry (22). In "Charles Olson and the 'Inferior Predecessors': 'Projective Verse' Revisited," Perloff claims that Olson's poetics were derived from Pound and Williams.

4. In a 1982 unpublished thesis, "Out of Me: Whitman and the Projective," the

poet Aaron Shurin, a student of Robert Duncan, describes Whitman's and Mallarmé's poetics as "projective."

5. I take the phrase "cool observation" from Fraser (*Translating* 127).

6. Both Pound and Agamben find Petrarch's love poetry to be deficient in contrast to the *dolce stil nuovo* poets who preceded him. Agamben reasons that Petrarch aims only to produce "fragments" of a "vernacular" rather than a primordial speech: "There could be no clearer way to say that the poetic universe that gave rise to the Provencal and Dolce Stil Novo [*sic*] projects had by now been left behind forever. . . . With a definitive movement away from the troubadour dictation, life now stands on one side, and poetry, on the other side, is only literature, mourning the irremediable death of Laura" (*End* 85). Pound thought Petrarch was a poet of "ornament" (*Pound's Cavalcanti* 208).

7. These are concepts developed at length by Jack Spicer and Robin Blaser. See Miriam Nichols's chapter on Blaser, "The Practice of Outside" (177–221).

Chapter 2

1. For example, Jessica Benjamin's theory of mutual recognition, however appealing, is a far cry from these writers' concepts of sexual love: "the need for *mutual recognition*, the necessity of recognizing as well as being recognized by the other . . . is crucial to the intersubjective view" (23).

2. In *The Psychic Life of Power: Theories in Subjection* (132–66) Butler explores in numerous ways how the other cannot simply be made into a vehicle for self-love or self-identification.

3. Bersani, taking on what he regards as Freud's most radical definition of sublimation, as a rerouting of sexual energy apart from object cathexis, emphasizes that sublimation is a burning away of the occasion, which allows for "free" intellectual and artistic play. While Bersani's primary terms here are sex and sexuality, and not love, his sense of artistic play is close to Irigaray's sense of an "endless becoming." Commenting on Mallarmé's poem "L'Après-midi d'un Faune," Bersani writes, "sublimation is not a transendence of desire, but rather a kind of extending of desire which has taken the form of a productive receding of consciousness. . . . The possibility of treating art as symbolic equivalents or disguises of sensual impulses is therefore ruined by the agitations of the 'symbolizing' consciousness itself. . . . The faun profoundly suggests that the reflection of his erotic fantasies in his music is a mobilizing project of his art" (*Freudian* 47, 48). Bersani finds that sexuality is not stimulated by others but rather seeks out others to trigger itself. Similarly, art does not record erotic experience so much as it seeks to produce it.

4. Luce Irigaray makes this distinction paramount to her discussion of the *Symposium* in "Sorcerer Love" (20–33).

5. Bersani has entertained the idea that "transcendence" may in some usages mark that which is exceptional rather than exceeding the earthbound.

Chapter 3

1. H.D. wrote several fictional and nonfictional accounts of her early paramours. See especially *HERmione, Bid Me to Live, Paint It Today*, and *End to Torment*.

2. While critics have been most alert to H.D.'s presumed devastation at Pound's withdrawal of his ambiguous marriage proposal, for the most part they have largely failed to note what Caroline Zilboorg documents as Pound's jealous response to H.D. and Aldington falling in love. Moreover, throughout this period Pound sought out the company of both H.D. and Aldington, and in 1915, to H.D.'s consternation, moved into a flat adjacent to her own. Pound critics tend to minimize H.D.'s importance to Pound and his poetics. For a corrective biographical account, see Korg. For discussions of the Pound, H.D., and Aldington triangle, see Zilboorg, "H.D. and R. A.: Early Love and the Exclusion of Ezra Pound"; Zilboorg, "H.D.'s Influence on Richard Aldington"; and Moody, *Ezra Pound: Poet* (180, 196). As for competitive relations, both Pound and T. E. Hulme claimed to have discovered Imagism; critics diverge in their assessments of these claims.

3. Many feminist critics have found limited value in Imagism. For Imagism as a "masculine" "straightjacket," see Laity (20–22); and McCabe (140). Janet Lyon finds Pound's Imagism primarily used by him for its manifesto value, serving to provide a group identity through which he promoted himself and his particular coterie of writers.

4. Gregory in *H.D. and Hellenism* reveals the extent of H.D.'s many Greek "translations" throughout her career. As already noted, both Gregory and Babcock emphasize the importance of Mackail's *Select Epigrams from the Greek Anthology*.

5. All of the Imagist poems in this chapter are from *Des Imagistes*.

6. H.D. recounts her early relationship with Pound and their shared reading in *End to Torment*. She notes how Pound brought her Balzac's *Seraphita*, a novel that addresses relationships between love and the occult, and muses, "The significance of 'first love' cannot be overestimated. If the 'first love' is an uncoordinated entity, Angel-Devil or Angel Daemon or Daimon, Seraphitus-Seraphita—what then?" (*End* 17).

7. In "Vorticism," Pound suggests that the only way he can get at what he is trying to convey about Imagism is "autobiographically," noting that his most vivid experiences have been "impersonal." See *Ezra Pound's Poetry and Prose* (1: 277–78).

8. Pound iterated these three principles in both "Imagisme" and "Vorticism," establishing them as his primary commitments. The only difference in the two versions is in the second rule—a change of the verb "did" to "does" (*Ezra Pound's Poetry and Prose* 1: 119).

9. Pound is quoting from the "chivalric code" in Latin. Pound remarks in his essay "Dante," "That *La Vita Nuova* is the idealization of a real woman can be doubted by no one who has, even in the last degree, that sort of intelligence whereby it was written, or who has known in any degree the passion whereof it treats" (*Spirit* 126).

10. "Counters" is a term used by Hulme to designate words used abstractly without "any sense of their relation to actuality" (Korg 29). Pound wrote in his notebooks, "Each *word* must be an image *seen*, not a counter"; "each sentence should be a lump of clay, a vision seen" (29).

11. Many of the prime examples of Pound's Imagist verse were written after the poems collected in *Des Imagistes*, including "In a Station of the Metro," "Alba," and "Heather" (*Personae* 111–12). The Eleusinian subtext of "In a Station of the Metro" interjects an erotic component.

12. Aldington's essay "Theocritus in Capri" is presumed to be about his travels with H.D. in Capri, although he never mentions H.D. directly, but rather evokes a

sense of their ecstatic experiences through descriptions of flowers and foliage (241–42). Louis H. Silverstein summarizes: H.D. "associates her love for Aldington with their travels and courtship in Italy" ("Herself Delineated," *Signets* 34). H.D. throughout her career utilized flowers as erotic icons.

13. This speculation about the poem's change in title is mine, based on Pound's sexual joking about Aldington as H.D.'s "Faun" (Carpenter 180).

14. Laity has elaborated on the importance of homoerotic references to hyacinths and swallows in H.D.'s writing, although she does not comment on this poem. She draws attention to how the repeating refrain in *HERmione*, "O sister, my sister, O fleet swallow," is meant to conjure H.D.'s relationship with Gregg (35).

15. Ruthven (62) suggests that "Doria" is about Dorothy Shakespear, as does Moody (163).

16. For an example, see Giles (101).

Chapter 4

1. A few critics make sexual love defining for Pound's work, although they do not link their observations to his poetics. Miyake in *Ezra Pound and the Mysteries of Love* claims that "Pound's life long urge [was] to pursue his paradise by shaping images that had the mysteries of love at their core" (20). Oderman writes that Pound "from very early on was preoccupied with the 'mediumistic' potentialities of sexuality" (xi).

2. Pound developed these concepts in multiple essays throughout 1917–1924. For a summary, see *Literary Essays* (25–26).

3. Oderman discusses Pound's emphasis on the importance of erotic secrecy (6).

4. The dates of these poems are somewhat uncertain, but Pound was likely working on both *Mauberley* and *Propertius* in 1918 (Moody 349).

5. Howatson and Chilvers (103–4).

6. Leon Surette, searching for a different explanation of Pound's work than rationalistic accounts, has suggested that what lies behind his poetics is a belief in occult palingenesis. In *The Birth of Modernism*, Surette engages the term "palingenesis," which he defines as "backward birth or rebirth," to suggest a dominant pattern in occult practices, which he finds in Yeats and Pound (15). According to Surette, what distinguishes the occult is a rite of initiation, through which the subject is awakened to "ultimate reality": "Contact with ultimate reality can be achieved either through a spontaneous mystical revelation or through some ritual initiation such as those of the mysteries at Eleusis. The possibility of illumination through initiation distinguishes the occult from mysticism and connects it to secret societies such as Masonry" (13). "Within the occult, mystical illumination permanently transforms the individual. The illuminated soul is henceforth superior to ordinary mortals in cognitive capacity and often possesses supernatural powers" (14). According to Surette, Ovid's *Metamorphoses* and *The Golden Ass* of Apuleius can be read as accounts of palingenesis. Pound remarks, "A great treasure of verity exists for mankind in Ovid and in the subject matter of Ovid's long poem, and only in this form could it be registered" (qtd. in Surette 15). An equally ubiquitous representation of palingenesis is the *hieros gamos*, divine marriage. Sexual copulation is a "backward birth" for the man, who reenters the womb of his female partner (16–17).

Chapter 5

1. H.D., "Compassionate Friendship" (28).

2. Many feminist scholars who study H.D. have concentrated on her work in prose, finding much to explore with respect to her interventions into dominant plot and representational conventions. See, for example, Friedman's *Penelope's Web* and Laity's *H.D. and the Victorian Fin de Siècle*.

3. Gregory comments on how the Dionysian cults maintained that the Olympian religion was overlaid upon an older form of worship involving "snakes and ghosts and underworld beings." The gods thus took on a dual aspect: while they bestowed gifts, they at the same time compelled painful initiation and service (*H.D. and Hellenism* 114–22).

4. For an excellent discussion that addresses H.D.'s envisioning as "projection," see Morris, "The Concept of Projection: H.D.'s Visionary Powers," in Friedman and DuPlessis, and a revision of that essay titled "Projection: A Study in Thought" in her *How to Live / What to Do* (89–119). See also Johnston.

5. Shawn Alfrey, utilizing Jessica Benjamin's work, extends Benjamin's concept of the intersubjective stressing its characteristics of "liminality" (87).

6. Laity (50).

7. For an excellent discussion of H.D.'s relationship with Hugh Dowding, see Hogue and Vandivere.

Chapter 6

1. In the late 1940s and early '50s, Duncan had personal meetings with Pound and Williams, with both responding that a chasm separated their work from his. When Duncan asked Pound whether he had read *Heavenly City, Earthly City* and *Medieval Scenes*, Pound wondered why the younger poet would go into that since he had already covered this ground before (Faas 240). On reading Duncan's manuscript "Domestic Scenes," Williams responded: "You speak of BREAKFAST, REAL ESTATE, BUS FARE, MAIL BOXES, etc. . . . In such bare words there is a suggestion of really modern *mood* but such a mood quickly disappears when the actual text of the poem is read. There's not another suggestion of it in THE LINES THEMSELVES. . . . It isn't what the words *say*, it's what the poem *makes*. Break it up—somehow." Duncan's expressions were heavy with "the wrong kind of reminiscence, the reminiscence of older manners—not perceptions—in the language itself" (Faas 232).

2. Jarnot notes that after three years of cohabiting with Collins, Duncan rebelled against bourgeois married life (*Robert Duncan* 129). She also documents the multiple affairs that Duncan pursued, sometimes with and sometimes without Jess's knowledge.

3. Maria Damon comments on Duncan's "ahierarchically arranged language. . . . each word . . . interacts across the spaces with other words to form images and sonic resonances" (190).

4. Michael Davidson remarks of Duncan's "Structure of Rime": "The poet 'makes' sentences only as he is made by them; he obeys a law of writing that he may write himself. The sentence is both an imperative . . . and a grammatical construct, just as the dream text is *beyond* yet *of* the dreamer" (*San Francisco* 132).

Chapter 7

1. Fraser served as the director of the Poetry Center at San Francisco State University and initiated its video archive, the American Poetry Archives, in 1973. She created the journal *How(ever)*, later overseeing its transformation into the electronic journal *HOW2*.

2. George Oppen, in correspondence with Fraser at this time, commended her early poem "Lust," but asked why she focused so much of her writing on "men" (Fraser and Oppen). The implicit sexism of this remark becomes evident by imagining Oppen writing a similar letter to Robert Creeley querying why there were so many women in his 1962 poetry volume *For Love*.

3. Cynthia Hogue uses the term "infectious ecstasy" to describe one of the effects of Fraser's writing (51).

4. Rich's poem "Trying to Talk with a Man" (1971) conveys a similar imminent, undefined sense of danger (48–49).

5. Carolyn Burke suggests that Fraser's later work marks her "preeminence" because of how it joins "form and content" (qtd. in Gregory, "Poetics" 20).

6. The project *ii ss* extended Fraser's writing of eros to a collaboration with the visual artist Hermine Ford, combining Ford's visual art with Fraser's text. For other late works that extend her experiments with the page, see *movable TYYPE*.

7. Gregory postulates that in the later poems "a private grief has been crystallized by particular external encounters" ("Poetics" 21).

8. Maeera Shreiber draws attention to the love letter as generative within "the love life," since a love letter assumes a responding lover, albeit one who is absent (1). As such, the letter as text is a means of "traversing the gap that separates would-be lovers" (2). While Shreiber stresses a negotiated gap between lovers, rather than an interpenetration of lovers or a mutual presencing of multiple lovers, her focus on letter writing provides a useful understanding of how writing conjures presence.

9. Gregory remarks that Fraser's angel draws on the trope of "an ancient messenger who breaks through the mundane and shatters its boundaries" ("Poetics" 26).

Chapter 8

1. Peter O'Leary in *Gnostic Contagion* defines Mackey's gnosticism through the attributes of loss and aspiration and of failure and aspiration. Gnosticism recognizes the failure that is our current life on earth, our current state of being, but it also posits a "scintilla of Spirit" that lives on. O'Leary quotes Jacques Lacarrière on the gnostics: "their native 'soil' is not the earth, but that lost heaven which they keep vividly alive in their memories: they are the autochthons of another world" (21). In writing this book, I have been much aware of *Gnostic Contagion* for a couple of different reasons. O'Leary's book, as does this book, attempts to locate poetry at a nexus of powerful human realities and bodily dispositions: for O'Leary, religious belief systems and the trouble of illness; for me, psychological processes and the writing of love. In reading O'Leary's book, I found myself asking, is it really "gnostic" contagion that links Duncan and his followers, or erotic contagion—a troubling question that may have far more significance in the trouble it initiates than in its answer. In any case, to separate out one aspect of Mackey's larger set of commitments to some extent falsifies his deeply syncretic work.

2. Mackey edited *Hambone* 1 (Spring 1974) and initiated the volume with Gerald Barrax's "That Men Should Do," a poem created in two columns: the sexual relations between blacks and whites in the first column and a listing of places where lynchings took place in the second.

3. Mackey elaborates on "abandonment" at some length in his essay "Sound and Sentiment, Sound and Symbol." He linked abandonment to "social death," a phrase he took from Orlando Patterson to describe "the orphan's ordeal—an orphan being anyone denied kinship, social sustenance" (*Discrepant* 231–36).

4. I discuss projective poetry as "this" is "this" in chapter 5 in reference to H.D.'s writing. In referring to novelistic ventures as writing that produces "this" is "that," I am drawing on Aristotle's ideas of mimesis and more recent theories of representation.

5. Paul Naylor engages the concept of the ecstatic, defining it through the Greek word *ekstasis* as referring to a "being put out of its place or standing outside of itself" (593).

6. From the back cover of *School of Udhra*.

Afterword

1. Creeley's statement makes way for a highly mutable language since different contexts and structures, forms and uses, can shift language into changed meanings.

2. In *Forms of Expansion*, Lynn Keller considers Sharon Doubiago as a projectivist poet (37), and Susan Howe and Rachel Blau DuPlessis as practicing composition by field poetics (207, 279).

3. For example, in "Propounding Modernist Maleness: How Pound Managed a Muse," DuPlessis writes that Pound dehistoricizes and despecifies his muse figure in "Portrait d'une Femme" (*Blue Studios* 122–36).

4. I was fortunate to meet and hear all three of these writers in the 1990s as they were working on or had just completed these books.

5. For Pound on "counters," see this book, chapter 3, note 10.

6. Maria Menocal uses the concept of "contagio[n]" with respect to love poetry throughout her *Shards of Love*. Hogue engages the concept of "infectious ecstasy" with respect to Fraser's poetry, as quoted in chapter 7 of this book.

Works Cited

Agamben, Giorgio. *The Coming Community.* 2 vols. Minneapolis: U of Minnesota P, 1993.

———. *The End of the Poem.* Trans. Daniel Heller-Roazen. Stanford: Stanford UP, 1999.

Aldington, Richard. "Theocritus in Capri." *Literary Studies and Reviews.* London: Allen and Unwin, 1924. 241–42.

Alfrey, Shawn. *The Sublime of Intense Sociability: Emily Dickinson, H.D., and Gertrude Stein.* Lewisburg: Bucknell UP, 2000.

Allen, Donald. *The New American Poetry.* New York: Grove, 1960.

Allen, Donald, and Warren Tallman. *The Poetics of the New American Poetry.* New York: Grove, 1973.

Altieri, Charles. *Painterly Abstraction in Modernist American Poetry: The Contemporaneity of Modernism.* Cambridge: Cambridge UP, 1989.

Babcock, Robert. "Verses, Translations, and Reflections from *The Anthology: H.D., Ezra Pound, and the Greek Anthology.*" *Sagetrieb* 14 (Spring–Fall): 202–16.

Barthes, Roland. *A Lover's Discourse.* Trans. Richard Howard. New York: Hill, 1978.

Bataille, Georges. *Erotism: Death and Sensuality.* 1962. San Francisco: City Lights, 1986.

Belsey, Catherine. *Desire: Love Stories in Western Culture.* Oxford: Blackwell, 1994.

Benjamin, Jessica. *The Bonds of Love: Psychoanalysis, Feminism, and the Problem of Domination.* New York: Pantheon, 1988.

Benjamin, Walter. "Surrealism." *Reflections: Essays, Aphorisms, Autobiographical Writings.* Ed. Peter Demetz. New York: Harcourt Brace Jovanovich, 1978. 177–92.

Berlant, Lauren. *Desire / Love.* Brooklyn: Punctum, 2012.

Bernstein, Charles, ed. *Close Listening: Poetry and the Performed Word.* Oxford: Oxford UP, 1998.

———. *Content's Dream: Essays 1975–1984.* Los Angeles: Sun and Moon, 1986.

———. "Introjective Verse." *Postmodern American Poetry: A Norton Anthology.* 2nd ed. Ed. Paul Hoover. New York: Norton, 2013. 926–28.

———. "The Klupzy Girl." *Postmodern American Poetry: A Norton Anthology.* 2nd ed. Ed. Paul Hoover. New York: Norton, 2013. 518–21.

————. *The Politics of Poetic Form: Poetry and Public Policy.* New York: Roof, 1990.

Bersani, Leo. *The Freudian Body: Psychoanalysis and Art.* New York: Columbia UP, 1986.

Bertholf, Robert, and Ian Reid, eds. *Robert Duncan: Scales of the Marvelous.* New York: New Directions, 1979.

Boland, Eavan, and Kathleen Fraser. "A Conversation." *Parnassus: Poetry in Review* 23.1–2 (1998): 387–404.

Brown, Lee Ann. *Polyverse.* Los Angeles: Sun and Moon, 1999.

Browne, Laynie. *Rebecca Letters.* Berkeley: Kelsey Street, 1997.

Bürger, Peter. *Theory of the Avant-Garde.* Minneapolis: U of Minnesota P, 1984.

Burke, Carolyn. "Thought Split Inward." [Review, *il cuore.*] *Poetry Flash: A Poetry Review and Literary Calendar for the West* 277 (June–July 1998): 17.

Bush, Ronald. *The Genesis of Ezra Pound's Cantos.* Princeton: Princeton UP, 1976.

Butler, Judith. *Bodies that Matter: On the Discursive Limits of "Sex."* New York: Routledge, 1993.

————. *The Psychic Life of Power: Theories in Subjection.* Stanford: Stanford UP, 1997.

Byrd, Donald. "The Question of Wisdom as Such." *Robert Duncan: Scales of the Marvelous.* Ed. Robert Bertholf and Ian Reid. New York: New Directions, 1979. 38–60.

Carey, Benedict. "Watching New Love as It Sears the Brain." *New York Times* 31 May 2005 nat. ed.: D1.

Carpenter, Humphrey. *A Serious Character: The Life of Ezra Pound.* Boston: Houghton Mifflin, 1988.

Carson, Anne. *Eros the Bittersweet.* Princeton: Princeton UP, 1986.

Catullus, Gaius Valerius. *The Poems of Catullus.* Trans. Guy Lee. Oxford: Oxford UP, 1990.

Creeley, Robert. *For Love.* New York: Scribner, 1962.

Damon, Maria. *The Dark End of the Street: Margins in American Vanguard Poetry.* Minneapolis: U of Minnesota P, 1993.

Dante. *The Divine Comedy: Purgatorio.* Trans. Charles S. Singleton. Princeton: Princeton UP, 1973.

————. *La Vita Nuova.* Trans. Barbara Reynolds. London: Penguin, 1969.

Davidson, Michael. *Guys like Us: Citing Masculinity in Cold War Poetics.* Chicago: U of Chicago P, 2004.

————. *The San Francisco Renaissance.* Cambridge: Cambridge UP, 1989.

Derrida, Jacques. *Dissemination.* Chicago: U of Chicago P, 1981.

Detloff, Madelyn. *The Persistence of Modernism: Loss and Mourning in the Twentieth Century.* Cambridge: Cambridge UP, 2009.

Dowling, Sarah. *Down.* Toronto: Coach House, 2014.

duBois, Page. *Sowing the Body: Psychoanalysis and Ancient Representations of Women.* Chicago: U of Chicago P, 1995.

Duncan, Robert. *Bending the Bow.* New York: New Directions, 1968.

————. *Fictive Certainties: Essays by Robert Duncan.* New York: New Directions, 1985.

————. *The First Decade: Selected Poems 1940–1950.* London: Fulcrum, 1968.

————. *The H.D. Book.* Berkeley: U of California P, 2011.

————. "Interview with Robert Duncan." By Ekbert Faas. *Boundary 2* 8.2 (Winter 1980): 1–19.

———. "Interview with Robert Duncan." By Steve Abbott and Aaron Shurin. *Gay Sunshine Interviews*. Vol. 2. Ed. Winston Leyland. San Francisco: Gay Sunshine, 1982. 77–94.

———. *Letters*. Ed. Robert Berthoff. Chicago: Flood, 2003.

———. *The Opening of the Field*. New York: New Directions, 1960.

———. *Robert Duncan: The Collected Early Poems and Plays*. Ed. Peter Quartermain. Berkeley: U of California P, 2014.

———. *Robert Duncan: An Interview by George Bowering and Robert Hogg*. Toronto: Coach, 1971.

———. *Selected Prose*. Ed. Robert Berthoff. New York: New Directions, 1995.

———. *The Truth of Life and Myth*. Fremont: Sumac, 1968.

———. *Writing Writing*. Albuquerque: Sumbooks, 1964.

———. *The Years as Catches: First Poems (1939–1946)*. Berkeley: Oyez, 1966.

DuPlessis, Rachel Blau. *Blue Studios: Poetry and Its Cultural Work*. Tuscaloosa: U of Alabama P, 2006.

———. "'Corpses of Poesy': Modern Poets and Some Gender Ideologies of the Lyric." Keller and Miller 69–95.

———. *Drafts 1–38, Toll*. Middletown: Wesleyan UP, 2001.

———. *Genders, Races, and Religious Cultures in Modern American Poetries 1908–1934*. New York: Cambridge UP, 2001.

———. *H.D.: The Career of That Struggle*. Bloomington: Indiana UP, 1986.

———. "Interview, Conducted by Jeanne Heuving." *Contemporary Literature* 51.3 (Fall 2010): 532–64.

———. *The Pink Guitar: Writing as Feminist Practice*. New York: Routledge, 1990.

———. "Propounding Modernist Maleness: How Pound Managed a Muse." *Blue Studios: Poetry and Its Cultural Work*. By Rachel Blau DuPlessis. Tuscaloosa: U of Alabama P, 2006. 122–36.

———. *Purple Passages: Pound, Eliot, Zukofsky, Olson, Creeley, and the Ends of Patriarchal Poetry*. Iowa City: U of Iowa P, 2012.

———. "Romantic Thralldom." *Signets: Reading H.D.* Ed. Susan Stanford Friedman and Rachel Blau DuPlessis. Madison: U of Wisconsin P, 1990. 406–29.

Easthope, Anthony. *Poetry and Phantasy*. Cambridge: Cambridge UP, 1989.

Eliot, T. S. *Collected Poems 1909–1935*. New York: Harcourt, Brace, 1936.

———. *Four Quartets*. London: Faber and Faber, 1945.

Faas, Ekbert. *Young Robert Duncan: Portrait of the Poet as Homosexual in Society*. Santa Barbara, CA: Black Sparrow, 1983.

Finkelstein, Norman. *On Mount Vision: Forms of the Sacred in Contemporary American Poetry*. Iowa City: U of Iowa P, 2010.

Foucault, Michel. *The History of Sexuality*. New York: Pantheon, 1978.

———. *The Order of Things*. New York: Vintage, 1973.

Fraser, Kathleen. "Barbara Guest: The Location of Her (A Memoir)" *Translating the Unspeakable: Poetry and the Innovative Necessity*. By Fraser. Tuscaloosa: U of Alabama P, 2000. 124–30.

———. "The Blank Page: H.D.'s Invitation to Trust and Mistrust Language." *Translating the Unspeakable: Poetry and the Innovative Necessity*. By Fraser. Tuscaloosa: U of Alabama P, 2000. 53–62.

———. *Change of Address*. San Francisco: Kayak, 1966.

———. *il cuore: the heart: Selected Poems 1970–1995*. Hanover: UP of New England/ Wesleyan UP, 1997.

———. *Each Next*. Berkeley: Figures, 1980.

———. "How did Emma Slide? A matter of gestation." *Translating the Unspeakable: Poetry and the Innovative Necessity*. By Fraser. Tuscaloosa: U of Alabama P, 2000. 39–44.

———. "Interview with Kathleen Fraser." By Cynthia Hogue. *Contemporary Literature* 39.1 (1998): 1–26.

———. *Little Notes to You, from Lucas Street*. Iowa City: Penumbra, 1972.

———. *Magritte Series*. By Fraser. *New Shoes*. New York: Harper, 1978

———. *movable TYYPE*. Callicoon, NY: Nightboat Books, 2011.

———. *New Shoes*. New York: Harper, 1978.

———. *Something (even human voices) in the foreground, a lake*. Berkeley: Kelsey Street, 1984.

———. *Translating the Unspeakable: Poetry and the Innovative Necessity*. Tuscaloosa: U of Alabama P, 2000.

———. "Translating the Unspeakable: Visual Poetics, as Projected through Olson's 'Field' into Current Female Writing Practice." *Translating the Unspeakable: Poetry and the Innovative Necessity*. By Fraser. Tuscaloosa: U of Ala. P, 2000. 174–200.

———. *20th Century*. San Francisco: a+bend, 2000.

———. *What I Want*. New York: Harper and Row, 1973.

———. *when new time folds up*. Minneapolis: Chax, 1993.

———. *WING*. Mill Valley, CA: EM Press, 1995.

Fraser, Kathleen, and Hermine Ford. *ii ss*. 2007. Art and poetry exhibit. Pratt Institute, School of Architecture, Rome, Italy.

Fraser, Kathleen, and George Oppen. Unpublished Correspondence 1966–1977. Kathleen Fraser Archive, Mandeville Special Collections Library, University of California, San Diego.

Fredman, Stephen. *Assemblage and the Erotic in Postwar Poetry and Art*. Stanford: Stanford UP, 2009.

Freud, Sigmund. *The Freud Reader*. Ed. Peter Gay. New York: Norton, 1989.

Friedman, Susan Stanford. *Penelope's Web: Gender, Modernity, H.D.'s Fiction*. Cambridge: Cambridge UP 1990.

———. *Psyche Reborn: The Emergence of H.D.* Bloomington: Indiana UP, 1981.

Friedman, Susan Stanford, and Rachel Blau DuPlessis, eds. *Signets: Reading H.D.* Madison: U of Wisconsin P, 1990.

Frost, Elisabeth, and Cynthia Hogue, eds. *Innovative Women Poets: An Anthology of Contemporary Poetry and Interviews*. Iowa City: U of Iowa P, 2006.

Gibb, Hamilton, and Alexander Rosskeen. *Encyclopedia of Islam*. Leiden: Brill, 1960.

Giles, Herbert A. *A History of Chinese Literature*. New York: Grove, 1958.

Greene, Roland. *Unrequited Conquests: Love and Empire in the Colonial Americas*. Chicago: U of Chicago P, 1999.

Gregory, Eileen. *H.D. and Hellenism*. Cambridge: Cambridge UP, 1997.

———. "'A Poetics of Emerging Evidence': Experiment in Kathleen Fraser's Poetry." *We Who Love to Be Astonished: Experimental Women's Writing and Performance Po-*

etics. Ed. Laura Hinton and Cynthia Hogue. Tuscaloosa: U of Alabama P, 2002. 15–27.

Grosz, Elizabeth. *Jacques Lacan: A Feminist Introduction*. London: Routledge, 1990.

Guest, Barbara. *Herself Defined*. New York: Quill, 1984.

———. *Selected Poems*. Los Angeles: Sun and Moon, 1993.

Gunn, Thom. "Homosexuality in Robert Duncan's Poetry." *Robert Duncan: Scales of the Marvelous*. Ed. Robert Bertholf and Ian Reid. New York: New Directions, 1979. 143–60.

Hardie, Philip. *Ovid's Poetics of Illusion*. Cambridge: Cambridge UP, 2002.

Harrison, Jane. *Prologomena to the Study of Greek Religion*. Cambridge: Cambridge UP, 1903.

Hayles, Katherine N. *Writing Machines*. Cambridge, MA: MIT P, 2002.

H.D. "Art and Ardor in World War One: Selected Letters to John Cournos." Ed. Donna Krolik Hollenberg. *Iowa Review* 16 (Fall 1986): 126–55.

———. *Asphodel*. Durham, NC: Duke UP, 1992.

———. *Bid Me to Live*. New York: Dial, 1960.

———. *Collected Poems 1912–1944*. New York: New Directions, 1986.

———. "Compassionate Friendship." H.D. Papers, Beinecke Rare Book and Manuscript Library, Yale University.

———. *End to Torment: A Memoir of Ezra Pound*. New York: New Directions, 1979.

———. "H.D. by Delia Alton." Ed. Adalaide Morris. *Iowa Review* 16 (Fall 1986): 180–221.

———. *Helen in Egypt*. New York: New Directions, 1979.

———. *HERmione*. New York: New Directions, 1979.

———. "Notes on Euripides, Pausanius, and Greek Lyric Poets." H.D. Papers, Beinecke Rare Book and Manuscript Library, Yale University.

———. *Notes on Thought and Vision*. San Francisco: City Lights, 1982.

———. *Paint It Today*. New York: New York UP, 1992.

———. *Sea Garden*. *Collected Poems 1912–1944*. By H.D. New York: New Directions, 1986. 3–42.

———. *The Sword Went Out to Sea*. Ed. Cynthia Hogue and Julie Vandivere. Gainesville: UP of Florida, 2007.

———. *Trilogy*. *Collected Poems 1912–1944*. By H.D. New York: New Directions, 1986. 505–612.

Hejinian, Lyn. *The Language of Inquiry*. Berkeley: U California P: 2000.

Heuving, Jeanne. "Gender in Marianne Moore's Art: Can'ts and Refusals." *Sagetrieb* 6.3 (1987): 117–26.

———. *Incapacity*. Portland: Chiasmus, 2004.

———. "Kathleen Fraser and the Transmutation of Love." *Contemporary Literature* 51.3 (Fall 2010): 532–64.

———. "Laura (Riding) Jackson's 'Really New' Poem." *Gendered Modernisms: American Women Poets and Their Readers*. Ed. Margaret Dickie and Thomas Travisano. Philadelphia: U of Pennsylvania P, 1996: 191–213.

———. *Omissions Are Not Accidents: Gender in the Art of Marianne Moore*. Detroit: Wayne State UP, 1992

———. *Transducer*. Tucson: Chax, 2008.

Hinds, Stephen. "Landscape with Figures: Aesthetics of Place in the *Metamorphoses* and Its Tradition." *The Cambridge Companion to Ovid.* Ed. Philp R. Hardie. Cambridge: Cambridge UP. 122–50.

Hogue, Cynthia. "Infectious Ecstasy: On the Poetics of Performative Transformation." *Women Poets of the Americas: Toward a Pan-American Gathering.* Ed. Jacqueline Vaught Brogan and Cordelia Chavez Candelaria. Notre Dame: U of Notre Dame P, 1999. 51–67.

Hogue, Cynthia, and Julie Vandivere. Introduction. *The Sword Went Out to Sea: (Synthesis of a Dream), by Delia Alton.* By H.D. Ed. Cynthia Hogue and Julie Vandivere. Gainesville: UP of Florida, 2007.

Homans, Margaret. "Syllables of Velvet: Dickinson, Rossetti, and the Rhetorics of Sexuality." *Feminist Studies* 2.3 (1985): 569–93.

Hoover, Paul, ed. *Postmodern American Poetry: A Norton Anthology.* 2nd ed. New York: Norton, 2013.

Howatson, M. C., and Ian Chilvers. *Concise Companion to Classical Literature.* Oxford: Oxford UP, 1993.

Howe, Susan. *The Europe of Trusts.* Los Angeles: Sun and Moon, 1990.

———. *My Emily Dickinson.* Berkeley: North Atlantic, 1985.

Irigaray, Luce. *An Ethics of Sexual Difference.* Ithaca, NY: Cornell UP, 1993.

Jackson, Laura (Riding). *Anarchism Is Not Enough.* Garden City, NY: Doubleday, 1928.

———. *The Poems of Laura Riding: A New Edition of the 1938 Collection.* New York: Persea, 1992.

Jarnot, Lisa. "from The Ambassador from Venus." *Fascicle* 2 (Winter 2005–2006): 1–11.

———. *Robert Duncan: The Ambassador from Venus.* Berkeley: U of California P, 2012.

———. *Some Other Kind of Mission.* Providence: Burning Deck, 1996.

Johnson, Mark Andrew. *Robert Duncan.* Boston: Twayne, 1988.

Johnston, Devin. *Precipitations: Contemporary Poetry as Occult Practice.* Middletown, CT: Wesleyan UP, 2002.

Keller, Lynn. *Forms of Expansion: Recent Long Poems by Women.* Chicago: U of Chicago P, 1997.

———. "'Just one of / the girls: / normal in the extreme': Experimentalists-to-Be Starting Out in the 1960s." *differences: A Journal of Feminist Cultural Studies* 12.2 (2001): 47–69.

———. "Measured Feet 'in Gender-Bender Shoes': The Politics of Form in Marilyn Hacker's *Love, Death, and the Changing of the Seasons.*" *Feminist Measures: Soundings in Poetry and Theory.* Ed. Lynn Keller and Cristanne Miller. Ann Arbor: U of Michigan P, 1994. 260–86.

Kelly, Robert. "H.D.: A Joining." *H.D. and Poets After.* Ed. Donna Krolik Hollenberg. Iowa City: U of Iowa P, 2000: 32–44.

Kennedy, Duncan. *The Arts of Love: Five Studies in the Discourse of Roman Love Elegy.* Cambridge: Cambridge UP, 1993.

Kenner, Hugh. "Blood for the Ghosts." *New Approaches to Ezra Pound.* Ed. Eva Hesse. Berkeley: U of California P, 1969. 331–48.

———. *The Pound Era.* Berkeley: U of California P, 1971.

Kern, Stephen. *The Culture of Love: Victorians to Moderns.* Cambridge, MA: Harvard UP, 1992.

Kinnahan, Linda. *Lyric Interventions: Feminism, Experimental Poetry, and Contemporary Discourse.* Iowa City: U of Iowa P, 2004.

Kipnis, Laura. *Against Love: A Polemic.* New York: Pantheon, 2003.

Kopelson, Kevin. *Love's Litany: The Writing of Modern Homoerotics.* Stanford: Stanford UP, 1994.

Korg, Jacob. *Winter Love: Ezra Pound and H.D.* Madison: U of Wisconsin P, 2003.

Kristeva, Julia. *Tales of Love.* Trans. Leon S. Roudiez. New York: Columbia UP, 1987.

Lacan, Jacques. *Ecrits: A Selection.* Trans. Alan Sheridan. New York: Norton, 1977.

———. *Feminine Sexuality.* Ed. Juliet Mitchell and Jacqueline Rose. Trans. Jacqueline Rose. New York: Norton, 1982.

———. *The Four Fundamental Concepts of Psycho-Analysis.* Ed. Jacques-Alain Miller. Trans. Alan Sheridan. New York: Norton, 1973.

Laity, Cassandra. *H.D. and the Victorian Fin de Siècle: Gender, Modernism, Decadence.* Cambridge: Cambridge UP, 1996.

Lang, Andrew, ed. *Theocritus, Bion and Moschus Rendered into English Prose.* London: Macmillan, 1889.

Lazer, Hank. "'Vatic Scat': Jazz and the Poetry of Robert Creeley and Nathaniel Mackey." *Lyric and Spirt.* Richmond, CA: Omnidawn, 2008.

Lipking, Lawrence. *Abandoned Women and Poetic Tradition.* Chicago: U of Chicago P, 1988.

Loy, Mina. *The Lost Lunar Baedeker.* Ed. Roger Conover. New York: Farrar, Straus and Giroux, 1996.

———. "Songs to Joannes." *The Lost Lunar Baedeker.* By Loy. Ed. Roger Conover. New York: Farrar, Straus and Giroux, 1996. 53–70.

Luhmann, Niklas. *Love as Passion: The Codification of Intimacy.* Trans. Jeremy Gaines and Doris L. Jones. 1986. Stanford: Stanford UP, 1998.

Lyon, Janet. *Manifestoes: Provocations of the Modern.* Cambridge: Cambridge UP, 1999.

Mackail, J. K. *Select Epigrams from the Greek Anthology.* 1906. London: Longmans, Green, 1910.

Mackey, Nathaniel. "Call Me Tantra: Open Field Poetics as Muse." Diss. Stanford University, 1975.

———. "Cante Moro." *Paracritical Hinge: Essays, Talks, Notes, Interviews.* By Mackey. Madison: U of Wisconsin P, 2005. 181–98.

———. "The Changing Same: Black Music in the Poetry of Amiri Baraka." *Discrepant Engagement: Dissonance, Cross-Culturality, and Experimental Writing.* By Mackey. Tuscaloosa: U of Alabama P, 1993. 22–48.

———. *Discrepant Engagement: Dissonance, Cross-Culturality, and Experimental Writing.* 1993. Tuscaloosa: U of Alabama P, 2000.

———. *Eroding Witness.* Urbana: U of Illinois P, 1983.

———. *Four for Trane.* Los Angeles: Golemics, 1978.

———. *From a Broken Bottle Traces of Perfume Still Emanate.* Vols. 1–3. New York: New Directions, 2010.

———. "Interview, Conducted by Jeanne Heuving." *Contemporary Literature* 53.2 (Summer 2012): 207–36.

———. "Limbo, Dislocation, Phantom Limb: Wilson Harris and the Caribbean Occasion." *Discrepant Engagement.* 162–79.

——. *Paracritical Hinge: Essays, Talks, Notes, Interviews.* Madison: U of Wisconsin P, 2005.

——. "Robert Creeley's *The Gold Diggers*: Projective Prose." *Discrepant Engagement: Dissonance, Cross-Culturality, and Experimental Writing.* By Mackey. Tuscaloosa: U of Alabama P, 1993. 104–20.

——. *School of Udhra.* San Francisco: City Lights, 1993.

——. "Sound and Sentiment, Sound and Symbol" in Mackey, *Discrepant Engagement.* 231–59.

——. *Splay Anthem.* New York: New Directions, 2006.

——. *Whatsaid Serif.* San Francisco: City Lights, 1998.

Mallarmé, Stéphane. *Selected Prose Poems, Essays, and Letters.* Trans. Bradford Cook. Baltimore: Johns Hopkins UP, 1956.

Marinetti, F. T. *Selected Writings.* Ed. R. W. Flint. Trans. R. W. Flint and Arthur A. Coppotelli. New York: Farrar, Straus and Giroux, 1972.

McCabe, Susan. *Cinematic Modernism: Modernist Poetry and Film.* Cambridge: Cambridge UP, 2005.

Menocal, Maria Rosa. *Shards of Love: Exile and the Origins of the Lyric.* Durham, NC: Duke UP, 1994.

Miller, Paul Allen. *Lyric Texts and Lyric Consciousness: The Birth of a Genre from Archaic Greece to Augustan Rome.* New York: Routledge, 1994.

Miyake, Akiko. *Ezra Pound and the Mysteries of Love: A Plan for the Cantos.* Durham, NC: Duke UP, 1991.

Montefiore, Jan. *Feminism and Poetry.* New York: Pandora, 1987.

Moody, A. David. *Ezra Pound: Poet.* Vol. 1. Oxford: Clarendon, 2007.

Morris, Adalaide. "The Concept of Projection: H.D.'s Visionary Powers." Ed. Susan Stanford Friedman and Rachel Blau DuPlessis. Madison: U of Wisconsin P, 1990. 273–96.

——. *How to Live / What to Do.* Middletown: Wesleyan UP, 2003.

Morrison, Toni. *Playing in the Dark: Whiteness and the Literary Imagination.* London: Picador, 1992.

Mullen, Harryette. *Muse and Drudge.* Philadelphia: Singing Horse, 1995.

Nakayasu, Sawako. *Hurry Home Honey.* Providence, RI: Burning Deck, 2009.

Naylor, Paul. "'Some Ecstatic Elsewhere': Nathaniel Mackey's *Whatsaid Serif.*" *Callaloo* 23.2 (2000): 592–605.

Nehring, Cristina. *A Vindication of Love: Reclaiming Romance for the Twenty-First Century.* New York: HarperCollins, 2009.

Nichols, Miriam. *Radical Affections: Essays on the Poetics of Outside.* Tuscaloosa: U of Alabama P, 2010.

Nielsen, Aldon. *Reading Race in American Poetry: An Area of Act.* Urbana: U of Illinois P, 2000: 49–101.

Oderman, Kevin. *Ezra Pound and the Erotic Medium.* Durham, NC: Duke UP, 1986.

O'Leary, Peter. *Gnostic Contagion: Robert Duncan and the Poetry of Illness.* Middletown: Wesleyan UP, 2002.

Olson, Charles. *Selected Writings.* New York: New Directions, 1966.

Olson, Charles, and Robert Creeley. *Charles Olson and Robert Creeley: The Complete Correspondence.* Vol. 1. Ed. George Butterick. Santa Barbara: Black Sparrow, 1980.

Ovid. *The Love Poems.* Trans. A. D. Melville. Oxford: Oxford UP, 1990.

Paton, W. R., ed. *The Greek Anthology*. Vols. 1–5. Cambridge, MA: Harvard UP, 1918.

Perloff, Marjorie. "Charles Olson and the 'Inferior Predecessors': 'Projective Verse' Revisited." *English Language History* 40.2 (1973): 285–306.

———. *Poetics of Indeterminacy: Rimbaud to Cage*. Princeton: Princeton UP, 1981.

———. *21st-Century Modernism: The "New" Poetics*. Malden: Blackwell, 2002.

Petrarch, Francesco. *Selections from the Canzionere and Other Works*. Trans. Mark Musa. Oxford: Oxford UP, 1985.

Plato. *Plato's Erotic Dialogues: The Symposium and the Phaedrus*. Ed. William S. Cobb. Albany: State U of New York P, 1993.

Poetry 1.2 (November 1912).

Poetry 1.4 (January 1913).

Poetry 1.5 (February 1913).

Pondrom, Cyrena. "H.D. and the Origins of Imagism." Ed. Susan Stanford Friedman and Rachel Blau DuPlessis. Madison: U of Wisconsin P, 1990. 85–109.

Pound, Ezra. *The Cantos of Ezra Pound*. New York: New Directions, 1983.

———. "Editorial Commentary." *Poetry* 1.4 (Feb. 1913): 120–22.

———. *Ezra Pound's Poetry and Prose: Contributions to Periodicals*. Ed. Lea Baechler, A. Walton Litz, and James Longenbeach. 10 vols. New York: Garland, 1991.

———. "The Growth of Three Cantos." *The Genesis of Ezra Pound's Cantos*. By Ronald Bush. Princeton: Princeton UP, 1976. 53–73.

———. *Hilda's Book*. Typed copy. Beinecke Rare Book and Manuscript Library, Yale University.

———, ed. *Des Imagistes: An Anthology*. New York: Boni, 1914.

———. *Literary Essays of Ezra Pound*. Ed. T. S. Eliot. New York: Garland, 1991.

———. *Personae: The Collected Poems of Ezra Pound*. New York: Boni & Liveright, 1926.

———. *Personae: The Shorter Poems of Ezra Pound*. 1926. New York: New Directions, 1990.

———. *The Pisan Cantos*. Ed. Richard Sieburth. New York: New Directions, 2003.

———. *Pound's Cavalcanti: An Edition of the Translations, Notes, and Essays*. Ed. David Anderson. Princeton: Princeton UP, 1983.

———. *Selected Letters*. Ed. D. D. Paige. New York: New Directions, 1950.

———. *Spirit of Romance*. New York: New Directions, 1968.

———. *Umbra*. London: Elkin Matthews, 1920.

Propertius. *Elegies*. Cambridge, MA: Harvard U P, 1990.

Quartermain, Peter. "Kathleen Fraser." *Dictionary of Literary Biography: American Poets since World War II*. 5th ser. Ed. Joseph Conte. Washington, DC: Gale Research, 1996. 106–15.

Rabate, Jean Michel. *Language, Sexuality, and Ideology in Ezra Pound's Cantos*. London: Macmillan, 1986.

Rich, Adrienne. *Adrienne Rich's Poetry and Prose*. Ed. Barbara Charlesworth Gelpi and Albert Gelpi. New York: Norton, 1993.

Rilke, Rainer Maria. *Letters to a Young Poet*. Trans. M. D. Hester. New York: Norton, 1934.

Ruthven, K. K. *A Guide to Pound's "Personae."* Berkeley: U of California P, 1969.

Said, Edward. *Orientalism*. New York: Vintage, 1979.

Schiesari, Juliana. *The Gendering of Melancholia: Feminism, Psychoanalysis, and the Symbolics of Loss in Renaissance Literature*. Ithaca, NY: Cornell UP, 1992.

Schulte-Sasse, Jochen. "Foreward: Theory of Modernism versus Theory of the Avant-Garde." *Theory of the Avant-Garde.* By Peter Bürger. Minneapolis: U of Minnesota P, 1984. vii–xlvii.

Sedgwick, Eve Kosofsky. *Epistemology of the Closet.* Berkeley: U of California P, 1990.

Selinger, Eric. *What Is It Then between Us?: Traditions of Love in American Poetry.* Ithaca, NY: Cornell UP, 1998.

Shaviro, Steven. *Connected, or What it Means to Live in the Network Society.* Minneapolis: U of Minnesota Press, 2003.

Shelley, Percy Bysshe. "A Defense of Poetry." *Shelley's Poetry and Prose.* By Shelley. Ed. Donald H. Reiman and Sharon B. Powers. New York: Norton, 1977. 480–509.

———. *Shelley's Poetry and Prose.* Ed. Donald H. Reiman and Sharon B. Powers. New York: Norton, 1977.

Shreiber, Maeera Y. *The Discourse of Love in the Lyric and the Letter.* Diss. Brandeis University, 1990. Ann Arbor: UMI, 1990.

Shurin, Aaron. *Involuntary Lyrics.* Richmond, CA: Omnidawn, 2005.

———. "Out of Me: Whitman and the Projective." MA thesis. New College of California, 1982.

Sieburth, Richard. Introduction. *The Pisan Cantos.* By Ezra Pound. Ed. Richard Sieburth. 1948. Reprint. New York: New Directions, 2003. ix–xliii.

Silliman, Ron. Afterword. *Close Listening: Poetry and the Performed Word.* Ed. Charles Bernstein. Oxford: Oxford UP, 1998. 360–78.

Silverstein, Louis H. "Herself Delineated: Chronological Highlights of H.D." Ed. Susan Stanford Friedman and Rachel Blau DuPlessis. Madison: U of Wisconsin P, 1990. 32–45.

Simmons, Thomas. *Erotic Reckonings: Mastery and Apprenticeship in the Work of Poets and Lovers.* Urbana: U of Illinois P, 1994.

Snediker, Michael. *Queer Optimism: Lyric Personhood and Other Felicitous Persuasions.* Minneapolis: U of Minnesota P, 2008.

Spivak, Gayatri. *Can the Subaltern Speak? Reflections on the History of an Idea.* New York: Columbia UP, 2010.

Staten, Henry. *Eros in Mourning: From Homer to Lacan.* Baltimore: Johns Hopkins UP, 1995.

Stein, Gertrude. "Patriarchal Poetry." *The Yale Gertrude Stein.* Ed. Richard Kostelanetz. New Haven, CT: Yale University Press, 1980. 104–46.

———. *Tender Buttons.* San Francisco: City Lights, 2014.

Stendhal. *On Love.* New York: Boni and Liveright, 1927.

Stewart, Susan. *Poetry and the Fate of the Senses.* Chicago: U of Chicago P, 2002.

———. "The State of Cultural Theory and the Future of Literary Form." *Profession.* New York: Modern Language Association, 1993. 93–97.

Surette, Leon. *The Birth of Modernism: Ezra Pound, T. S. Eliot, W. B. Yeats, and the Occult.* Montreal: McGill Queen's UP, 1993.

Swensen, Cole, and David St. John, eds. *American Hybrid: A Norton Anthology of New Poetry.* New York: Norton, 2009.

Teare, Brian. *Sight Map.* Berkeley: U California P, 2009.

Terrell, Carroll. *A Companion to the Cantos of Ezra Pound.* Vol. 1. Berkeley: U of California P, 1980.

Vernant, Jean-Pierre. "One . . . Two . . . Three: Eros." *Before Sexuality: The Construction of Erotic Experience in the Ancient World*. Ed. David M. Halperin, John J. Winkler, and Froma I. Zeitlin. Princeton: Princeton UP, 1990: 465–78.

Vickers, Nancy J. "Diana Described: Scattered Woman and Scattered Rhyme." *Writing and Sexual Difference*. Ed. Elizabeth Abel. Chicago: U of Chicago P, 1982. 95–110.

Wilde, Oscar. "The Critic as Artist." *The Artist as Critic: Critical Writings of Oscar Wilde*. Ed. Richard Ellmann. Chicago: U of Chicago P, 1968. 341–407.

Williams, William Carlos. *Asphodel, That Greeny Flower and Other Love Poems*. 1938. Reprint. New York: New Directions, 1994.

———. *Paterson*. 1946. Reprint. New York: New Directions, 1995.

———. *Spring and All*. 1923. Reprint. New York: New Directions, 2011.

Wolsak, Lissa. *Squeezed Light: Collected Poems 1994–2005*. Barrytown, NY: Station Hill, 2010.

Yeats, W. B. *The Collected Poems of W. B. Yeats*. New York: Macmillan, 1956.

Zilboorg, Caroline. "H.D. and R. A.: Early Love and the Exclusion of Ezra Pound." *H.D. Newsletter* 3.1 (1990): 26–34.

———. "H.D.'s Influence on Richard Aldington." *Richard Aldington: Reappraisals*. Ed. Charles Doyle. Victoria, Canada: University of Victoria English Dept., 1990.

———. Introduction. *Richard Aldington and H.D.: The Early Years in Letters*. Ed. Caroline Zilboorg. Bloomington: Indiana UP, 1992. xv–liii.

Index

Collins, Jess, 115, 124, 195n2 (chap. 6)

Coltrane, John, 161, 163, 165; "A Love Supreme," 163; *Sun Ship*; 165

Creeley, Robert, 5, 10, 147–48, 157, 163, 180, 184, 189n1 (Intro), 196n2, 197n1 (Afterword); *For Love*, 164

Dante: 54, 57, 133, 189n1 (intro.); *La Divina Commedia*, 1, 31, 56–57

Daniel, Arnaut, 26

Davidson, Michael, 184

da Vinci, Leonardo, 37, 39, 40

Deleuze, Giles, 15

Derrida, Jacques: *Dissemination*, 41–42

Des Imagistes, 12, 52, 58–59, 62–63, 193n11. See also H.D.: "Acon"; H.D.: "Sitalkas"; Pound, Ezra: "After Ch'u Yuan"; Pound, Ezra: "Doria"; Pound, Ezra: "Fan-Piece, for Her Imperial Lord"; Pound, Ezra: "The Fault of It"; Pound, Ezra: "Liu Ch'e"; Pound, Ezra: "The Return"

de Tegea, Anyte, 55. See also H.D.: "Hermes of the Ways"

Dieterlen, Germaine: *The Pale Fox*, 166

Djamil, 171, 172

Doubiago, Sharon, 197n2 (Afterword)

Dowding, Hugh, 90, 103, 107, 195n7

Dowling, Sarah: *Down*, 186

duBois, Page: *Sowing the Body*, 190n3

duende, 160–62; *cante moro*, 160, 174

Duncan, Robert, ix–xi, 1, 2, 6, 9, 13–15, 22, 26, 32–33, 47, 110–36, 137, 141, 149, 156, 161–62, 181–82, 184–85, 192n4, 195nn1–4 (chap. 6), 196n1 (chap. 8); "An African Elegy," 117–19, 136; "An Apollonian Elegy," 118–19, 122; "The Beginning of Writing," 125–26, 128; *Bending the Bow*, 111, 116, 128, 133–36, 162; Berkeley poems, 119–21; "The Collage, *Passages 6*," 135; "The Dance," 111, 129–30; "Descriptions of Imaginary Poetries," 126; "Domestic Scenes," 195n1 (chap. 6); "Eros," 112–14; "5th Sonnet," 135; *The H.D. Book*, ix, 2, 36, 110, 112–14, 116, 121; *Heavenly City, Earthly City*, 195n1 (chap. 6); "The Homosexual in Society," 13, 112, 117; "Imagining in Writing," 125–26; "The

Law I Love is Major Mover," 130; *Letters*, 110, 116, 123, 126–27; *Medieval Scenes*, 119, 121–23, 125, 195n1 (chap. 6); "Often I Am Permitted to Return to a Meadow," 11, 22, 27, 129, 133; *The Opening of the Field*, 6, 11, 15–16, 26, 110, 112, 116, 121, 123, 127–33, 136, 150; "A Poem Beginning with a Line from Pindar," xii, 130–33, 184–85; "Sonnet 4," 135; "The Structure of Rime I," 127, 130–31, 195n4 (chap. 6); "The Torso, *Passages 18*," 135–36; *The Truth of Life and Myth*, 33, 126, 131; *Writing Writing*, 15, 110, 116, 123–26

DuPlessis, Rachel Blau, 16; 190n4; 197n2 (Afterword); "Corpses of Poetry," 73; *Drafts*, 184; *H.D.*, 102–3; "Propounding Modernist Maleness," 197n3 (Afterword); *Purple Passages*, 184; "Romantic Thralldom," 91–92, 145; "Writing," 184–85

Eliot, T. S., 124, 191n8; *Four Quartets*, 28, 101; "The Love Song of J. Alfred Prufrock," 28; *The Wasteland*, 28

Elmslie, Kenward, 154

enchantment, 12, 38, 46–47, 68, 69, 71, 80, 86, 111–12, 137, 161

Encyclopedia of Islam, 171–72

eros 3, 7, 41, 48 112–114, 116, 132, 124, 181–82; erotism, 7, 182, 191n6; jouissance, 7, 47

Euripides, 92; *Helen*, 104

Faas, Ekbert, 124, 130

fascism, 29, 87, 154

Fenollosa, Ernest, 59

Finkelstein, Norman, 17

Ford, Maddox Ford, 57

Foucault, Michel: *The History of Sexuality*, 9; *The Order of Things*, 32

Fraser, Kathleen, ix–xi, 1, 9, 13–16, 27, 111, 137–55, 181, 186, 189n3, 192n5 (chap. 1), 196n1 (chap. 7), 196n5, 196n9, 197n6 (Afterword); "Barbara Guest," 139–40; "The Blank Page," 137; *Change of Address*, 3, 138, 142, 145; "Day and Night," 143–44; *Each Next*, 145–46; "Energy Unavailable for Useful Work in a System Undergoing Change," 141, 147–49; "Etruscan Pages,"